Mothering Without a Map

ALSO BY KATHRYN BLACK

In the Shadow of Polio:
A Personal and Social History

KATHRYN BLACK

Mothering Without a Map

*The Search for
the Good Mother Within*

VIKING

VIKING
Published by the Penguin Group
Penguin Group (USA) Inc., 375 Hudson Street,
New York, New York 10014, U.S.A.
Penguin Books Ltd, 80 Strand, London WC2R 0RL, England
Penguin Books Australia Ltd, 250 Camberwell Road, Camberwell,
Victoria 3124, Australia
Penguin Books Canada Ltd, 10 Alcorn Avenue,
Toronto, Ontario, Canada M4V 3B2
Penguin Books India (P) Ltd, 11 Community Centre, Panchsheel Park,
New Delhi – 110 017, India
Penguin Books (N.Z.) Ltd, Cnr Rosedale and Airborne Roads, Albany,
Auckland, New Zealand
Penguin Books (South Africa) (Pty) Ltd, 24 Sturdee Avenue,
Rosebank, Johannesburg 2196, South Africa

Penguin Books Ltd, Registered Offices: 80 Strand, London WC2R 0RL, England

First published in 2004 by Viking Penguin, a member of Penguin Group (USA) Inc.

1   3   5   7   9   10   8   6   4   2

Grateful acknowledgment is made for permission to reprint a selection from *Tortoise Voices* by
Dorian Haarhoff. Used by permission of Mercer Books, Cape Town, copyright © 2001.

LIBRARY OF CONGRESS CATALOGING-IN-PUBLICATION DATA
Black, Kathryn.
Mothering without a map : the search for the good mother within / Kathryn Black.
p. cm.
Includes bibliographical references and index.
ISBN 0-670-03266-2
1. Mothers.   2. Mother and child.   I. Title.
HQ759.B583 2003
306.874'3—dc21   2003057198

This book is printed on acid-free paper. ∞

Printed in the United States of America
Set in Adobe Garamond   Designed by Francesca Belanger

For Ian and Willy, of course

ACKNOWLEDGMENTS

This book would not have been possible without the women who shared their stories with me, allowing me to delve into the individual experience of mothering and being mothered. I've disguised their identities to protect their privacy, but their words are unchanged, and their words made all the difference. I'm deeply grateful to all who participated in my research.

My profound gratitude goes as well to my "village women." They inspire and aid me, and without them my child-rearing would not be as rich and rewarding or nearly as much fun as it is. I'm blessed with a wide circle of village women, but my pillars are Pamela Patrick Novotny, who attended both births, Theresa Beck, Mary Ellen Vernon, Krystyna Poray Goddu and Chiquita Woodard.

I'm grateful also to the many people at Viking Penguin who worked on this book, especially Pamela Dorman, who brought her supreme professionalism, her stimulating insights and her own thoughtful mothering to the project. Susan Hans O'Connor also offered her unfailing editorial eye and patient guidance.

Thanks, too, to Pat Whitaker, George Clark, Jaye Zola and Brooke Davison; and to Kelly Moore for her research assistance. And many thanks go to Evelyn Bassoff, Ph.D., who helped me over important emotional and intellectual hurdles midway through the project.

Gail Hochman is the dream agent: smart, connected, fast,

wise, honest, supportive—and great fun to be with besides. Laura Goodman spans the categories of village mom, dear friend and editor extraordinaire. She stood by me from idea to final manuscript, offering wise counsel and clarity of mind.

Above all, I thank my husband, Jens Husted, and our sons, Ian and William, who give everything I do meaning and joy, every day.

CONTENTS

ACKNOWLEDGMENTS — *vii*

CHAPTER ONE: The Beginning — *1*

CHAPTER TWO: Mothers Matter — *9*

CHAPTER THREE: Uneasy Attachments — *42*

CHAPTER FOUR: Ghosts — *75*

CHAPTER FIVE: Exceptions — *102*

CHAPTER SIX: Reclamations — *131*

CHAPTER SEVEN: Mother Lore, Mother Love — *165*

CHAPTER EIGHT: The Mother Within — *201*

NOTES — *243*

SELECTED BIBLIOGRAPHY — *261*

INDEX — *265*

in the beginning fluid,
I, a snail thread
on a sea bed of time
heard the universe sound
"this one. yes."

—Dorian Haarhoff,
Tortoise Voices

Mothering Without a Map

CHAPTER ONE

The Beginning

. . . and what a priceless gift—to hold like a wild young animal another's safety in one's hand, or to place your soul in just such jeopardy, and still to be loved.

—William Gass

The journey toward motherhood for any woman begins with conception. But whose? Did my maternal path begin when my first child was conceived? The casual answer to that question is *yes*. But the true answer, I think, is that the journey began long ago, with my conception, or my mother's, or her mother's or even further back in the chain of mothers before us. For me, as for every woman, all the incidents of my life, all that makes up my character and personality, my DNA, what I read and experience, where I've traveled from and to, all of it led me to motherhood. And all of it affects how I mother. Nothing, however, exerts an influence on how a woman raises a child as powerfully as does her own mother. For some women, the maternal route traces a clean trajectory from a childhood of being watched over by a loving and consistent mother to later parenthood whose foundation rests on Mother's solid template.

For others of us, the maternal experience is far different. My mother disappeared into hospitals when I was four years old and died when I was six. From her I came to know the cavern of grief the absent mother creates. I also know what it is to be mothered by someone who can't see you, who can't recognize or respond to the needs of your deepest self. That was the kind of care I found in mother substitutes—stepmothers, but mainly my maternal grandmother—who held dominion over me after my mother's death. These experiences, which underlay my identity, kept me from the comfortable assumption that I would mother my children with ease, relying on the patterns, practices and confidences conveyed from mother to daughter. For a long time, my childhood privation kept me from motherhood altogether. My first marriage was to a man who wanted nothing to do with fatherhood, and that suited me just fine. I wanted a career and an arena of cities and adventure, not the stifling limits of a life I assumed would be bound by shopping malls and schoolyards. I feared the suffocation of motherhood.

At age forty-one I married again, this time to a childless man who wanted children with the same fever that had by then overpowered my fears. Together we created a family, with two sons born to us in quick succession.

Once a mother myself I began to search for assurance that I could nurture my children more joyfully, deliberately and lovingly than I had been reared. Long excluded from the hallowed covenant between mothers and daughters, I knew I had missed something essential, something mothers impart to daughters about becoming women and mothers, something women who have or had intimate mothers know and use to raise happy, well-adjusted children. I sought evidence that maternal care, though perhaps best or most easily acquired at the breast of one's own mother, can be learned elsewhere.

Mothers are so vital to children that renowned pediatrician and psychoanalyst D. W. Winnicott put it this way: "There is no such thing as a baby." He meant that a baby must be considered not in isolation but in relationship to the someone nearby whose eyes and ears are "glued to it." Infants cannot exist without the care of another; they are bound by biology to the adults responsible for them. Cornell University anthropologist Meredith Small says that evolution has arranged mothers and babies this way so that "the mother will feed and protect the infant and the infant will remain close by to be fed and protected."

Parenthood, the intricate weave of biological, psychological and cultural resolve, extends further into the human offspring's life than it does for any other animal. Intense parenting is, in fact, one of the most distinguishing features of the human species. The care parents provide their children, however, varies widely. It ranges from optimal—exactly what nature meant and the baby requires—all the way to destructive. For those of us who received nurturing that fell short of ideal, the knowledge that adult caregivers—usually but not exclusively mothers—are essential to children is a two-edged sword. We live lives made more complex by having missed first-rate care in childhood, and we face the momentous task of mothering without a worthy model to follow.

My quest to understand what becomes of the under-mothered when they have children and to discover whether flawed mothering can be overcome in the next generation led me to the fields of psychiatric and psychoanalytic research, developmental psychology and social work as well as biology and anthropology. In the writings of experts in those fields I found answers to my questions about the purpose of mothers in the lives of children. There I also found explanations for why children cling, often far into adulthood, to inadequate mothers and why humans tend to repeat in adulthood patterns experienced in childhood, even when those patterns of behavior and relatedness don't bring them what they want or need. There, too, I learned what developmental psychologists have discovered about why some people are able to overcome troubled childhoods and lead satisfying lives, and others are not. I found answers and reassurance in the work of such experts, but comfort and wisdom have come from the women, ages twenty to seventy, who have told me their mother stories—in person, on the telephone, via e-mail and through questionnaires. I've heard from them of the many ways the path nature intends for us—being suckled, nurtured and protected by a responsive caregiver—can go wrong. Mothers sometimes go crazy, desert us or die young. Others stay but are inept or cold, mean or wounded, distant or perpetually distracted, well intentioned but needy, possessive or overprotective, alcoholic or otherwise unpredictable. Whether these women are at fault or are victims of their fates, the result is girls who grow up without having been well mothered. The voices of many of the more than fifty women who participated in my research illustrate the experience of being under-mothered and of becoming mothers who strive to provide for their own children something different from what they themselves received. Along the way, I've come to see that while scientists help us understand the past and its effects, it's often other mothers who point the way as we walk into the future with our children.

For some women the route to becoming an under-mothered mother can be clearly, if not easily, described or explained, as it is for women like me whose protectors disappeared too soon. In my interviews I sometimes heard chilling stories. One woman's mother tried to give her away to a friend when she was just a year old, and then relented a few months later, only to desert her again. I heard of alcoholic and drug-addicted mothers. I heard of mothers who were physically abusive or stood by while their husbands abused their daughters.

Most often, however, I heard of the subtle shortcomings of maternal care. Women told me of family lives that seemed fine, or at least adequate, but in which something invisible yet critical was askew. As I spoke to more and more women, the idea of "growing up without a mother" took on wider meaning. Often I heard of the particular torment of having a mother physically present, though aloof or irresponsible, preoccupied or inattentive, intrusive or fretful, strident, suspicious or even hostile. One woman spoke of that yearning for the person who is there, but not there, this way: She remembers being about six and settled on the floor near her mother who sat knitting on the sofa. Her mother shifted and her leg came to rest against the girl's back. The girl froze, drinking in her mother's accidental touch, feeling her weight and presence, knowing that if she moved and reminded her mother of their closeness, she would pull away.

My mother always had dinner on the table, the house cleaned up, the laundry and ironing done. I suppose that's one way of assessing quality of care. I would not, however, call her a good mother. She was missing the heart of mothering, the ability to impart the essential feeling to a child that she is seen and heard, that she is known and loved, that she is cared for and cared about.

The daughters of those women who couldn't demonstrate, or perhaps even feel, love and approval, who didn't provide warm, consistent care, told me of facing the uncertainty and difficulty of parenting their children while fearing they would repeat the mistakes of their mothers.

I think I'm a good mother, but that doesn't stop me from asking again and again: Am I good enough?

I grew up with no sense that life was about seeking joy or fulfilling curiosity. I felt as if I never had anything beyond that day. When my daughter was in preschool I began to worry about my ability to instill the wonder of life in her. Does it just happen? Do you plan for it every day? And now that she's a teen, I'm terrified that maybe I'm treating her the same stingy way I was treated and don't even know it.

I don't have a firm idea about what a mother is supposed to do. I have such a hazy picture of what my mom's role was.

From conversations with women who missed out on a childhood made rich by the devotion of a benevolent, competent figure, I heard how hard-won confidence, especially in one's self as a mother, can be. I also heard from women who've been able to fashion from their tainted pasts a richly satisfying and fulfilling motherhood.

It was at my mother's knee that I learned first that I was not worthy. And it has taken many years for me to understand how and why she could tell me that in so many subtle and not-so-subtle ways, and many more years to work toward undoing the effects of that message. But now I feel good about myself as a mother and see that I am a good one. I see it in my children and I hear it from them. I also see my relationship with each of my children growing and changing as they change and grow, which pleases me and gives me confidence that we are all on the path toward being adults together, toward having adult relationships. Along with my relationship with my husband, being a mother has been the most wonderful, life-affirming, fulfilling thing in my life.

Whatever the particulars of their childhoods, women often expressed the same painful ambivalence I felt in stepping forward to say, "I was not well mothered."

In a paradoxical way, my mother's legacy to my children is that I have been a good mother to them, in part because I learned from her what it was to be a lousy mother. I wince as I say that, because I know she never intended to be a lousy mother.

Neither of my parents ever mentioned the degenerative brain disease my mother suffered from, even though she was sometimes hospitalized for months at a time. Our housekeeper told me, when I was grown, that my mother had told her, "When the children come home from school, sit and listen to them because I can't." My mother was frail, inconsistent, inadequate—but also devoted.

I keep asking myself whether I qualify as a motherless mother. I feel like one, but all those years there was the flesh-and-blood woman who gave birth to me. And if anyone were to ask her if she loved her child, I know she would answer, honestly, "Yes." What was going on to make me doubt a mother's love?

A mother's love for her child is so sacred, culturally and psychologically, that to question it can bring confusion and shame to those who didn't feel it. I interviewed one woman who assured me she had "a good mother," but as our conversation continued she told me she grew up feeling "left out." "My mother opened her heart to many people and was very socially adept," she said, "but she wouldn't sit down and read a book to us. I don't ever remember being held or rocked." Another woman who volunteered through an e-mail network to fill out my questionnaire eventually called to say she couldn't do it. A sense of guilt and betrayal overcame her every time she approached questions that asked her to describe or evaluate her mother's care of her as a child.

Other women told me that expressing their thoughts and feelings about their mothers as role models was cathartic. They saw it as an opportunity to sit with and work through snarls in the weave of their lives. Again and again women showed me that an inadequate mother can sometimes be the hard stone on which a fine person and parent is polished.

Often I left interviews full of respect for the women I talked to, for what they have overcome and created in their lives, for their resolute courage and integrity. They revealed not only their pain but sometimes their good humor. One night, at an Italian restaurant, I had dinner with a small group of women, most of them strangers to me, and we talked of mothers. One spoke of her "me, me, me" mother who was unable to acknowledge the problems, concerns and joys of others. "Hey," piped up another, "we should get our moms together and let them talk over each other." The women who participated in my research showed me again and again that there's no formula for what it is to be a motherless mother.

We get one chance at a secure childhood with our mothers and if that fails, for whatever reasons, the only sure thing is that we can't retrieve it. But I have learned that we can turn around, away from the past and toward a future with our own children. Many of the women I spoke to have moved beyond the wounds, blatant and subtle, of childhood to take on mothering as a positive life development. They no longer identify themselves as wounded daughters but as healing mothers. They have released their potential to become the mothers they wish to be and the ones their children deserve.

Searching for an answer to the question, "How do I become a good mother to my children without having been well-mothered myself?" has kept me on the journey toward freedom from the past. It's a journey that requires looking back, looking inward and looking ahead. It leads to finding the smart mother within who can parent with love and thought. And the blessing is this: In mothering our children well, we find healing for ourselves.

CHAPTER TWO

Mothers Matter

... there she was, in the very centre of that great Cathedral space which was childhood; there she was from the very first.
—Virginia Woolf

I have a memory from my teenage years of lying on the bathroom floor suffering from severe menstrual cramps. Too ill to stand and certainly too ill to go to school, I lay pale-faced and clammy, curled in a fetal position, waiting for the pain to pass. My grandmother, with whom I lived, opened the door and stood looking at me, her face pinched with concern. "Are you okay?" she asked. I murmured, "No." She stood another moment and then went away.

My grandmother seldom touched me. She seldom, in any situation, offered warmth or comfort. Anxiety, above all else, characterized her caregiving. She had nursed her only child, my mother, during the last months of her life as she lay immobile, unable to draw a breath unaided. My mother then died one restless April afternoon, while my brother and I sat at our desks in school. Our father fled soon after her funeral, and our grandmother was then charged with rearing me and my brother.

The last time my mother held me in her arms I was four. She was twenty-eight when polio rendered her paralyzed from the neck down. I didn't see her for a year while she struggled in hospitals, beyond rehabilitation and hope. When she came home to us, kept alive by breathing machines, she was placed in the dining room. From there she watched the fractured lives of her children, parents and, on occasion, husband, carried out in the kitchen and living room. One of the particularly cruel aspects of polio is that it steals motion without taking sensation. My mother could feel my breath on her arm as I stood next to her high bed, she could feel her own menstrual cramps, but she could not respond. She could not touch me and I was forbidden, by my grandmother, to touch her, for fear I would cause her pain.

These peculiar circumstances took from me a mother's touch. When I became a mother myself, I considered the meaning of this deprivation and others accumulated during the years my mother lay out of reach, along with those that came later, when I lived under the sway of my grandmother and the two stepmothers who made brief appearances in my life. I saw that I could not rely on my own experiences as a child to guide me with my children. My fear was that the distorted images and experiences of "mother" from my childhood would lead me to fail my children in critical ways. Might I, too, miss the mark with something fundamental, something as rudimentary as touch? I knew I had to search beyond my own experience for answers to my questions about what mothers are meant to be and do.

At its most basic level, the role of mother (or her substitutes) is biological: Her close attention to her newborns keeps them alive. Born before their brains are finished, human babies require intense care for a protracted time. One primate anatomist and paleontologist claims that human gestation is twenty-one months—nine in utero and a year outside. *Nine months in the womb, nine months in the arms* is what other mothers, none of them paleontologists, instructed me when my first child was born. Through evolutionary design babies are meant to be part of "an intimate physical dyad with an adult," says Cornell anthropologist Meredith Small. "Cross-cultural studies, observations of non-human primates, and historical fact all combine to paint a portrait of a human infant entwined with a parent."

This entanglement of mothers and babies isn't, of course, merely physical. While babies are fed and kept warm in the protective arms of mother, they're learning what it is to be human and to be in relationship with others. Daniel Stern, a psychoanalytically trained psychiatrist, has been in the forefront of research on infant behavior. He says that at six months the infant emerges as a social human being, learning in those first months such moves of social interaction as how to invite his mother to play and how to avoid her attention. A woman nursing her four-month-old leans her head toward the child, who drops the nipple and meets her gaze; then the two begin an exchange of smiles, noises, imitations. After a couple of minutes, the baby's eyes droop and he turns back to the nipple. Stern and his colleagues filmed many mothers and infants in such typical situations and then analyzed the interactions and developing relationships in slow motion. Stern contends that these everyday moments of "free play" are crucial experiences in teaching the infant to join in human events. "This biologically designed choreography," Stern wrote, "will serve as a prototype for all his later interpersonal exchanges."

That first relationship between mother and baby, with all its minute and mundane detail, provides the basis for the child's learning to relate to society and points the infant toward the uniquely human task of becoming "I." And in that first relationship the seeds of lifelong discontent can also be sown.

Over the course of a long afternoon I listened as a woman named Kit Bishop revealed keen insight into herself, her mother and her two school-age children. Those insights, gleaned from years of effort in therapy, have helped her make sense of her relationship with her mother. Kit grew up in one of those outwardly trouble-free families: handsome colonial house in a good neighborhood, stay-at-home mom, three kids, Dad a well-paid executive. But beneath the pleasant surface, Kit's mother was cold, rigid and strict. "My husband once told me," Kit said, "that my mother doesn't have a maternal bone in her body. And he's right."

Kit arrived for our appointment wearing a slouchy sweater in a shade of pink that red-haired women like herself usually steer clear of, but it suited her well. That, along with her soft leather mules and quirky eyeglasses, made her look every bit the sophisticated, Ivy League–educated woman that she is. A corporate trainer, Kit drastically cut back on her work when her children, who are less than a year apart in age, were infants. Sitting across from me in a comfortable chair in her home office, she confessed she'd been wary about being interviewed for a book. She and her mother, she said, had been getting along pretty well lately and the prospect of her mother reading Kit's complaints about her was disconcerting. "I was stewing about this at home last night," Kit said, "and my husband, ever the realist, pointed out that though my mother is an avid reader the chances that she'd pick up a book on mothering are mighty slim."

Kit, the eldest of three children and the only girl, said that her mother had not connected with her from the very beginning. "I've never known her to be passionate about anything," Kit said, "including her children. All the time I was growing up my mother simply couldn't see what people needed from her. She always put her own needs first. She told me once that when I was a baby she would lock me in my bedroom so I would be 'safe,' and then she'd take a nap while I screamed." Kit crossed her legs and took a sip of her coffee. Her face tightened as she seemed to collect her thoughts before going on.

"She came to visit us soon after our son was born. One day I was nursing him while she sat on the couch watching, and pretty soon she was crying. I asked what was wrong and she said, 'I wasn't a good mother. I did so much wrong.'

"So I pressed her, 'Like *what?* Get specific. I want to know these things!' And she told me she couldn't even remember giving me and my brothers bottles. 'I must have held my babies in my arms,' she said, 'but I don't remember it. I can't bear to think of that, watching you.'

"Now almost every time she's with us, she says something like that, like, 'I can't believe I didn't do that.' Watching me breast-feed is what got to her the most, but just watching me in my everyday interactions with my children can sometimes turn her maudlin. I suppose it might be gratifying to think she's learning something from me about how to relate to people, but truthfully, I'm horrified. It just cements for me an awareness of all I didn't get from her."

What Kit didn't get from her mother, from that crucial first relationship, was the warm, consistent, responsive care that rests at the core of good mothering.

Mothers, Babies and Love

In a fascinating paper first published in 1939 just before her death at age forty-one, Hungarian psychoanalyst Alice Balint, herself a mother, distilled the mother-child relationship to a single significant idea. She made a distinction between the love mothers and babies hold for each other. Balint, who has been called a forerunner of Winnicott, wrote that the infant's love is remote from reality. To the infant "the ideal mother [has] no interests of her own." Balint was not saying that a mother shouldn't have interests of her own, but that the infant's love rests on complete harmony between parent and child. A young child might be distressed if her mother becomes ill, not because the child is concerned for her, but because the child's well-being requires the mother's presence. The infant's life depends absolutely on some other human being who wants to keep that child alive. This dependency is nothing exotic, but what any of us observes between babies and their caregivers on buses and park benches.

The love the mother holds for the child, according to Balint, is the *almost* perfect counterpoint to the child's love for the mother. Just as the mother is to the child, the child is to the mother an object of gratification, beginning with the infant's dependency on the mother's body, which pleases them both. The two enjoy a mutuality rooted in biology and psychology. And like love for the mother, mother's love has a foot set firmly in fantasy. "[J]ust as the child does not recognize the separate identity of the mother, so the mother looks upon her child as part of herself whose interests are identical with her own," wrote Balint. Think of a mother with her little one strapped to her chest as she moves through the grocery store, her heartbeat and the baby's mingling.

This early devotion between the tiny child and the mother gives rise to idealized notions of maternal love. When all goes well, there is a time, as psychologist Robert Karen says, when "all the corny things ever recited about mother-love seem to glow with a truth untarnished by the ironies, failings, and complexities of later years." Change must come, however, to even the most idyllic mother-child pair, because they are *not* one, because their needs *are* different. That's why Balint calls mother love the *almost* perfect counterpoint to the child's love. The essential, and heartbreaking, difference between mother love and love for the mother is that the child has but one unique, irreplaceable mother, but a mother can spread her love among multiple children. Though it would be a rare mother indeed who considered any of her children to be expendable, from the child's point of view she *acts* as if she does when she turns her attention elsewhere—when, for example, she jumps up from playing with a toddler to tend the baby who has awakened from a nap.

Even after that first mutuality wears thin—when a sibling arrives or the mother goes to work or otherwise demonstrates that this child is not the whole of her universe—the child continues to cling to her, knowing no other love. Hating her or abandoning her is no solution to the heartbreak because the child needs her. Instead, reality enters the child's emotional life, as the child faces the task of loving and being loved in new ways.

While interviewing a woman whose children are young adults now, I heard her make a comment that Balint herself would likely have made. I asked this woman how she would describe a good mother, and after a moment she said, "There's the child's side and the mother's side of that question." That's Balint's theory in a nutshell. This mother went on to elaborate: "When children are small they want what they want, and you're good if you give it to them. But as they get older the most difficult aspect of mothering becomes drawing a line between nurturing, protecting and supporting on one side, and helping them establish independence and responsibility. The balance with every child is different."

In Alice Balint's distinction between the mother's love and the child's love, I found a thought that has come to guide me in my reflections on the mothering I received and the mothering I try to provide my children. It's nothing more than the simple but essential truth that in all situations, from the child's birth on, there are always two points of view: the mother's and the child's. Children can't be expected to appreciate this distinction, but mothers can. A crucial missing piece for me in the care I received from my grandmother was that she couldn't see my point of view. Her thinking simply didn't run in the direction of wondering, "How do you feel? What does this mean to you? How do my actions affect you?" I don't know whether trying to see the world from my vantage point didn't interest her, whether it felt too risky and intimate, or whether it simply never occurred to her. I wonder now if coming upon me on the bathroom floor that long-ago day triggered memories of the helplessness she felt in the face of my mother's dire illness. I don't know. I only know that under her care I heard in countless subtle and often unspoken ways that I must *do* and *be* according to her dictates, not mine. Balint said that *both* mother and child eventually must come to see their desires and themselves as distinct. I think that my grandmother didn't want me to be separate. I think she saw me as an appendage—a recalcitrant, unruly appendage. And I, as a confused and needy child, wanted to comply but could never quite twist myself into the mold she desired.

No one looking in on us in those years, however—my grandparents, my brother and me, the four of us living in our red brick bungalow—would have thought anything was wrong. As is often the case, what can be seen on the outside doesn't necessarily reflect what is felt by a specific child inside the family.

What Children Need

A woman who had just become a grandmother for the first time was looking back with satisfaction on her child-rearing years when she said to me, "I had three goals in mind: my children would feel safe at home; they would feel loved; and they would feel good about themselves." I don't know whether this woman, a musician, had read in the field of human development, but I recognized in her goals for mothering the familiar hierarchy of needs identified by Abraham H. Maslow. A pioneer thinker in humanistic psychology, Maslow ranked five sets of needs—physiological, safety, love, esteem and self-actualization—as the primary motivators for behavior. He contended that when a need is fairly well satisfied, the next higher one becomes the focus of a person's drives.

When looked at through the lens of mothering, Maslow's hierarchy becomes a short answer to the question, "What does a mother do?" It's this: She ensures that her child's lower needs are met so that the higher ones can emerge, and then she helps fill those. In the end, she sends into the world adults who, on their own, can reach for self-actualization. I find this five-part rubric appealing and very useful in trying to tease out just what was amiss in the care I and so many of the women in my research received as children.

In Maslow's model the lowest needs are physiological, such as for food, drink and rest. From the moment of birth, a child's urgent need for suckling and swaddling is obvious.

The next requirement is for safety, which in adults is generally sought through choosing the familiar over the unfamiliar. Science, religion and philosophy, which provide organized views of the universe, can also satisfy safety-seeking for adults, by assuring them that order, not chaos, reigns. Children, however, need physical safety first—protection from being dropped or handled roughly or exposed to sudden or harsh stimulation. Most children also seek the safety of routine, which persuades them of the world's predictability and orderliness. Faced with injustice and inconsistency, children become anxious. They want to know they can count on life around them to unfold without unexpected, unmanageable or dangerous events happening. If that fails, they want the assurance of all-powerful parents who will shield them from harm.

Children need safety so desperately that even if parents don't shield them from harm, even if the parents themselves are the source of pain, children persist in looking to them, especially mother, for protection. It has been more than ten years since I first read *Necessary Losses*, Judith Viorst's psychoanalytic exploration of what we must give up in order to mature, and yet I still remember the haunting illustration of this blind persistence that opens her book. She tells of a boy lying in a hospital bed and crying for his mother, frightened and in pain, with burns covering almost half his body. Someone has doused him with alcohol and then set him on fire. That someone is his mother. "Separation from mother is worse than being in her arms when the bombs are exploding. Separation from mother is sometimes worse than being with her when she is the bomb," Viorst writes. "For the presence of mother—our mother—stands for safety. Fear of her loss is the earliest terror we know."

This loyalty derived from a primal fear helps explain the anxiety that arises in many women when they contemplate the shortcomings of their mothers. Mother is needed so powerfully that sometimes it's easier to invent her than to see her clearly. One woman I interviewed described a childhood of growing up in a large, poor family in which both her parents were overworked and exhausted. As a girl, she faked illnesses to get attention. "I felt invisible," she said. As we talked about her childhood and her relationship with her children now, I asked her to tell me more about her mother. She sat silently a moment and then said slowly: "I had an odd reaction to that request. I thought, 'Should I think of my romanticized mother or my real mother?'" The attentive mother of her imagination stood, in her mind, alongside the real mother of her experience.

Love needs, which include giving and receiving love and affection and having a sense of belonging, come after physiological and safety needs. An infant's first passion is for mother, and from this early, intimate attraction the child begins to learn the ways of love. Fulfilling the need to love and be loved can be the most daunting, complex task of a life. "In our society," wrote Maslow, "the thwarting of these needs is the most commonly found core in cases of maladjustment and more severe psychopathy." When circumstances are right, however, the most straightforward of human experiences is to love a child and to accept the child's love. One woman's eight-year-old son put it this way on his Mother's Day card: "I learn to love when you take care of me." Love requires not perfection from mother or child, but openness and willingness. "The miracle is that your children will love you with all your imperfections if you can do the same for them," says Harriet Lerner, a psychologist and mother of two grown sons.

We knew we were loved. My mother listened to me when I needed to talk. She made me feel good about myself. During junior high school I was skinny, with frizzy hair and ugly glasses, but she kept telling me how cute I was. As I grew up she supported my ambitions and activities. When I married a man outside my religion, some family members temporarily disowned me, but she stood by me.

I was very close to my mother, though I didn't tell her everything. I felt she was always there. I could go to her and fall apart and say 'Everything is going wrong and I'm messing up,' and she would just love me.

After physiological, safety and love needs comes the desire all humans have for self-respect and a sense of being respected by others. Satisfaction of this need, according to Maslow, leads to a sense of worth, of capability and of being useful and necessary. Thwarting of these needs produces feelings of inferiority and helplessness. A child, above all, needs to feel valued and respected by primary caregivers. I used to be puzzled by the underlying insecurity of a man I once knew who was outwardly accomplished; he was artistic and kind, a fine businessman who had accumulated enough wealth to retire at midlife, and was handsome besides. And then I met his mother. Not ten minutes into our acquaintance, she began criticizing her son. We were in a summer home he had renovated in what I found to be a magazine-perfect way, yet his mother pulled me around showing me all she didn't like, saying he'd never finish this project or that, and could I believe he had chosen *that* floor covering? I felt I understood my friend better after that surprising encounter. He couldn't feel good about his accomplishments with his mother chipping away at them and him.

My friend's experience contrasts starkly with that of a woman who told me that her mother, whom she loves, respects and knows well, "took the fear out of my life. Mother encouraged me and supported me. I always heard, 'You're going to be great, go ahead and do it! Hang in there.'" And a twenty-three-year-old extolled "the world's best mother," her own: "I can truly say that she is my best friend. I cannot go a day or two without talking to her. She's the person I confide in. She's my support."

People who have been satisfied in their needs throughout their lives, but especially in the first two years, tend to develop a healthy character and to remain secure and strong in the face of whatever threatens. With those lower needs answered, they experience a desire for self-fulfillment, a pull toward what Maslow called self-actualization. They long to be and strive toward being all they are capable of becoming. Self-actualized people are human beings at their best.

Most people, however, live their lives only partly satisfied in the first four needs. For some, the deprivations are such that they spend adulthood searching for the love and approval they didn't get as children, struggling to feel safe or respected.

I heard threads of these deprivations in the stories told by a woman named Hannah Frank. On the winter morning I showed up at her Colorado home to interview her, she greeted me at the door and ushered me into the entry hall of her spacious house. As I followed her past the living room, I glimpsed art and artifacts that appeared to be gathered from faraway places, a concert grand piano, lots of books and a massive flagstone fireplace. Once in the kitchen, Hannah went back to clearing and stacking the breakfast dishes, all the while chatting with me and introducing her husband, an affable retired college professor. Her soft, ample figure, the lines on her face and her wash-and-wear clothing gave Hannah a relaxed air, but her sparkling, intelligent eyes looked straight into mine when we sat down to talk at her dining room table.

Warmed by slanted sunlight and the view out to a tawny mountainside, I listened as Hannah, mother to four biological children and three stepchildren and grandmother to twelve, began to tell me her history. I already knew, from the woman who had suggested I meet Hannah, that she had grown up without her own mother and had become a dedicated, loving parent to her many children. Hannah told me that after her parents divorced, when Hannah was five, her father gained custody of her and her brother, and her mother disappeared.

"The Depression," she said, "kept my father away for long periods of time. My brother and I lived mainly in informal foster families and a boarding school. I only saw my mother three or four times after she ran off, each time briefly. Once, when I was seven or so, my mother came to visit the farm where my brother and I were living. When I saw her, I climbed a tree and pretended not to know her, but I knew who she was." Here Hannah chuckled and gestured with her hand the twisting of a knife. Recounting her checkered childhood, she told me a story about getting into trouble when she was in eighth grade and living in a Catholic boarding school.

"One Sunday afternoon a bunch of us, boys and girls, took off and caused a scandal by breaking two rules at once: being unsupervised with the opposite sex and leaving without permission. The nuns brought us back, and later one of them took me aside to scold me and said, 'All you care about is a pair of men's pants and what's underneath them!' "

I expected Hannah to grin at this memory, but instead she leaned her chin on her hand and smiled wanly, saying: "And I've been thinking that maybe Sister Josephine was partly right. I spent a lot of my young adulthood looking not for sex from the men in my life but for the affection I didn't get from my mother." Unlike Hannah, some people who were wounded in childhood go all through life searching for that love but never realize the root of their discontent.

In her book *The Drama of the Gifted Child*, first published under the more apt title *Prisoners of Childhood*, Alice Miller addressed that need children have to be the focus of their mothers' attention. Miller asks us to consider what a different world it would be "if the majority of babies had the chance to rule over their mothers like *paschas* and to be coddled by them, without having to concern themselves with their mothers' needs too early." I find it hard to picture what that world would be, but I know I have often wondered for myself who I might have been and what I might have done had I not spent so much energy trying to fill holes left empty by childhood. And I've heard other women, including Hannah, say something similar. In her seventies now, with her first marriage (to the father of her four biological children) far behind her and with her career as a social worker completed, she's nestled into that gracious home with her husband of thirty-five years whom she calls "this wonderful man." She's educated and widely traveled and lives a life rich in deeply satisfying family relationships. Still, she looks back, wondering what her life might have been like with a mother to watch over her. "Maybe I wouldn't be a happier person, but I might have accomplished more," she said. "No one ever talked to me about goals, so I never had a goal. I see all the things that women accomplish now and I think I might have done more with my life. I also wonder whether I might have made a better choice about a first husband. But a very insecure childhood limited me."

Even though Hannah considers herself a happy person, and by all outward signs she leads a fulfilled and fulfilling life, these many decades after her mother left home, she's still aware of the love, security and respect she missed in childhood.

I was reminded in a powerful way of the range of circumstances that confront mothers and the breadth of what might be considered "providing for one's children" when reading James McBride's memoir *The Color of Water*, in which he relates growing up in New York City the eighth of twelve children born to a twice-widowed woman. McBride describes a wild and chaotic home life. "It was kill or be killed in my house," he wrote, "and Mommy understood that, in fact created the system. You were left to your own devices or so you thought until you were at your very wits' end, at which time she would step in and rescue you." The children hid food from one another, ate from jars and cans, bought junk food when they got money, shared a single washcloth and toothbrush and lived with a German shepherd who bit them all and freely used the house as his toilet. His mounds of feces would sit until dried, then someone would kick them under a radiator. And yet, McBride writes, "we thrived on thought, books, music, and art, which she fed to us instead of food."

Those dozen McBride children needed more to eat than they got, needed more order and physical comfort; but children can clearly get by with far fewer comforts than are provided in most middle-class American homes. How little love and respect they can survive on is harder to determine, and must bend to individual differences. What each of us needs, Maslow took pains to point out, can vary. Some people, for instance, strive more for esteem than for love; some powerfully creative people strive toward their art despite lack of other satisfactions. And, certainly, some people get stuck at the very basic needs for good reasons. A chronically homeless person, for instance, might eventually strive no further than to find today's meal and a warm place to sleep.

When a parent fails to provide food, shelter and safety from physical harm, most anyone looking in can see her deficiencies. But the spectrum of what an individual child can tolerate in unfulfilled needs is wide and seldom obvious. Many women who feel under-mothered are confused by their dissatisfactions and criticisms of their mothers, because the care they received looked appropriate. Unlike James McBride's mother, their mothers provided toothbrushes, did their best to house-train the dog and served dinner at the table.

No matter what else a mother might provide, however, if she skimps on the subtle, invisible needs of love and respect, her children suffer. Often that suffering is compounded by the discrepancies between the visible, surface care the children received, which was good or at least adequate, and what it *felt* like to be that particular child of that particular mother.

* * *

My grandmother was a commendable housewife who enjoyed the role and dedicated herself to perfecting her homemaking skills. She gardened, cooked, baked, sewed, decorated, crocheted, cleaned and rearranged furniture with unflagging energy. When I was in elementary school she made matching dresses for me and my best friend and taught me to sew. I tossed my dirty clothes down the laundry chute, and they soon reappeared in my closet clean, pressed, mended and ready to wear again. She painted my bedroom lavender and white. When she baked pies she saved the scraps of dough, then baked them with cinnamon sugar for me.

She made a home with every detail in place except for this: I didn't feel safe. She shopped, cooked and set the table, but I sat through many meals pointedly ignored, given the "silent treatment," often for days, often not knowing precisely what my transgression was. Now I know that it was always some version of my having left her, such as going to a slumber party with my girlfriends, dating one boy, dating lots of boys, spending all day at the swimming pool. I would creep down the hall after a night out with friends to tell her I was home, and she would turn her back to me. In the morning we would eat toast and grapefruit in silence.

She set this pattern for us soon after my mother died. One late afternoon the next winter, when I was seven, she took me with her to a downtown department store. I grew bored and wandered away, attracted by the greeting card aisle. After what must have been a long while I realized that I didn't know where my grandmother was and that it had grown dark outside. I rushed around the store, searching, and circled back to the door we had come in. I'll never forget catching sight of her white, grim face, luminous in the car window as she slowly drove down the street. I rushed out, cowed and trembling, to flag her down. She let me in and drove home without a word.

No number of red roses in the garden or oatmeal cookies in the jar made me feel secure with her. I was always aware that she could put me out—of her home, her affection, her awareness—at will. Living with her was like living with a menacing, fickle animal. I had to be alert to her moods and emotions. I had to tend to her, stroking, wooing, always demonstrating my allegiance. This is clear to me now, but only now. All the years I lived with her, and for many afterward, I couldn't make sense of the dissonance between what I saw and what I felt. She had friends who thought her kind and helpful, and to whom she *was* kind and helpful. She gave me the quarters she won in her bridge games. I never heard her speak a cross word to my grandfather. She drank only the occasional cocktail and seldom went out at night for any purpose. Every Sunday she went to Mass, dipping her fingers in the holy water, accepting the communion wafer, murmuring the responses in the liturgy. I, too, went to Mass and to confession, but it was *her* forgiveness I wanted. Our silences ended with my going to her, offering capitulation, but without the maturity or understanding to articulate the question to which I so badly needed an answer: "Why is it so hard to be kind to me?" Instead, I would ask: "May I do your hair for your luncheon?" She would sit at the bathroom sink under the fluorescent light with me behind her, teasing her soft gray and white hair into a smooth crown. With my fingers I would beg her to forgive me, to turn her face to me, to see me.

Attachments

One day an elderly woman, leaning on her daughter's arm, came into my husband's photography lab. She carried an old, faded picture of a large group of people. Could he, she wanted to know, single out this one tiny head, a woman, and enlarge it? A relative had unearthed this long-lost photo that included the woman's mother, who had died giving birth to her. "I have never seen my mother's face," the old woman said, and began to weep there at the counter, holding the photograph.

* * *

The unfolding understanding of the complex attraction between mother and child took a leap forward in the second half
of the last century with the work of attachment theorists, both
clinicians and researchers, who delved deep into the mechanics
and purpose of the mother-child relationship. Attachment in
psychology refers not to the popular concept of affection, but to
a unique connection the child has to one or more caregivers.
During infancy and early childhood, the attachment figure is the
child's "solution" to potentially life-threatening circumstances,
the one or ones the child depends on with that absoluteness Alice
Balint described.

Viewed in the context of Maslow's hierarchy of needs, attachment theory demonstrates how and why and whether a
caregiver is able to meet a child's need for safety, esteem and,
most especially, love. Love gone awry is attachment gone awry.

The originator of attachment theory was British psychoanalyst and child psychiatrist John Bowlby, a seminal thinker in
the field of human development. Through studying mothers
and babies and looking at what happens to them when separated, he changed the way people thought about what children
require for emotional development. Bowlby was the first to link
anthropology and psychoanalytic thought, and when he made
that link he was able to demonstrate that infants come into the
world biologically primed to seek a trusted other who will rescue them from their extreme vulnerability. They don't want to
be alone; they want to be held and kept safe; they want a caregiver who will make them feel loved. This inclination toward
creating intimate bonds with specific others is basic to human
nature, beginning at birth and continuing to old age.

In the early 1960s, Mary Ainsworth, a Canadian psychologist who had worked with Bowlby, began research on babies at
Johns Hopkins University. She observed mothers and children
in the diverse locations of Baltimore and Uganda, paying atten-

tion to how mothers responded to their infants with feeding, crying, eye contact, cuddling, smiling. What she learned dramatically shifted ideas about the mother-child nexus in psychology, psychiatry and psychoanalysis and brought Bowlby and attachment theory into mainstream thinking. With her research, Ainsworth provided the first scientific evidence for what had only been theory before: that the warm, sensitively attuned and reliable mother provides her baby with a "secure base," which allows the child to go forth and explore the world. Ainsworth demonstrated that this secure attachment between parent and child is crucially important to the child's psychological development. A sensitive, responsive and dependable mothering style, she found, leads to emotional health and allows the child to be confident, secure and able to form satisfying relationships with others. (The term *secure,* whether in reference to an infant, child or adult, describes the person's confidence that a protective, supportive figure will be accessible and available.) A child with a secure base is one whose love, esteem and safety needs are being met.

By the end of my morning with Hannah Frank we had covered her seven decades of life, including her fifteen-year first marriage, her remarriage, her going back to college to finish her bachelor's degree, her completion of a master's degree in her early forties, her regrets and joys, and then circled back to her mother. I asked whether she had any photographs of her. Hannah had described her mother as unstable, a beautiful, vague woman who seemed "not really present." Hannah had remained close to her father, despite his frequent absences, but she saw her mother only a few isolated times. Once was that day she spied her from a tree perch. Another came decades later when her mother came to visit Hannah as an adult.

"She took my hand and said, 'At last, I've found my little girl!' I wanted to throw up, it was so inappropriate, so sentimental,"

Hannah said. "My mother had been living in a nearby town for *years* without ever letting me know she was there."

While Hannah went to collect photographs, I sat at her dining table, soaking in the comfort of her home and chatting with her husband, who had come by to see how we were doing. Soon Hannah was back with a handful of old photos, including a large portrait of her mother, taken in about 1940, several years after her mother ran off with her husband's best friend. It showed a woman studied in her glamour. I searched for resemblance between gray-haired Hannah, who exudes ease, nurturance and a natural elegance, and the woman in the picture, who wore a high-necked dress, buttoned down the back, her slick, wavy hair swept from her face. She was in profile, looking back over her shoulder, not at the camera but literally down her gorgeous, patrician nose. Her beauty made believable the other story, or "legend," Hannah had heard about her, that she and her lover had fled to a ski resort and there she met a Frenchman who was on his honeymoon; she took him as a lover and ran away again. Hannah had a couple of other photos from her childhood, but only one of her with her mother. She handed that to me, and after a glance, I shot her a questioning look.

"I don't want to read too much into this," she said. Her mother stands facing the camera, in pumps and a suit. She's holding the baby Hannah in one arm, open and away from her body. It was hard to say whether she was showing her child to the camera or was truly as awkward with an infant as she appeared. As Hannah and I bent forward to study the picture, our shoulders touched and together we sighed. I wondered whether she was thinking, as I was, that nobody who had but one photo of herself and her mother would choose this one. No one can know what Hannah's mother had been thinking or feeling about her baby the day that picture was snapped, but as time went on she proved herself unwilling or incapable of being Hannah's secure base.

Before I left, Hannah pulled out one more picture. It was a typical formal family portrait with its smiles, Sunday clothes and tidy hair, with one startling difference. Hannah and her younger brother, perhaps seven and eight then, sit side by side in front of their father, who is arranged awkwardly to one side. Next to him, behind the children, is a looming white space. Hannah calls this "the missing mother photo." Earlier she had talked to me of "that hole in you where something is missing" and had said, "There's a part of me that's always incredibly sad. I'm very aware of it, and I can get to it immediately."

As I was leaving, Hannah and I stood at her front door chatting just a bit more, when she asked, head cocked, "Why a book about mothers?"

"My mother died when I was six, from polio, and I was reared by my maternal grandparents."

She put a hand on my arm, lifted her eyebrows and said, "Et tu, Kathryn?"

Yes, me too. After leaving Hannah's home, I thought about how women such as Hannah and me share the "missing mother" photo, but also how in our unusual stories of actual mother loss there exist emotional similarities to women whose mothers "walked out" by becoming depressed, distracted, withdrawn, overwhelmed, unwilling or inadequate. I thought about how the message, "I am not here for you," can be said through physical absence, but also through a mother's treatment of her daughter, as with the distance Kit Bishop's mother kept between them. There are many routes, I thought, to becoming a woman who feels like a motherless mother.

For some women the route is little understood, shrouded by deceptive external details. But the emotion is clear. One such woman, an only child, told me that she had been cleaning out her widowed mother's basement in preparation for helping her move to an apartment and had found a dusty box of eight-millimeter film cans.

"I took them home and watched reel after reel in amazement. There I was looking happy, thriving, bubbly. And there was my father, and there was my mother with her endearing mannerisms. She was so cute and perky with her perfect little body, well dressed in put-together outfits, cigarette in hand. There's a whole reel of me riding my horse. Think of it—parents standing in fields taking movies of their daughter on her horse. It looked so *right,* idyllic even. But what you can't see is the underlying emotion.

"At what point did the wheels fall off our little family wagon? Or were they ever on? You can't see in these films the way my mother constantly let me know that I was a big mistake, that her life wasn't suppose to include me. You can't see in these films the point at which I came to be so well aware that I had to be on my guard against being like her when I was grown up. It happened gradually, daily, over time."

Another woman whose mother was physically present throughout her childhood and who is still alive said this:

"My husband and friends are great support to me, but I'm sometimes nagged by a feeling of missing out on something important. You know how sometimes you're a little depressed over some turn of events or for no good reason, and you want to talk but not to a friend because you know you should be able to handle this alone? Well, some people have a *mother* they can go to and say, 'You know, Mom, this is going on and I feel like a failure.' And she'll say, 'No wonder you feel that way. I'm here for you, I love you and never forget you're a good person who makes good decisions.'

"You know you're being ridiculous, but it's okay because it's *Mom* you're talking to. I do this for my children all the time. And once in a while, I wish I had a mom to do it for me."

Many of us carry around some version of "the missing mother photo," the symbol of Hannah's enduring sense of loss. We missed out on the full measure of love and approval we needed from our mothers. For some of us, the sturdy foundation that childhood is meant to be forms instead an unreliable structure, an insecure base.

The repercussions of secure attachment extend far into an individual's life. Children who are securely attached to a caregiver are often friendly, cheerful, resilient and confident and become adults who create stable marriages and who have access to a wide range of emotions and memories. They are flexible rather than rigid, and thus have the ability to acknowledge having more than one emotion at a time, to imagine how feelings might change and to recognize that different people can feel differently in the same situation. Children who grow up without a secure base, however, find life more difficult, especially when it comes to relationships.

Although attachment theory first focused on infancy, Bowlby contended that parent-child attachment continues to be important throughout childhood and into early adulthood, saying that "an unthinking confidence in the unfailing accessibility and support of attachment figures is the bedrock on which stable and self-reliant personalities are built." A central point in Bowlby's concept of parenting is that parents provide a secure base that a child can move away from and return to knowing she will be welcomed, "nourished physically and emotionally, comforted if distressed, reassured if frightened." Much of the time the role of the parent is a waiting one, especially as the child reaches adolescence and her excursions range wider and for longer time periods, but, in the words of Bowlby, "it is none the less vital for that."

Research has shown that secure adolescents regard a parent, usually the mother, as their primary attachment figure and can communicate well with her. They can discuss potentially stressful and contentious topics more constructively than insecure teens, and when they disagree with their mothers they are able to concentrate on problem solving, rather than on attacking her or accusing her of attacking them. One study of college students suggests that a secure base at home goes on helping young adults by giving them the strength to take risks, to face challenge and change, to form new attachments and to become a secure base to their own children.

Is there a mother who can learn about attachment and not wonder about her bond with her children? Likely not. I certainly found myself trying to remember how my toddlers behaved. Did they, like the securely attached children in the studies, show confidence in my availability, watch me leave with distress and greet me eagerly on my return? Were they readily comforted by my embrace? Mostly, I'd say, but not infallibly. And who can learn of attachment theory and not wonder about her attachment to her own mother?

Secure mother-child attachment is just one of three patterns Ainsworth identified. The other two fall under a general shorthand of "anxious" or "insecure." The behavior of anxious mothers, as summarized by psychologist Karen, ranges "from mean-spirited to merely cool, from chaotic to pleasantly incompetent." Some mothers who are unable to be a secure base for their children are, nonetheless, nice, well-meaning people who take pride in their babies and express love. Some are "good playmates or teachers"; some are "delighted by the positive qualities" they see in their children. These mothers may appear to be parenting well, and actually may be hitting some of the right notes, but what these mothers who foster insecure attachments have in common is "difficulty responding to the baby's attachment needs in a loving, attuned, and consistent way." These insecure attachments compound as the babies, not getting what they need, become more demanding and distressed, or whine and cling, and the mothers, unable to satisfy their children, become more annoyed and overwhelmed and a vicious circle ensues. Sometimes power struggles result and bring out a hostile and rejecting side of the mother. As many under-mothered women have experienced, a child becomes as definitively attached to an inadequate parent, even a battering one, as to a sensitively responsive one. The trouble is, the attachment is insecure, with all its attendant ills.

Attachment theory has become a significant factor in the effort to determine what shapes emotional health, but it has its opponents. Some detractors separate nature and nurture and come down firmly on the side of nature; others find infants supremely adaptable and resilient. Some feminists have objected to Bowlby's emphasis on the mother's role in establishing the child's psychological health, even though Bowlby repeatedly said his theories refer to a "mother figure," not necessarily the biological mother. And by no means does subscribing to attachment theory count fathers out. No reputable theorist in psychological development would question the profound importance of men as fathers and husbands. They, too, act as role models to their children and with their love and affection engender in them a sense of being valued, protected and competent. Specifically from attachment research we know that husbands, with the emotional support they give their wives, affect the quality of the child's relationship to the mother. The percentage of children who are securely attached to the father is about the same as that of those attached to the mother, and children can have a secure attachment to one without the other. Children who are securely attached to both parents, however, tend to be the most confident, competent and empathetic.

And yet, mother is the child's first love, the lodestar; she's there at the beginning no matter what else follows. In my own experience of losing both my parents in childhood, I've always felt a greater tragedy in mother loss. Her absence has driven my life. Is that because my father didn't die when I was child, as she did, but only moved away? Perhaps I yearn for him less because he lived long enough to disappoint me. He stayed on the periphery of my life, married repeatedly, and struggled with alcoholism. I lost him with my mother's death as surely as I lost her, and yet nothing he did or didn't do was ever as painful as the unrequited love I've held for my mother. Every mother is both an individual and the bearer of an archetype. No matter who she is individually, she also embodies home, security, love, wisdom, nurturance.

The Ordinary Devoted Mother

Mother's role is so immense, Winnicott argued, that "every man or woman who is sane, every man or woman who has the feeling of being a person in the world, and for whom the world means something, every happy person, is in infinite debt to a woman." He contended that recognition of the contribution mothers make is withheld in part because people fear the dependence that mothers (and women in general) represent. It's easier to discount her influence and power than to admit a need for her.

Winnicott, who brought pediatrics, child development and psychoanalysis to bear on popular concepts of child care, concerned himself mostly with the mother's relationship to her baby in the first few months after birth. "I am trying," he said late in his life, "to draw attention to the immense contribution to the individual and to society that the ordinary good mother with her husband in support makes at the beginning, and which she does simply through being devoted to her infant." What this early, ordinary devotion does is allow the mother to be a catalyst in the child's development and to help the child become increasingly independent. Winnicott's life work was driven by the urge to speak to and appreciate the "ordinary good mother."

"Ordinary good mother" and "ordinary devoted mother" better express what children need, I think, than Winnicott's more famous phrase "good enough mother." It's obvious that no mother need be or can be perfect (though how much of her imperfection an individual child can tolerate is a matter of great debate). The phrase "good enough," however, can imply not only imperfect but minimal and can be easily brokered by those who want to shrug off the significance of mothers. The terms "good mother" and "devoted mother" set a higher standard and are, to my mind, better ones for mothers to focus on. Winnicott did not wish to induce gratitude, praise or guilt in or for mothers. He did, however, want to make clear the importance of a mother's devotion to her child.

One woman told me with a laugh that after the first few days of walking her daughter to kindergarten and walking back again to meet her at the end of the morning, the little girl came out the school door and asked, "Mommy, do you wait here for me?" Ordinary devotion creates the secure base and teaches the child to take her mother's dependability for granted. Mother is present in a way that provides comfort and safety to the child, not in a way that requires the child's attention and management.

When I asked women who identified themselves as daughters of good mothers to tell me what made them so good, I often heard of the prosaic, the "ordinary" devotion that Winnicott advocated.

It's hard for me to really put my finger on any one thing that made my mom such a good mom, and she still is. I think it boils down to just that my brother and I were about the most important thing in the world to her. I remember being shocked once in high school when I heard how a friend's mother talked to her. It was as if she just didn't care about her kids, like they were a bother to her.

My mother gave me the confidence to find my own way. She always stood behind me and made me feel like I could do anything. She also showed me that I didn't have to do things her way. Her religious beliefs were very strict and profoundly felt for her, but she didn't push it on others. She believed there were many ways to the truth and that spirituality is deeply personal. Her goal was that we be happy. I don't think she had other expectations for us.

How a mother goes about being that ordinary devoted mother, filling the child's basic needs, seems relatively straightforward when the child is an infant. But as the child grows, what it means to provide physical comfort, safety, love and respect becomes more vague, varied, complex and seemingly without end. The choices mothers make change with age, maturation and life situations, but, according to psychoanalyst Therese Benedek, "they do not end so long as the mother is in active interaction with her child."

A woman I interviewed who is still very much involved with her adult children is Melinda Morales. She is mother to seven sons, all grown now. Talking with her, I couldn't help but think that she looked far too young, with her plump, friendly face and thick black hair, to have brought so many children so far. This loquacious, high-energy woman, who ran a gas station to support her children after divorcing her husband of twenty years, has been rearing boys for nearly thirty-five years. I asked about her life since her youngest child recently moved out, expecting her to heave a sigh of relief. She did sigh, but it was resignation, not relief, I saw in her face. After three-plus decades, so far, of nurturing sons, it's becoming clear to her that she's in it for life. Though only fifty-three, she thinks longingly of retiring to a mountain cabin with space and time and quiet all around her, but she knows she'll never be able to live in isolation. "Oh, I'm *never* going to be done. Until the grave, you're it," she said. "Adult children aren't so very different from four- to six-year-olds. They need your love, sympathy, comfort and support."

Just before I interviewed her, Melinda had spent several days with one of her thirty-something sons and came home reminded of the fact that motherhood is forever. "He needed me to see everything new, do everything with him, put my stamp of approval on his family, activities and accomplishments. They always need their mother to say 'You did good.' " She considers herself to be still "working on" her sons, keeping them in line and educating them through her sassy humor and by developing relationships with their wives and girlfriends.

Relating colorful stories to me about life with her sons, Melinda evoked Alice Balint and her theories, reminding me that with any mother-child pair, two viewpoints, not one, frame their past together. In defining love of the mother, which rests on complete harmony of interests, Balint coined the phrase *naive egoism* to describe the infant's narrow view of mother. To the infant, recognition of the *actual* mother is superfluous, she says, because the infant's view is, " 'anyway, it wants the same as I do.' " This naive egoistic attitude, Balint went on to say, persists in most adults toward their own mothers. Even people who are "otherwise quite normal and capable of an 'adult,' altruistic form of love which acknowledges the interests of the partner" often go on seeing their mothers as the need-filler, rather than as a separate person with needs of her own.

I heard this view expressed about Melinda when she said that one of her sons casually mentioned recently that she should have gotten more education than her one year of college. Telling me this, she rolled her eyes and flung out an arm mockingly, "Gosh, you mean my whole life might have been about me! I could have stayed single, lived a decadent life in the south of France and had decent-looking thighs!" Clearly, that was not her destiny. Motherhood overwhelmed whatever else she might have wanted for herself, but at least one of her sons seemed to have missed that she'd been mighty busy for the past thirty years rearing and supporting children. Throughout that time, her house brimmed with her growing children and their friends, and she found that "everyone wants a mother—it's like sunshine to flowers." Even the children who were getting plenty of attention in their own homes lapped up her motherliness. And they still do.

In my reading and research I've kept an eye out for descriptions of how the "ordinary devoted mother" appears to the child, for glimpses into what it would have been to be the girl or woman standing on a secure base. Robert Karen summed up the mother's role for older children this way: "To be understood instead of punished, to express anger and not be rejected, to complain and be taken seriously, to be frightened and not have one's fear trivialized, to be depressed or unhappy and feel taken care of, to express a self-doubt and feel listened to and not judged— such experiences may be for later childhood what sensitive responsiveness to the baby's cries and other distress signals are for infancy." For the adult child's viewpoint, I turned to Kay Redfield Jamison, a professor of psychology at Johns Hopkins University School of Medicine and an expert on manic-depressive illness who wrote a now-famous book, *An Unquiet Mind*, about her personal journey with the disease. Jamison wrote that her mother had an absolute belief that it's not the cards one is dealt in life that matter, but how one plays them. "Mother is, by far," she wrote, "the highest card I was dealt. Kind, fair and generous, she has the type of self-confidence that comes from having been brought up by parents who not only loved her deeply and well, but who were themselves kind, fair, and generous people."

During Jamison's bouts of depression, her mother fed her, did her laundry, paid her bills and endured her bad moods. "Without her I never could have survived. . . . Often the only thing that would keep me going was the belief, instilled by my mother years before, that will and grit and responsibility are what ultimately make us supremely human in our existence. For each terrible storm that came my way, my mother—her love and her strong sense of values—provided me with powerful, and sustaining, countervailing winds."

During my interviews, I often asked women to tell me about a time when they felt they were being the "ordinary good mother." It was then that I heard of women in their everyday lives being those powerful, sustaining, countervailing winds for their children. One woman, named Laura, told me of a trying time with her oldest child who was then in eighth grade, and in this story I heard a mother who was able to keep her focus on her child. Laura came upon her daughter, Cindy, sobbing on her bed, "truly and completely devastated." She had not made the volleyball team, and all her friends had.

"My first impulse was to make it all go away," Laura said, "Cindy's hurt and disappointment, the arbitrary coach, the whole situation. My next was that I wished I could make it not important to her because it hurt me to see her hurt so badly.

"Instead, I drew a deep breath, laid down on the bed with her and just tried to be with her in her pain. I rubbed her back while she cried, and listened to her, held her and told her how sorry I was that it didn't work out this time.

"It was a great lesson to me, because once she'd had enough comforting, she and I sat together and went over her options. We decided Cindy would play on a lower-level team in hopes of being moved up. She did that for many months, working steadfastly without complaint, but she never did make the team.

"Even so, the story has a happy ending, because as time passed, Cindy came to look back on the long, painful episode with pride. She's impressed with the strength of character she showed in a difficult situation. And while I don't claim credit for her strength of character, I do think that the firm foundation of love and support my husband and I gave her, as well as my ability and willingness to see her needs over my own in that awful moment, were both key."

Another key, I think, is that Laura and her husband retold this tale many times, helping their daughter interpret it and incorporate it into her view of herself. Cindy has come to remember the event not as a failure, but as evidence of her determination.

For any woman, mothering in a thoughtful, deliberate way presents challenges. But for those who lack a positive role model and live with the wounds childhood may have inflicted, parenting presents additional obstacles. In my interviews I talked to many women whose own needs, sometimes even the lowest of them, were not satisfied early in life, and yet who feel both the desire and the duty to provide fully for their children. Although certain specific demands must be met in the child, a wide range of pathways can end in a healthy, successful adult. No one gets a perfect childhood, and no one gets to be the perfect mother. We all must make do, and make peace, with what fate and circumstance provide.

Melinda Morales, who describes her own mother as alternating unpredictably between "*Mommy Dearest* and a weeping little girl," grew up focused on the perfect mother ideal, complete with aprons and a white picket fence. She wanted first to have as her mother Donna Reed, the stay-at-home mom in the wholesome early sixties sitcom, and later to be Donna Reed. But from television she got, of course, only surface. "It was the picture of the cake," says Melinda, "not the recipe. I didn't know how to do this for my family. I wanted to be patient and cheerful. I wanted softly modulated voices, reasonable statements, hugs and kisses." But that can't be done when you marry a "loon," as Melinda says, have seven children with him and then divorce, knowing he won't help with child support. What she provided her children, by necessity, was far different from what could be seen in a television sitcom.

The essence of what children need in order to thrive intellectually and emotionally, Robert Karen says, summarizing the whole complex knot, is simply the parent's availability and responsiveness. "You don't need to be rich or smart or talented or funny," he says; "you just have to be there, in both senses of the phrase. To your child, none of the rest matters, except inasmuch as it enables you to give of yourself."

That's precisely what was missing in my childhood and in the childhoods of many of the women I interviewed. Our mothers or their substitutes, for whatever their individual reasons, couldn't open their hearts to us and stand fast. In discovering what mothers are meant to be and do for their children and where our own mothers floundered *as well as* where they flourished, we begin to take the steps that allow us to do more for our children than was done for us. For many of us, the route to providing a secure base for our children begins with a look at the past. Examining our histories may well require a dive into dark waters; but by exploring those waters, as we shall see, we can leave them and the fear they evoke behind. We can give ourselves the opportunity to create lifelong, fulfilling relationships with our children. This exploration begins with examining the nature of our relationships with our own mothers.

CHAPTER THREE

Uneasy Attachments

Who is ever weaned?

—Frank McCourt

My husband was four when his mother died a week after falling ill with polio. I was four when my mother disappeared into an iron lung. My father was four when his father, refusing an operation that could have saved him, died of gallstones. The day my younger son turned five, with all of us—myself, my husband and our two boys—alive and healthy, I sat down and wept. We had escaped, at least, that family legacy.

With my mother's death I learned, too soon, that love and loss are inseparable, that every beginning has an ending. Hardly a day goes by that I don't think of death. Too often I dwell on the knowledge that motherhood has made me vulnerable to suffering a loss even greater than the loss of my mother—the death of either of my children. I also fear the early death of my husband or myself which would sentence our sons to a life framed by sorrow.

The message I took from my childhood—*I lose what I love*—hovers over my mothering. Throughout my first pregnancy, fears about all that could go wrong in the womb and in birth plagued me. I couldn't trust that I would be allowed a child. Later, when both of my sons were born robust and perfect, a new chasm of dangers opened. I came to tread carefully through my days, never far from the knowledge that my family is fragile, like glass. This thinking, this anxiety, is part of my mother's bequest.

I know that my fears can teach my children to fear their lives. I know I am not the only mother who worries. I know also that a Freudian might like to suggest that my "fears" are actually a coverup for unconscious, repressed hostility, of unknown origin, toward my loved ones. But the fact is that my mother's death changed me, as too-early encounters with death always change children. The loss of a parent, through death or otherwise, shatters a child's core belief that the world is safe and secure, orderly and predictable. On the day my mother fell ill I learned that disastrous events happened not "out there" to someone else, but to me. The lesson that everything we love changes, that life is change, usually comes gradually, incrementally, allowing for perspectives to broaden, allowing us to take in over time the mixture of good and bad. For me that lesson landed whole, one day at the age of four, and I bring it to my mothering.

For each mother, what she bears from the past into parenthood differs, and for good or ill, it all affects her children. Some women bring a dread of intimacy that causes them to protect themselves even from their children. Fearing rejection, having been rejected by those she loves, a woman enters relationships cautiously, held aloof, habitually pushing away first, lest she be pushed, holding back until unequivocally invited. And so, even with her infant, she averts her eyes to break a mutual gaze, she ignores the baby's signals that ask to be picked up or put down. She's unable to smile unless the baby smiles first.

A woman I interviewed who has two young boys described her mother as one who could not comfort or hug or encourage. "Her mothering," she says, "was nothing about nurturing the spirit of a child. It was about order and control." As a result, the daughter grew up protecting herself from closeness and the vulnerability it brought, and she approached her first infant the same way. She could not bear to hold him, look him in the eye or breast-feed him. "I would prop him in a car seat with towels and wedge a bottle into his mouth," she recalls. "I couldn't bear the intimacy of breast-feeding. Feeling those powerful tugs of love and maternity frightened me, and I pushed them away."

Other women learned as children to minister to their mothers: *She needs me; I can't leave her.* And then they turn their children into parent figures, hoping unconsciously to recover what was lost in their youth. A mother comes home at the end of a long workday, tired and cranky. She snaps at her four-year-old who then strokes her hand, saying: "That's okay, Mommy. You had a bad day. Do you still love me?" Some women develop a sense that trails them all through life of being behind schedule or otherwise out of sync, no matter what they've accomplished. Those hurt in childhood sometimes sit on the sidelines of life rather than risk additional losses or the possibility of further pain or disappointment, preferring security over passion. Others grow up with a naive faith that love in adulthood will cure any lack of love in childhood, and they search for the ideal mate to heal them. Some shut down emotionally and decide they can get along without love. Still others are rattled by recurrent anxiety and depression. My mother's death and father's abandonment shattered my sense of safety early on, and then my grandmother reinforced my insecurity by keeping me guessing about her tie to me. The attachment between caregiver and child can misfire for any number of reasons, and when it does, there's trouble for both.

Mother Love, Love for Mother

One significant way love can go wrong and the wrong can reverberate through the child's life is when the mother fails to move

beyond Alice Balint's concept of "initial archaic love," the period when mother and child are bound by mutual gratification
and common interests. Sometimes a mother is so tangled with
her child that she can't fulfill the adult role in the mother–child
duo; she refuses evidence that her infant is a separate being with
independent emotions and motives. She confuses her baby with
herself. She might, for example, assume her baby's crying or ex-
ploratory behavior indicates the baby needs time away from her,
when actually it's *she* who wishes to be away from her infant.
When a mother gets stuck here, she persists in thinking her
child's needs are identical to her own. Instead of letting the child
grow, she clings to the idyllic moments when mother and infant
meet with shared gratification, such as immediately after birth
or in ideal nursing circumstances. She insists on seeing her child
through the myth of oneness. Later in her child's life she may be
the mother who can't recognize her child's experiences if they
differ from her own. "I'm cold," says the child. "You can't be
cold," the mother replies. "It's warm in here." One woman told
me that her mother made her wear to high school "these god-
awful saddle oxfords that were popular when *she* was in school!"

A mother can become so determined that her child have no
separate needs that she may reject the growing child who tries to
express a self. She can do this in various ways, including by trying to delay the child's development, by not allowing the child
to have opinions or interests different from hers, or by replacing
the child with another infant and then expecting independence
from the older one, who may be but a toddler.

I heard an example of this pushing away from a woman
named Sheila, who was pregnant with her second child when I
interviewed her. "Growing up," she said, "my sisters and I
would say to each other, 'You know, I don't think our mom was
really meant to be a mom.' As a child I just craved physical attention, hand-holding, being told 'I love you. You're a good person,' and that didn't occur."

Sheila waited until her first child, a daughter, was four before getting pregnant again. Although this thirty-eight-year-old lawyer knows that her career and that of her husband contributed to the wait, she also says that her reluctance to dislodge her daughter from her top spot stemmed directly from her own memory of being the oldest sister.

"Once my sisters were born, I was pushed out," Sheila said. "I didn't want to repeat that for my daughter.

"When I was two my mother abruptly went away and left me in the care of an older woman in the building where my family lived in New York City. From what others have told me, I quit eating and refused to get out of bed until my mother returned home a week later. Trouble is, she came home with a baby! I must have had no idea what to expect or even that she was pregnant. My father was doing his residency then and wasn't ever home.

"I vaguely remember life becoming a lot of TV-watching while my mother cared for the baby. A couple years later my second sister was born and my mother said to me, 'You're the big girl. You can take care of yourself.' And I did. I was only six when I learned to cross Park Avenue by myself to get to school on Madison Avenue. We lived on the ninth floor of our building and my mother didn't want to have to bundle up the baby and my middle sister to get me to school, so she taught me to do it myself. I'd walk to school and home for lunch every day. I liked it when the older sister of a friend who lived down the street would walk with us.

"By seven or eight I was riding the bus to visit school friends and spend the night. It was better than being home and being told, 'You're in the way.' "

Sheila suspects that her mother, who has tended toward depression much of her life, felt overwhelmed by her daughters and the care they demanded. But whatever the reasons, Sheila has never felt she had a secure place in her family. She and her

mother somehow missed forging the reciprocal relationship between mother and child that allows each her individuality while
maintaining intimacy.

Sometimes these failures at love cause the child to be angry,
but because they're usually subtle, the child experiences her rage as
unfounded and confusing. The child's rage remains unconscious
and her guilt deepens as she tries to express her anger in behavior
that's considered by everyone around her to be unexplainable.

Susan Wiseman, a wry, fast-talking woman from the Pacific
Northwest, told me a story of growing up as that angry child.
Now a married, stay-at-home mother to children aged ten and
eleven, Susan grew up the youngest in a stepfamily and the only
child born to both parents. Sitting in her usual jeans and shirt,
wearing no makeup, her turned-up nose giving her an impish
air, she looked nothing like the wild youth she described herself
to have been. Even before she reached high school, she said, she
was smoking marijuana and drinking alcohol daily.

"My mom and dad told me every day that they loved me and
I believed them," she says, "but I just couldn't accept the way
they showed their love. There was so much going on that con-
tradicted it." Her parents behaved conventionally by day, but at
night secluded themselves to drink—and argue. The confusing
push and pull of her mother's inconsistent behavior baffled Susan. Once Susan had been put to bed, she wasn't allowed to go
to her parents' room, even as a very young child.

"I don't care how scared you were," she remembers, "or how
much you thought you needed them, you couldn't bug them
once they were in their gin nest. I was often afraid and lonely.

"In the early evening, though, my mother and I would
sometimes sit in an overstuffed chair, the two of us watching
Mod Squad, The Streets of San Francisco and others of our favorite television programs together. It meant the world to me to
sit all mushed up in the chair with her, and she'd distractedly
rub my hand with her thumb. I would feel loved by her and as

close to her as I could with no one else." But then Susan would be sent out of the room, and her parents would begin their nightly drinking.

Like some others who missed out on the consistent care of a devoted mother, Susan turned her rage both inward and outward. She sank into depression in her teen years and finally ran away from home. "Even in the depth of my depression and anger as a teen," Susan says, "I believed my parents loved me and I understood they weren't hateful people." But for Susan, this understanding and hearing "I love you" weren't enough to overcome the loud message of her mother's rejecting actions.

Insecure Attachment

Just as secure attachment echoes throughout a life in healthy relationships and behavior, insecure attachment (sometimes called anxious attachment) can reverberate far into adulthood, resulting in low self-esteem, unhealthy relationships and failure to mature. Insecure attachment happens when the mother is unable to respond adequately to her infant's individual characteristics and specific needs. This failure to respond can be subtle and even well-intentioned, as illustrated by one clinician who observed an eighteen-month-old boy stand on a kiddie chair and stretch his arms out to his mother, clearly wishing to be taken onto her lap. The mother reached her hands out, palms up, and when the boy put his hands in hers, she led him back to the floor and off to the side, instead of pulling him up into her arms. The boy stood dejected, head lowered, his sadness undetected by his mother. When the primary caregiver *repeatedly* fails to notice her child's signals or notices them only sporadically, and when her responses are inappropriate or tardy, the pair fails to become securely attached.

I interviewed a mother of two teenage girls who expressed the pain of insecure attachment, saying this of her childhood experiences: "What I had was surface. The picture looked good, the sun was out, the lace curtains waving in the breeze, but underneath was mayhem. When there's no emotional depth, you're left with a hole." She paused and then added, "Sometimes I feel like I fall in that hole; there's no support. That's my biggest sadness."

Research indicates that about one-third of middle-class American children experience insecure attachment, which tends to be transmitted from one generation to the next. The percentage in poor homes is higher.

Robert Karen suggests that misattachment can come from various difficulties, such as:

- Trying circumstances, for example, an overtaxed, under-supported mother not having the time or the peace of mind to be sensitively and consistently available to each of her children
- Ignorance, which might cause otherwise caring parents to let a baby cry for prolonged periods, to leave a baby repeatedly for too long a time or to train the child prematurely for independence
- Unhappy events (deaths, separations, sibling rivalries) that the parent cannot handle
- Parental psychology, which easily works its way into and complicates the other conditions; indeed, what begins with ignorance, unfortunate circumstances or infant need is often prolonged by the parent's psychology.

Sadly, when insecure attachment develops in a child's early life it often generates behaviors, such as the child being either clingy or aloof, that exacerbate problems in the parent's psychology. And if the parent's psychology has contributed to the anxious attachment in infancy, the faulty bond between them is likely to continue through the child's life, unless the parent changes. In addition, the child learns from the parent a model of relating to others and tends to perpetuate that model.

Throughout our conversation, Susan Wiseman expressed fears that she may be repeating her mother's contradictory behavior and her mistake of thinking that she's giving love, while the love is actually missing its target. "I worry that I'm not warm enough with them, especially when they're needy," she said. "I try to say 'I love you' lots and hope that all my verbal affirmations override any messages from my body and attitude that say I *don't* support them."

Other women told of the puzzling state of feeling lonely and unloved by a mother who voiced love or acted in ways that seemed loving. One cause, I suspect, is a failure of openness in the mother, an inability to let love and gratification flow in a reciprocal relationship. If a woman cannot receive, she cannot give. For emotionally healthy women, a balanced give-and-take brings a sense of well-being and leads to maturation, according to psychoanalyst Therese Benedek. The healthy mother consciously and deliberately provides for her child, giving food and love. This "motherliness," Benedek contends, is drawn from a reservoir of motherly behavior that is being continually filled by the emotional gratification a mother receives from her child. The mother is "filled up" by watching the child thrive and respond to her care. If the mother can't receive from her child, because of her emotional immaturity, then she isn't refilled and has nothing to give. The healthy cycle of give-and-take is interrupted, to the detriment of mother and child.

One young mother spoke of suffering as a child from the "huge discrepancy" between what she felt from her parents and what they said. She once told her mother, "I feel like a burden in your life," but her mother only denied it. "There was something toxic in that space between what I felt was true and what my parents said was true. Kids feel what is real," the woman declared.

Not having a secure base in the early stages of life doesn't necessarily breed future trouble, but it is a liability for the child and the effects can be far-reaching. Infants whose needs haven't been met learn that others can't be trusted and that care isn't available, which makes later bonds hard to forge.

Sheila, who began being pushed out by her mother at age two, says that she never felt safe at home. Growing up in a well-to-do family in New York City, she thought abuse was only physical; but in her family, she says, "We verbally beat each other up all the time. Nothing we ever did was good enough for our parents. Almost straight A's on my report card wasn't enough. They wanted to know why it wasn't all A's. My mother was constantly after me about my hair and clothes and makeup. They wanted us to look like the fairy-tale family. But in our house we were five people living very separately.

"In high school I had three close friends who were from more blue-collar families and they'd tell me about their parents' drinking and yelling, grabbing their arms, and they'd say to me, 'Sheila, you have it so good. Your dad's a doctor and your mom's always home.' And I'd tell them, 'It looks good, but I'm totally neglected in other ways.' By then I'd been aware of the isolation for a long time."

As soon as she left home for college, Sheila entered a relationship with a young man who abused her physically, emotionally and sexually. She dropped out of college and spent more than four years with him before making her break.

Insecure attachment doesn't bode well for self-esteem, either. Researchers have repeatedly measured the self-worth of securely and insecurely attached children at various ages and have found unmistakable differences: Secure children score higher in all measures of self-esteem, no doubt because getting consistent and reliable care makes a child feel worthy of love. The child whose intense love for her parents is somehow not accepted comes to think something is wrong with her.

One woman, born the only child to a mother whose approval

was dispensed "with a warning not to slack off," learned as a girl, she said, "to hide my life and my feelings from her as much as I could. I was very sneaky about many things that other people took in stride, like the food I ate, the people I knew in school, even the clothes I wore. I'd hide shoes I was afraid she wouldn't like in my locker at school and change there. And I didn't confide in her *ever* because I never knew how she'd end up twisting something around."

Over time, the conditional, exiguous approval from her mother taught her to doubt herself. "If I took a test," she says, "I was sure I'd failed. If I went on a date, I was sure he wouldn't like me. Those insecurities are still very much with me, despite years of therapy. It's not as bad as it used to be, and I tend to shrug it off. But before I shrug it off, I think about it."

Insecure attachment comes in two main types, termed *ambivalent* and *avoidant;* each type is manifested by typical, specific behaviors in the mother and the child.

Ambivalent Attachment is characterized by inconsistent, incompetent or chaotic parenting that leads children to be uncertain of their caregivers, overtly anxious, perpetually seeking to appease their mothers, and fearful about exploring the world. These mothers are often attentive but are out of step with their children. They're sometimes available and helpful, but other times not; they might threaten abandonment as a way of controlling the child. Mostly, they can't read and respond to their children's needs and emotions, except perhaps fear. Robert Karen says that the behavior of these preoccupied mothers suggests a lack of involvement with their children, but in fact they may be "haunted by different demons." He goes on to describe these mothers in a way that was familiar to me. I could recognize my grandmother here, along with many of the mothers of women I interviewed. "A mother who has never worked through her own ambivalent attachment," he writes, "has probably been struggling all her life to find stable love. When she was a child, she may have been pained by the competent, steady caring that she saw friends' parents give to them. As an adult she may be prone to a nagging, uncontrollable jealousy in any close relationship where she feels cause for doubt. She may want to love deeply and steadily, but it is hard for her because she's never been filled up enough with patient, reliable love to be in a position to give it. When she becomes a mother, such unresolved, tormenting issues may play havoc with her emotional life."

In my research, I heard of many varieties of maternal deprivation, from the subtle to the blatant, and I also saw that those individual variations fell into patterns. Despite the particulars of any woman's childhood—being the oldest of eight, the child of immigrants, growing up with a single mother or in an intact family—the ways in which attachment became distorted and in which parents failed to provide for their daughters' physical care, safety, love and esteem needs fell into categories. Two of three general themes I heard described variations of the ambivalent mother; I call them *present-but-absent* and *too-present* mothers.

PRESENT-BUT-ABSENT. In research that would ultimately provide strong underpinnings of attachment theory, psychologist Harry Harlow, who was a specialist in animal learning at the University of Wisconsin and president of the American Psychological Association, described the mother who shows up, but who withholds love or approval, is inept or neglectful or otherwise provides distorted care. His classic paper published in 1958 and called "The Nature of Love" reported on experiments Harlow had devised with infant rhesus monkeys. He took the babies from their mothers at birth and raised them alone in cages with two inanimate surrogate mothers. One was padded and covered in terry cloth, the other was made of wire mesh. He found that the baby monkeys clung to the cloth mothers most of the time, even if the wire mother was rigged up to do the feeding. This was the first scientifically sound blow to the long-held psychoanalytic belief that a baby's ties to its mother were based on her being the source of food.

In his experiments Harlow found little difference between how much milk the baby monkeys drank from the wire mothers and how much they drank from the cloth ones, or in their weight gain. But he did find that the wire-mother infants had softer feces, a physical indication of the greater stress and anxiety they experienced. "The wire mother is biologically adequate but psychologically inept," he wrote. ". . . Certainly, man cannot live by milk alone."

In his paper, Harlow described an encounter with a "charming lady" who had once heard him describe these experiments. "When I subsequently talked to her, her face brightened with sudden insight: 'Now I know what's wrong with me,' she said, 'I'm just a wire mother.'" Harlow then added this jovial comment: "Perhaps she was lucky. She might have been a wire wife." I can't guess what this woman's husband thought of her, but I suspect that her children found her neither charming nor lucky. I interviewed many women who had what I've come to think of as the "wire mother"; she provides physical sustenance but little more cuddling and nurturing than Harlow's inanimate mothers. It's important to note that the cloth mothers in Harlow's experiments were beloved by the infant monkeys, even though they were completely passive, returning no hugs, relating not in the slightest. His experiments showed how very important it was for the infants to have *someone,* no matter how inadequate, to attach to.

When I was a child I was very attracted to my mother. I was always seeking something I couldn't get from her—snuggling, nurturing— but she wasn't that type.

My mother never worked while I was growing up, but I often have thought, "Where was she?" For so many important events she wasn't there—my prom, my performances at school. But what was she doing? She was at golf tournaments, I guess.

I grew up in a home where keeping the kitchen scissors in place was more important than having a conversation. If something was misplaced it set my mother off. She was much more interested in whether I left a dirty dish in the sink than how my day was. Even now, if you try to look her in the eye and reveal something personal, she immediately goes off to fluff something.

Women told me of passive, not-there mothers, but also of growing up in homes permeated with a negativity that conveyed the messages of not being listened to or heard, not loved or close to anyone, where empty feelings of not being noticed haunted childhood. Whether neglect came from ineptitude or irresponsibility or even hostility, it was deeply felt. One woman, a nurse who is now mother to three children herself, will never forget her first day of school. She was the youngest of six and her mother sent her off to school with her older siblings, but it turned out that kindergarten didn't start until the following day. The girl, just four then, walked home by herself. Had this been one incident in an otherwise happy, loving home life, it would be a far different memory. Instead, it stands as a pointed illustration of the message the woman heard all the years she was growing up: "You don't matter."

TOO-PRESENT. In my interviews and reading I learned of another type of ambivalent mother I call too-present. She's one whose love or need for her children overwhelms her ability to see them clearly, who insists that her place is at the center of their lives, or who uses her children to fill her own emptiness or to bolster her shaky self-esteem. These excessive mothers, sometimes called "smothers," may try to control their children or make them perfect, and in doing so, they interfere with their children's abilities to develop separate selves. Winnicott called this using of the child an "impingement" on the child's psyche. Other theorists have called continuing entanglement "boundary distortions," which can show up as intrusive, overprotective and role-reversal behavior that stifles the child's autonomy. Smothers often are the ambivalent mothers whose own "rankling needs," as Robert Karen describes them, make it hard for them to be consistently available to their children. They may try to keep their children from separating so the children stay nearby, filling their mothers' attachment needs. A woman who feels deprived of love is pained at seeing her child become autonomous. Particularly frightening for a child is feeling truly responsible for looking after parents, not merely playing at being "a big girl." One woman told me that "role reversal was my childhood." She said she always had to look after her mother. "She told me too much," she said. "She didn't want to be a parent but a friend, and she put me in that role of taking care of her. She even admitted it once."

Smother behavior can look very good. The overinvolvement can be interpreted as caring and warmth, but since it's focused on meeting the parent's needs rather than the child's, it is very different from true affection and warmth. Far from being overindulged, the child in the "inverted" relationship, as Bowlby characterized it, is burdened with having to take care of Mother, often at the expense of developing her own social life.

The motives of smothers can lie in a variety of sources, including the wish to protect the child as they had not been protected as children, the compulsion to honor their own mothers by repeating their over-the-top behaviors, the mother's helplessness and low self-esteem that cause her to elevate the child too high or the conviction that with effort she can be the perfect mother to the perfect child. Sometimes smothers become hypercritical and overbearing in their efforts to control and mold their children.

When we were growing up my mother always insisted that we children look a certain way when we went out, and then she'd introduce me saying, "Here's my daughter. Normally she looks better."

I think my mother saw me as part of herself and that this time she was determined to get it right. She never saw me as an individual. What she saw was imperfection and her own failure. Her need for me to be perfect was overwhelming and so all I heard was what was wrong.

Whatever the source of the behavior, smothering prevents the child from separating and prolongs emotional enmeshment far beyond what the child needs. The child then comes to think that being independent means that love and protection won't be there. The girl growing into a woman may feel crowded out of her own life by her mother, who wants to be in the driver's seat.

Few women I interviewed told me directly that they had "smother mothers." They understood only implicitly that the love their mothers provided was conditional, that the hugs, kisses, gifts and words of praise came with a price tag. They grew up knowing that mother's love required an intangible return, such as unwavering loyalty, admiration and gratitude, or perhaps the submersion of their own ambitions in favor of what their mothers desired for them. But they weren't necessarily able to identify or articulate the conditions their mothers had demanded. That's why, I suspect, when women I interviewed revealed their mothers to be smothers, it was usually unwittingly. One woman, for example, who described herself as a "loving, supportive and enlightened mom" to her two sons, said that she had been in therapy on and off for thirty years, struggling with "feelings of inadequacy." She said, "I felt I could never meet my mother's expectations of me." She also described her mother as "a very good mother, very affectionate and caring."

She elaborated on her mother's caregiving this way: "She provided a great many opportunities for my sister and me, such as lessons, clubs, camps, as well as teaching us how to cook, sew and do the things she loved to do. She told me how proud she was of us and let us know that we could do anything we wanted, but the message that also came through was, 'I'm here to catch you because you can't do it by yourself.' Appearances are important to her, so we always had to do the 'right' thing, based on her value system. My sister and I both married late in life, and having two spinster daughters was very troublesome to her, even though as single women we were well-educated professionals making good salaries." Clearly, this woman's mother provided for her in many helpful, caring ways; and yet those strains of "live for mother, not for yourself" and "you can't do it without me" so typical of smothers ring as well.

Another woman, Wendy, an air traffic controller and mother to a teenage boy, says that until she was about thirty she would have described her mother as terrific, but in the last ten years her view has changed drastically.

"Growing up," she said, with the hint of a drawl, "I felt I had a perfect family. My father owned a thriving business that put us among the wealthiest in our blue-collar town. And my mother sparkled in the June Cleaver role. When my brother and I came home from school at the end of the year it was to a banner our mom had hung reading 'Welcome home for the summer!' Mom baked bread, picked up after us and took us all to church every Sunday. She made it clear that her children were her whole life."

Cracks appeared in the picture when Wendy reached high school, and she began to notice how much her parents fought. "I would see Mom crying," she says, "and hear my dad yell, and I was convinced she was the innocent one." And then Wendy began to resist her mother's assumption that Wendy would fulfill traditional women's roles, when all Wendy's interests leaned toward those of her father, especially riding motorcycles and flying airplanes. Life in college and experience in the wider world caused Wendy to doubt her mother even more. "I started to see how sheltered and unrealistic a life she leads."

Later, when Wendy married and had a child, her mother criticized Wendy's parenting, saying that Wendy was ruining her child by working. "She hovered around my son and wouldn't al-low him to do *anything* for himself, including pick up his own toys. She wouldn't even let him walk down the stairs. He had to bump down on his bottom to minimize the risk of falling! I now wonder whether my mother's 'over-mothering' came because she never had anything in her life except me and my brother. She tried. Too hard. My mother is about as loving as they come, but to the point of almost alienating my brother and me. I felt loved as a kid, and I give her credit for that. And I don't doubt she loves me now, but she doesn't allow any independence from those she loves. If you strike out on your own, it's like a betrayal to her."

The child of an ambivalent mother—whether present-but-absent or too-present—becomes hooked by her unpredictability and develops unconscious strategies for dealing with her neglect, control or inconsistency. The result, Robert Karen writes, is that these children become "wildly addicted" to mother and to their efforts to change her. One woman told me she learned early that if she tried to meet her mother's needs, "if I was feeding her in some way," then her mother could be pretty reliable. The chil-dren of such ambivalent relationships easily become enmeshed with their mothers in unhealthy ways and may later shift that addiction to other attachment figures, writes Karen, "but through it all they do not believe they have what it takes to get what they need from another person." And that may be exactly the child the mother wants: an immature, dependent girl who is eager to please, who clings to and constantly demonstrates a need for mother. These children are drawn to relationships, but don't have the social skills of securely attached children; they don't have a sense of self-worth and of being capable around their peers.

Avoidant Attachment, the second main type of anxious at-tachment, is characterized by a parent who is harsh or dismissive or otherwise deflects the child's efforts at closeness. While am-bivalent mothers are often maddeningly unpredictable, avoidant ones are considerably more rejecting. They are often unavailable emotionally and tend to dislike neediness and praise independence. In clinical studies of mothers and babies, the avoidant mothers showed less emotional expression than others; they seemed to be containing anger and irritation. Some even mocked their infants, spoke sarcastically or stared them down and often avoided physical contact. Robert Karen theorizes that the aversion to nurturance that these mothers demonstrate is an outgrowth of the neglect they likely experienced as children.

"Needs and longings that were painfully unmet have become a source of hurt and shame for her," he writes. "Having cut herself off from them, they make her angry, depressed or disgusted when she sees them in her child." The woman who told me she couldn't look her infant in the eye or nurse him must have been experiencing something like this.

REJECTING. The theme of rejection was the third path to being under-mothered that I heard from the women I interviewed, along with too-present and present-but-absent. These rejecting, or avoidant, mothers refuse the role, whether through their own doing or not, whether maliciously or not. They may be ill, immature, irresponsible or, as some of their daughters told me, "not mother material." Whatever the reason, they don't provide consistent care and are often physically absent. I put my own mother here. I also put in this category a friend's mother, who suffered mental illness and spent much of her children's early years hospitalized. As my friend and her sisters grew older the hospitalizations were fewer, but their mother couldn't bear the stimulation and tumult of family life and kept her children away from her. Her fragility kept her in bed till noon and prevented her from performing even simple tasks like making a trip to the grocery store. Her children grew up knowing she loved them, yet deprived of mothercare.

In a way, every mother is a rejecting mother. As Anna Freud said, just as "no child is wholly loved," every mother rejects her children; or, more accurately, her children will feel rejected by her. This can happen at certain times of the day or the week, when mothers are preoccupied with their own lives, or during some particular stage of a child's development. Most children can weather a bit of this, but the child suffers greatly when rejection dominates the mother-child relationship.

I always felt that I was an intrusion in her life. After being told by two separate doctors that she'd never have children, my mother neither expected nor wanted me. My appearance nine months and two weeks after her wedding wasn't exactly welcome. My birthday is the day after hers and for years she told me the story about how I made her throw up her birthday dinner.

My mother really didn't want to raise children. She doesn't like little kids. Which is something I didn't know until I had my own.

Some mothers reject their children through their unwillingness to perform mothering duties. "[T]he relationship of a mother to her infant is an exacting one," wrote Anna Freud. "It is too much to expect that she will fulfill her task if she has not taken on the role of motherhood voluntarily, if it has been forced upon her." Some such mothers abandon their children to others and go on with their lives. One woman's mother grew up in a large family caring for her younger siblings and then became a mother in her teens. She had three children by age twenty, and as her daughter said, "I really don't think she could handle it." So she walked out.

In some ways the truly unwilling mother, the woman who refuses her role altogether, isn't the one who inflicts the most damage on her child. When she deserts completely, she at least leaves the door open for a mother substitute to step in and take over. "It is the mother who wavers between rejection and possessiveness who does the more irreparable harm," Anna Freud wrote, "by forcing her child into an unproductive partnership in which he fails to develop his capacities" to love others.

The book and movie *Mommie Dearest*, about the actor Joan Crawford mothering her adopted daughter Christina, provides a glimpse of an extreme example of rejection and possessiveness. Like many daughters of difficult mothers, Christina could not abandon her mother and save herself. Instead she would say "I love you" and throw her arms around the mother who had tried to strangle her. What made Joan Crawford, as depicted in the film by Faye Dunaway, so terrifying was her inconsistency. Was she going to lash out in vicious physical violence or merely be manipulative or perhaps even tender?

You would think you were getting along fine but then you would say something she didn't like and she would snap and be nasty. BOOM! The rug is pulled out—and it hurts doubly bad because you thought everything was okay. And she was always the one who decided it was over. There'd never be any "I'm sorry I behaved badly." And I'd never have a chance to say "That really hurt my feelings." She'd just be nice again. No resolution, ever.

Some wavering mothers, for whatever individual reasons, are unable or unwilling to step aside and let others meet the needs of their children. "Apathetic mothers," as Therese Benedek called them, sometimes have enough ego strength to protect themselves from the shame and guilt of actually abandoning their offspring. Instead they put emotional distance between themselves and their children. They might, for instance, train the oldest child to take care of the younger ones and thus avoid any obligation to their children beyond infancy. But they find other ways, as well, to shield themselves from their children's needs and love.

I had way too much responsibility as the oldest. In effect, I had no childhood. I have many memories of waking up in the middle of the night, from age eight or ten, and comforting siblings because our parents weren't home. I guess they thought we wouldn't wake up and notice that they had gone to a party.

My mother was quite handicapped in her ability to show love to her children in physical ways such as touch. She has always seemed unhappy. Meals were a huge chore, and she showed little joy or pride in our scholastic accomplishments.

She was well respected and honored in her career in human relations at a university. Her job was to help people, and she kept doing it even after she retired. But she never seemed to want to take care of us.

In a survey of 1,100 mothers aged eighteen to eighty published as *The Motherhood Report*, Eva Margolies and Louis Genevie found that 4 percent of mothers wouldn't do it over again if they had the choice. Two of the women I interviewed, Rachel and Kim, suggested their mothers were among that group.

Rachel's mother sounded like one of those "apathetic mothers" described by Therese Benedek who don't want to be mothers, but who also don't want to abandon their children and suffer the social consequences. From the time she was two and her parents divorced, Rachel lived with her mother, though her mother didn't seem to want her. When Rachel was thirteen her mother announced that she was moving to another state to live in a commune. "Do you want to come?" she asked. Although Rachel was reluctant to leave her school, she followed her mother, not knowing where else she'd go.

"Then when I was sixteen," Rachel continued her story, "Mom decided to move across the country to go to secretarial school. She said I could come with her, but when I got there she had only a little room to live in. I don't think she really had expected me to come along.

"Pretty soon I found a family I could live with in exchange for baby-sitting. Then a man who was thirty-one wanted to date me. I remember wanting so very much for my mother to forbid it, but she didn't. I now think my mom probably saw this guy as a way to be free of me for good.

"People really like my mother, and if she wasn't my mom I might really like her, too. But she just didn't have the mother thing. I think that if she had not had social pressure to marry and have children she never would have. She's perfectly happy living alone now with no responsibilities."

Unlike Rachel, Kim grew up in an entirely conventional southern family, but she, too, heard a loud and clear message that she was "a bother" to her mother.

"My mother was always pushing me away," Kim says. "She was always too busy to hug me or play with me. One evening, when I was eight or so, she was sewing at the dining room table making a dress for herself. I wanted to be with her and to get some attention, but about the third time I tried to give her a hug, she physically pushed me away and snapped, 'Stop traumatizing me!' Rejection doesn't feel very nice from anyone, but when it comes from your own mother it's especially hard to take."

As babies, avoidantly attached children appear quite insecure at home, showing extreme separation distress. The child is angry at the mother for repeatedly rejecting the child's bids for love, but she can't show her anger because that only drives the mother further away. In order to cope, the child becomes deaf to her own love needs and may become isolated and withdrawn or defiant and aggressive. Whereas the ambivalently attached child is always looking for love, the avoidant tries to live without love and support and may develop an attitude that says "I don't need you; I can do it on my own." These children often look good, being independent and engaging, but a few of them are cold and cruel. The child of an avoidant attachment can grow into an adult who is cut off from her own emotions, particularly hurt and anger, as she tries to become emotionally self-sufficient. Rejected by her mother, a girl may grow up to dismiss the significance of her childhood experiences and her need for love, and to avoid self-reflection. She may even idealize her parents and childhood but have no memories to back up those feelings.

I interviewed a woman named Carolyn who seemed almost entirely cut off from her past. One afternoon, we slid into a semicircular booth together at a chain restaurant near her home and ordered iced tea. She avoided my eyes and fidgeted as we got started, but relaxed when I asked about her two young teenagers, smiling and laughing in a husky way that made me think she must have been a smoker.

As we talked, I learned that her mother had run off with a lover and left Carolyn and her siblings to be reared by their father and other relatives. Carolyn's mother showed up every few years, but mostly kept out of her children's lives. Throughout the interview I kept trying to steer Carolyn to the past, to try to firm up a chronology of events in her childhood. I wanted to know, for instance, how old Carolyn was when her mother left; around two it seems, but I couldn't pin down that or numerous other details. "I don't remember," "I'm not sure of that," "I don't know," were her replies, as she twirled her spoon in her glass of tea. My efforts to straighten out contradictions and to find out, for example, how old she was when her mother took her in for what was apparently a brief time only led to dead ends.

At one point I asked whether Carolyn had come to terms with her childhood, and she said steadily, "I didn't have a bad childhood. There was just something about their divorce that always gnawed at me, especially with my mom." I studied her face, searching for evidence that she did know what would gnaw at a little girl whose mother had walked out, but saw nothing. She spoke of her own mothering with clarity and pleasure, but her childhood seemed to lie behind a curtain.

Later we talked of the struggle she has had trusting her live-in boyfriend. Her ex-husband, whom she had been with since a teenager and who is the father of her children, left her for another woman when their boys were just starting school. Carolyn said she finally went to see a counselor because she felt so miserable every time her boyfriend wanted to go anywhere without her.

"I had this, like, uh, what's the word? I had this feeling like he would just not come back. What's the word I'm looking for?" She frowned, then said, "Abandoning. Abandoning me. So I did go see a counselor once or twice just to say, 'What? Am I crazy? Why would I feel this way?' "

"And what did the counselor say?" I asked.

Carolyn replied: "No." She barked a dry cough, and then said, "I think it referred back to my ex, who wasn't there for me. I don't want to go down that road again."

She told me she dropped the counseling after a short time. "I quit going," she told me, "when the counselor said, 'You have a lot of walls built up and we need to break those down.' And I thought, 'Well, I like those walls! I want to keep those. They're my security blanket.' "

The Odd "Category D"

To the original two insecure categories (ambivalent and avoidant), Mary Main, Ph.D., professor of psychology at the University of California at Berkeley and a former student of Ainsworth, later added "category D." When I first read of this research, I expected to find nothing more than a footnote to the other two categories, but I came to see that "category D" had particular significance in my own life, as well as in the stories of some of the women I interviewed.

In a longitudinal study of middle-class families begun in the mid-1970s, Main found a group of children who were "clearly more disturbed than others" and who didn't fit the original categories of attachment. The behavior of these infants toward their mothers showed such distortions as these: The infant appears to be in a good mood, but strikes or pulls at the mother's face or eyes; the infant approaches the parent but then falls in a huddled position or flings her hands in front of her face; the infant freezes when mother approaches and adopts a dazed or trance-like expression. The mothers of these "category-D" infants exhibited behavior toward their babies that seemed likely to frighten the child either by being directly frightening or by showing the mother's fright.

Such behavior included greeting the baby with an ominous or haunted tone of voice or abruptly dropping the voice in intonation or pitch; moving suddenly toward the infant and looming with her own face or another object; displaying conflicting signals such as calling the infant while standing with hands on hips and jaw jutting; handling the child with extreme timidity or unpredictable intrusions, such as suddenly putting hands on the child's face. Main labeled these attachments "disorganized/disoriented" and found in subsequent research that some of these mothers were the children of abuse, which doesn't seem surprising. What she also found, however, was that some were children of mothers who harbored unresolved loss or trauma. Main and her associates determined that these disturbances included the deaths of close family members or experiences like a brush with death. In particular, mothers who had lost parents in their youth and had not resolved that loss were likely to attach in this "category-D" way, which might be a result of pervasive anxiety and fearfulness that are communicated to the baby. The mother is frightened, frightening or both.

Any journalistic objectivity I might have maintained about attachment research vanished when I learned this. I found it stunning that a woman whose mother had died too soon, a woman like me, might relate to her child in ways similar to that of a mother who's physically abusive. The reason, Main and her colleagues suggest, is that a parent suffering unresolved mourning may still be frightened by her loss experiences and, as a result, she might communicate anxiety and fearfulness that could be frightening to her child. The researchers were quite clear that it wasn't loss itself that led to category-D attachments, but the lack of resolution following a loss.

This could explain the fearfulness some women I interviewed showed about their seemingly innocuous mothers. "I can't visit her by myself; I have to take along my son or husband," said one woman, with a shiver. Her mother, whom she described as entirely satisfactory in physical caregiving but emotionally vacant, lost her own mother at age four. I can't help but wonder whether the daughter's reluctance, which she calls "the fear I can't characterize," is similar to the fear an adult might always harbor toward a parent who had once physically abused her.

Another woman, who describes herself as "a hippie, a dreamer," is at fifty still struggling to create some structure in her life and finds being a parent "very challenging." Her mother survived a Nazi concentration camp as a child, and later, as a mother, often frightened her children. Her daughter said she led the Brownie troop and put clean clothes in the drawers, but "she blew up a lot. You had to be very careful about upsetting Mom."

And I am one of those mothers who suffered early trauma that went unresolved for decades. I know without a doubt that my children are not "clearly more disturbed than others," as Main described children with category-D attachments. I hope that the years of therapy I had before becoming a mother allowed me to resolve my childhood losses. And yet, I recognize myself in that "frightened" mother. I don't have a corner on worry; it's familiar territory to mothers. But I also suspect that few people have the morbid default thinking that I do. *I'm not going to be able to keep him* often comes to me. *This is how it ends,* floats through my head at any threat. One fall morning my husband set out early to go fishing in the mountains nearby, and some hours later I noticed his wallet sitting on his dresser. *They won't be able to identify his body.* My worries aren't vague and free-floating. They're specific and unimaginative given what became of my mother: I'm afraid my sons or husband will die or become paralyzed. I don't want to have these thoughts, these fears. Above all, I don't want to pass on that anxiety. I bite my tongue on "Be careful" when they leave home, but I hear my own dreads and wonder whether I'm successfully keeping them to myself.

In my own attachment history I can see, as research indicates, that attachment can vary over time and can be complex. I want to think that my mother and I were securely bonded before her illness. I've found evidence in letters and from stories told by friends and family who knew her that she was mentally stable and took pleasure in her children and in her role as mother. And long ago my father, in a rare moment of unguarded remembering of our early days together, told me that before she got sick, my mother and I were a "happy twosome." I hang on to that and to a single, shimmering memory of walking hand in hand with her on a warm summer evening, listening to her high heels click on the sidewalk, feeling special and protected. I treasure these memory shards from the ruins of our short time together and hope that the love my mother had for me rests at my core and feeds me still, like a time-release drug, protecting my children from the burdens of my past.

I want my mother to have been loving, kind and secure. And yet, I don't know what kind of attachment she had to my grandmother. My mother was her only child, born after a string of miscarriages. Did my grandmother's anxiety begin there, rather than at my mother's death? A large portrait of a lovely young girl lay in a basement closet all the years I was growing up. It was of Alice, my grandmother's sister, who died in childhood. There was a story there, but I never heard it. I don't know the secret sorrows of my grandmother's heart. I'll never know whether she was able to nurture my mother with more calm, loving care than she could me. I only know that, for me, when my mother disappeared abruptly from my four-year-old world, she became unavailable and rejecting and demanding of my independence in a most literal way, as only a severely avoidant mother would. My grandmother, who was profoundly affected by my mother's death and unable to grieve, may have related to me as a category-D parent when I went to live with her. Sifting through the descriptions of uneasy attachment, however, I keep coming back to ambivalent, specifically the present-but-absent "wire mother," as a fit for my grandmother and for myself as the dependent, anxious, appeasing child.

The women I interviewed often revealed similar complex overlappings of categories. Kit Bishop, the woman who grew up in an outwardly conventional family but who described her mother as "cold, rigid and strict," said that she had tried hard, in therapy and by talking to her mother, to understand the nature of their relationship when Kit was growing up, and to discover why her mother behaved as she did.

"My mother had a difficult childhood," Kit offered. "Her father died before she was two, and she was reared by a severe, racist mother who often farmed her out to relatives. She eloped at seventeen, and I was born soon after that. My mother had nothing to draw on for a model for her mothering but something concocted by a teenager who had not been well nurtured and who, in fact, had suffered a lot of neglect."

Kit sees in her mother prolonged avoidance of emotional attachment, as illustrated by a disturbing dream told to Kit years ago. Her mother dreamt that children—her own grandchildren—were crawling all over her and when she could bear it no longer she began flinging them away and beating them with sticks. "My mother told me this dream and sounded truly horrified by it. But then she also said, 'You know, I'm not one to get real close.' " Despite this evidence of avoidance, which Kit felt all through her growing years, Kit says ambivalent better describes the overall mothering she received.

Kit paused for a long moment, combing her fingers through the waves of her red hair, and then said, "My mother's message to me as a girl was: 'I'll comfort you right now, but maybe not again.' She was, above all, inconsistent. You just never knew with her."

The type of relationship a girl has with her mother can change over time as external and internal circumstances change. Sometimes a mother's life alters and with it her treatment of her children. One young woman, a graduate student, remembers her mother as being "very loving and compassionate" until her parents divorced, when she was eight. "After that," she told me, "my mother became very distracted with her new husband, and she was increasingly neglectful, leaving us with irresponsible caregivers for a week or two at a time. She'd forget important events or be gone for them. She became less nurturing and more threatened by independence."

Sometimes a girl reaches a developmental stage that triggers negative reactions in the mother and changes the attachment. The mother-daughter relationship might go relatively smoothly until the child reaches an age at which the mother expects the child to fail, because that's where the parent had trouble. The anxiety that arises can lead the parent to become overly strict and watchful or to give up and leave the child to her own devices. Neither option, of course, works for the child.

From the time of my mother's death, my presence was a constant, unwelcome reminder to my grandmother of all she had lost, but our difficulties intensified when I became a teen and wanted to date and move further out into the world. One night, my grandmother was already in bed when I got off the phone with a boy who had asked me out on what was a true first date. I told him I had to ask my grandmother. She was still awake and

I explained our plan. In response, she rolled over and with her back to me said, "I went through this with your mother, and I'm not going to go through it again."

I now know that from my grandmother's point of view, everything had gone wrong with my mother's dating. Her daughter had broken an engagement to a promising young physician and dropped out of nursing school to elope with a blue-eyed ex-Marine, who moved my mother away from her home where she contracted the disease that ended her life. I can now imagine how powerfully my grandmother would have wanted to spare herself another teenage girl's dating. At the time, of course, I knew none of that. As I stood by her bed that night I felt a familiar, disconcerting warring between my desire to please her and my need to assert myself. And this time, perhaps because her position just felt so blatantly wrong, I understood that I was going to go on dates with or without her blessing.

For Jeanne Beauvais, who lives in the Southwest and is mother to two girls, her teen years collided with her family's financial woes. She had had what she considered a "normal life" until about age twelve, when her father's business failed and the family declared bankruptcy. They sold the house they had built and moved to a small rental. Jeanne knows that the worst of this for her wasn't the sudden slip in social standing, but that her mother turned on her. "She was constantly after me about how I looked," Jeanne remembers. "She often made comments like, 'Doesn't your daughter look sexy tonight?' I felt horrible. I didn't want people to notice me sexually, especially my father." By the time Jeanne was eighteen her family's finances had turned around, but the pressure from her mother kept up. She wanted Jeanne to abandon her college ambitions and marry her boyfriend.

"She made it clear that she didn't want me to rise above her," Jeanne says. "She saw me as a threat, as competition. Things got worse and worse when it became clear that I wasn't going to follow her. My mother fought with herself, I know, but her overwhelming need was for me to justify her life. I didn't understand any of this as a young woman, but there was no mistaking my mother's animosity. I think she came to hate me, to truly hate me. I don't think she hated me as a baby, but she hated me when I was a teenager. I came to represent something she despised."

Jeanne now thinks that when her mother reached middle age and lost the "cuteness" and charm she had relied on to get by, she must have felt replaced by her daughter. Recently Jeanne found a photograph of her mother as a young woman of about twenty that helped explain this to her. The photo shows her mother sitting, legs crossed, "dressed to the nines," Jeanne says, in a broad-brimmed hat that framed her face, a little black dress and pumps with open toes. She's looking at the camera, holding a drink in a hand with carefully polished nails.

"Her expression," Jeanne tells me, "says 'Look at me. Aren't I something?' I was sitting on the floor staring at this photo and it came to me, 'That's her. This is who she was, who she wanted to be. She always wanted to be the center of attention, certainly not a middle-aged mother to a teenage girl.' "

Attachment doesn't wholly or solely shape a person. It doesn't govern a child's intellect, for example, and one's psychological makeup rests on many variables and complexities. Nor is attachment the only component of the infant-parent relationship, just as love is not the only need a child has. Caregiving and attachment go together, but as Bowlby emphasized, parents also support the development of their children in other ways: They teach, play, discipline, provide financial support and serve as role models, among other things.

"Nevertheless," writes Robert Karen, "to a growing number of developmentalists, the quality of early attachment stood out, like the key in which an otherwise complicated piece of music is played, imbuing the personality with a characteristic inflection that is present from movement to movement." All of us learned about relationships from the way our attachment figures treated us as children. And, as we shall see, powerful influences encourage those of us who lived much of our early lives in a minor key to pass on our experience of distorted attachment to our children. As we shall also see, however, a mother can change the patterns set in the past and compose a new tune, set in a new key, for the life she leads with the family she makes.

CHAPTER FOUR

Ghosts

No past is dead for us, but only sleeping, Love.

—Helen Hunt Jackson

As a child and then a teenager, I absorbed an image of motherhood that served as a powerful deterrent to having a child myself. No one in my grandparents' home spoke of my mother after her death, and I grew up knowing little about her. I knew none of the facts about her death or my father's disappearance. I knew no details of their lives, not the names of my paternal grandparents or when and where my parents married or even mundane facts such as what musical instrument my mother played in high school. No one, however, could hide the intense emotion around our shared history. I learned well our family taboo against expressing sadness, pain and vulnerability. I knew implicitly never to ask questions. Without ever having heard about theories of intergenerational transfer, I acquired the unconscious conviction that to be a mother meant I would have to repeat the experiences of my mother and grandmother. And through them I saw maternal life as fraught with physical and mental pain as well as being unbearably restricting. In the last two years of her life my mother couldn't leave her bed, and my grandmother couldn't leave her daughter's side. After my mother's death, I watched my grandmother continue to move only within the confines of the known and safe. I wanted a life as unlike this one as possible.

Lacking the money, imagination and courage to go away to college, however, I entered the university in my hometown, still living with my grandparents in my childhood bedroom. Later I moved into a series of apartments, but often went home to do laundry and eat my grandmother's meals. I passed up an opportunity to study abroad in my junior year, and when I replay the memory of telling the professor who had helped me apply for and win a spot in a program in England that I would not, could not go, I'm grieved for the confused girl who sat there weeping. I told my professor that my grandparents were getting old, and I was afraid I had too little time left with them. I'll never know whether he saw this as tender filial devotion or whether he could see what I didn't say, and didn't know in any way I could have put into words, which was that I couldn't leave them because I was afraid that they would die without my vigilant attention and that without them I would die. Staying risked imprisonment; going meant I would fly off loose in the world, lost and alone.

Two weeks after graduating from college I married an anchor—a man slightly older than I, destined for law school and a stable job. He was bright and ambitious, had a savings account, wanted to leave Colorado, did not want to have children and, although he had a sensitive nature, refused intimate conversation. At the time, that all seemed perfect. Immediately after our wedding we moved to another state, where we put each other through graduate school and then headed to New York City to work.

I had been afraid that Boulder, the town my great-grandparents had moved to in the early part of the twentieth century, would be the sum of my life. Now I had broken free, to no less than New York. And, it seemed, I would dodge motherhood as well.

My reasons for rejecting parenthood were sub rosa, unknown to myself. I thought I chose the "child-free" life because I preferred the excitement and fulfillment of a career over the drudgery of caring for children. I couldn't picture discussing toilet training and couldn't hide my supercilious air toward those who did. Soon after I first married, *Ms.* magazine was born and I had the full force of the women's movement behind my decision to choose career over maternity. Too busy denying and dissembling, I lacked self-knowledge, unlike one forthright woman who told me that at twenty-eight she inadvertently got pregnant, and though she was married, she promptly had an abortion. "Thanks to my upbringing," she said, "there was no way I was going to bring a child into the world and have history repeat itself."

And yet history does repeat itself. In my first marriage I unconsciously re-created the home I had had with my grandparents. Though the external details were entirely different—my husband and I had advanced degrees, lived in New York City, traveled, persisted in our childlessness—the internal environment was as emotionally constrained as that of my childhood. We were dependent on each other and enthralled with our marriage, but we didn't know each other. We never discussed my past, which was deeply buried, or any of the traumas in his life, including his tour as a foot soldier in Vietnam and his father's suicide just before our wedding. Order, control, safety: That's what I wanted, nothing as messy or risky as intimacy or independence.

The extent to which I tried to duplicate in adulthood the pattern of my past suggests how firmly tethered to it I was. Unlike children who are reared in safety and love, I couldn't leave home. I couldn't mature beyond my unfulfilled childhood needs. In adulthood I re-created the relationships I had had in childhood—impersonal but enmeshed, bound by secrets— because I didn't know there was another way.

* * *

That we tend to repeat in our adult lives what we have experienced in childhood is obvious. As Daniel Stern has said, "What else is there for you to fall back on?" Freud called it the "repetition compulsion," observing that despite conscious efforts and protests, people often prefer relationships that repeat earlier ones, even if they are unsatisfying. Bowlby explained this bias by saying that no matter how painful or disappointing the past may be, it provides the second-rate security of being familiar. The patterns of earlier relationships turn up with marriage partners, bosses, friends, extended family and, of course, children. This unconscious leaning toward repetition well serves those whose early relationships were loving, empathetic and nurturing. But what of others, women like me, whose data banks are crowded with "wrong way" examples? Are we destined to burden our children with the limitations of our childhoods? The answer, I found, is complex.

A woman named Annie told me that she has struggled against repeating her mother's way of mothering, and related a story of growing up in a small beach town. One of Annie's after-school chores was sweeping the kitchen floor.

"One day, my mother came home from work, inspected the floor and without a word pulled the broom from the closet and swept up a pile of dirt and sand. I picked it up and threw it out. Then I took the broom and swept and gathered up another small pile.

" 'See,' I told my mom, 'no matter how many times you sweep, there's always more to find.'

"Well, my mother glared at me and silently fixed dinner. She served the meal and then went to another room to read the newspaper. My father and brothers and sisters all sat down, looking at each other saying, 'What was it this time?' 'Who did it?' 'Not me!' I let it go on for a little bit and then confessed."

Today Annie, a mother of grown children, says that as hard as her mother's silent disapproval was to endure, she preferred it to the "bad" words, the critical ones.

"My mother never yelled or cursed, and she certainly wasn't angry all the time, but she could not compliment. She didn't get the warm, fuzzy treatment from her own mother and didn't give it to us. And I've had to fight that in my own mothering.

"I heard myself saying the same critical things to my daughter when she was a teenager that I had heard from my mother, even though I vowed not to. I had to *force* myself to praise my children. And now, I see my grown daughter about once a week, and I don't greet her or say good-bye with a hug, even though I feel like it. I haven't been able to overcome that particular hurdle, but both my children are now in their thirties and are self-sufficient, decent human beings. I know I mothered them and continue to mother them successfully."

Ghosts in the Nursery

"In every nursery there are ghosts," wrote child psychoanalyst Selma Fraiberg. "They are the visitors from the unremembered past of the parents; the uninvited guests at the christening." Under the best circumstances, the ghosts are banished by the bonds of love between the baby and parents, and the "magic circle of the family" protects the child. Other families, however, become possessed by their ghosts. "The baby in these families is burdened by the oppressive past of his parents from the moment he enters the world," writes Fraiberg.

Considerable research supports the idea that a mother creates a relationship with her child out of the psychological residue of her family history. Human behavior is complex and influenced by many, often immeasurable, factors; still, specific traits carry from one generation to the next. Children of depressed parents (who make up as much as 20 percent of the adult population), for example, are more likely to be depressed, and at an earlier age, and to suffer substance abuse, compared with other children. Reading this, I thought of Susan Wiseman, who began abusing drugs and alcohol in her early teens. I don't know whether her mother was ever diagnosed as depressed, but her mother's alcoholism, along with life circumstances that included a difficult divorce when she had five small children, would point in that direction. Another woman said: "Depression runs in my family. We have each in our own ways learned how to shut each other and the world out."

In a study of the transfer of child abuse, researchers found that 70 percent of parents who were abused as children were suspected of being abusers of their own children. And, conversely, all but one of the mothers in the study with a history of supportive and loving parental care provided adequately for their children. Interviewers asked the parents who were abused as children whether they would raise their children differently, and all but a small fraction said yes, vowing that they would not mistreat their children. And yet, the vast majority of them did abuse their children. The abusers don't intend to pass on the trauma. They just do. One woman whose children are now grown told me she was hit "too much" as a child (though she never thought of herself as an abused child) and when her first-born was two years old she flew into a rage and hurled him across the room onto a bed. She had not known she had such violent fury in her and spent many years in counseling trying to curb it.

In an effort to tease out answers to questions about whether maternal care is repeated, researchers at the University of Texas looked at three generations of women—grandmother, mother and infant—in forty-nine families. The researchers asked the grandmothers whether they raised their daughters in a way similar to or different from how they were raised. Eighty percent said *differently*. But their daughters had something else to say. Most of them, when asked what they wished had been different in their upbringing, described the same complaint about their childhoods that their mothers had made about theirs. One grandmother, for instance, said, "My mother smothered me and would not let any of us go out and have fun. I raised my daughter differently. I let her have the freedom I never had." That woman's daughter, when asked to describe her biggest complaint about her mother when growing up, said this: "We always had to stay home. My mother never let me go out."

Although many of the relationships between the mothers and grandmothers were not the same as in childhood—they had changed, for better or worse, over time—the mother's early pattern with her mother rose up to influence her own parenting. Specific, sometimes long-past behaviors of the grandmothers, such as being overprotective or intrusive or distrusting of outsiders, were repeated by the mothers in the care they gave their infants. When it comes to mothering, as Stern has said, "we have mounting evidence that intergenerational forces are hard at work, and powerfully influence the new mother as she begins to relate to her baby."

Occasionally I find myself doing or saying something that is like her. If my daughter or husband is around I'll usually hear about it immediately. "Ooooh, you sound just like Nana!" They both have standing orders never to say that in jest.

Mother was a yeller. My sisters and I knew that in the mid to late afternoon we should stay as far away from her as possible. I'm also a yeller. I try not to do that with my daughter, but I'm having trouble with it. I'm pregnant now and have no patience. My daughter pushes my buttons.

I try not to hover, nag, be fearful and worry, and I try not to keep silent about what I need and then get angry when I don't get it, like my mother did. I'm making progress, but honestly, these are lifelong struggles.

Passing On Attachment

Do attachment patterns flow predictably to the next generation? Many recent studies tell us that the answer is "usually." The pattern of attachment a mother forms with her baby—the way she and the baby act toward each other and feel about each other as they separate and reunite—is largely determined by the pattern of attachment she had with her mother.

Alan Sroufe, a leading figure in developmental psychology, once said: "If you're in a relationship, the relationship is part of you, there's no way around it. . . . How do you get an empathic child? You get an empathic child not by trying to teach the child and admonish the child to be empathic, you get an empathic child by being empathic with the child. The child's understanding of relationships can only be from the relationships he's experienced." If, for example, a mother can hear and accept a child's negative emotions, such as jealousy, anger or hurt, without being dismissive or overreacting, her child learns to express and cope with pain. Her child becomes confident that negative feelings can evoke a sensitive response.

Reflecting on her interviews of pregnant women, attachment researcher Arietta Slade once said, "It's so interesting that a mother who felt controlled by her mother her entire life is already preoccupied with whether she can control her fetus. Or that a mother whose own mother pushed her aside is already convinced that her child won't have any needs, won't change her life, and will be autonomous early on. Chills go up and down your spine when you hear these things."

During my interviews with mothers I, too, had occasion to experience those chills as women told me their mothering stories. The phantoms of their uneasy attachments seemed to hover around us as we talked. One woman spoke of the difficulties and insecurities she was having as a mother of two grown sons who make no effort to be with her. "I don't know what it is, and it's very hard for me," she said. "They're polite, but perpetually busy when I ask to see them." Groping for an explanation, she offered that she's very different from them and is opinionated about health, nutrition and politics.

"I do think my habit of stating my opinions, whether requested or not, can be a challenge for them, and especially for their wives," she said. I felt a shiver a moment later as, talking about what she had tried to do differently from her own mother, she said, "I've tried to avoid my mother's tendency to think she knew what was best for me." It seems quite possible to me that stating her opinions "whether requested or not" might be interpreted by her children as telling them what she thinks is best for them—her very complaint about her own mother.

Echoes of the past also sounded through the descriptions of her parenting given by young Alexandra Reed, who became pregnant as an unwed teen. She struck me as a brave, intelligent, responsible parent who's consciously striving to give her daughter more than was given to her. Of her own mother she says, "I'd never in a million years pick her as my mom, but as a friend she'd be fine. She's fun and enjoys art and music and nature, but I needed a grown-up."

Her mother plainly failed Alexandra by refusing even basic parenting obligations; she was inconsistent and repeatedly abdicated responsibility for her daughter. Alexandra, in contrast, has shown strong determination to provide for her daughter. At sixteen she rose at 4:30 a.m. to get on a bus and take her infant to day care and herself to work. Today, at twenty-one, she's held the same job as an office manager for a stock brokerage firm for three years. And yet, the past casts a shadow. Alexandra's daughter will have her own story to tell, one day, of being brought up by a too-young, single mother, about not knowing her father, about roommates and relatives who turned up suddenly or left abruptly. Her story surely will be a happier one, but not without its tribulations.

During our conversation, Alexandra's daughter, a blithe four-year-old who dances rather than walks across a room and who has her mother's straight brown hair and pointed chin, kept interrupting. Soon Alexandra sent her off to play a video game that simulates driving a car.

"To me, parenting is like baby-sitting," she said. "You think of something to keep them distracted until they fall asleep." This notion of mother as baby-sitter—emotionally uninvolved, not ultimately accountable, transient—may flow from further back than her own upbringing. Alexandra's maternal grandmother married eight times, moved even more often and professed no interest in children, though she had five. While striving to do better for her daughter, Alexandra knows she doesn't have the right images in her head.

"If you don't know any different, you don't know any better," she said. "I can't picture what it would be like to have a mother and a father and everything being handy-dandy. Nothing close to what I see on TV. I just can't picture what it would feel like to be in a family.

"I don't really feel like a mom, probably because I started too young, but still it hasn't changed now that I'm older. I don't feel like I'm the best mom. I just treat her like I'd like to be treated.

"One time I found hair all over the place and when I found her, she had a giant bald spot in front where she'd cut her own hair. Deep inside I felt, 'How could you do this!' But then I thought about it and remembered that when I was young I cut my own hair. So I just said, 'How do you like it?' And she said, 'Are you mad?' 'Nah, I'm not mad,' I said. 'But next time let someone else cut it.' A lot of parents would have gotten mad.

"My daughter acts like a kid, but she's also a little adult. She takes care of herself now, which sounds bad, I know, but it's true. She's very independent. She gets up in the morning and gets dressed, and I have breakfast ready for her. She needs very little guidance, just a slight order like, 'Brush your teeth, then go to bed,' and she does it."

Throughout our conversation I heard a strain of detachment. She wants to treat her daughter "like a normal person, not like my baby," and she encourages her to be independent, just as Alexandra was from too early an age. Later, she repeated the theme of her mothering: "I decided I would treat her like I did kids when I was a baby-sitter. Give them some love, tuck them in. This is a full-time baby-sitting job."

In the 1980s, developmental psychologist Mary Main advanced attachment research significantly by devising a way to link a parent's memories of childhood with her current behavior as a parent. By analyzing their answers to questions about their childhoods, Main was able to divide the adults in her study into categories that corresponded to Ainsworth's attachment types. These were Ainsworth's "children" grown up and acting on the attachments of their childhoods.

DISMISSING. Adults labeled by Main as *dismissing* were guarded and vague and often had trouble remembering specifics of their childhoods; they were terse and deflected discussion of the past. They were like the woman I interviewed who couldn't say "abandonment" and who couldn't relate the chronology of her girlhood, the one who dropped counseling when she was told that she had "walls built up." Often these adults spoke of their parents in idealized, glowing terms, but then couldn't support their views with examples. Frequently, as the interview progressed, these people would contradict themselves, for example, revealing they had been afraid to go to a parent when badly hurt. Dismissing adults correlated to Ainsworth's avoidant children. Now grown up, they still appear indifferent to hurt or rejection and are still cut off from the longing for love. Adults in this category have repeatedly been found to have children who are avoidantly attached to them.

PREOCCUPIED. A second group of adults called *preoccupied* matched ambivalent children, and the vast majority of them have children who are ambivalently attached. For them, the hurt, disappointment and anger of the past, often thirty or forty years past, lived on. As children, they tried hard to please their parents, and as adults they still sought parental approval. They often talked of their childhood memories in confused and incoherent ways and would get lost in feelings of resentment during the questioning. The past held its grip, as it did for a woman I talked to whose resentment of her "manipulative, passive-aggressive" mother threaded through our conversation. "I'm forty and she treats me like I'm ten," she snapped. "She wants forgiveness, but goes on doing the same unforgivable things." The only reason, she said, she hasn't entirely cut off her mother, as her siblings have, is that she doesn't want to model "rejecting mother" for her own children.

SECURE-AUTONOMOUS. This third group, also called *free to evaluate*, could relate to the researchers a coherent narrative of their parents and childhood experiences. They were objective about the good and bad aspects of their parents and comfortable reflecting on themselves and the past. Secure adults appear to value attachment relationships and regard them as influential, but seem relatively objective about any particular relationship or experience. Free to explore thoughts and feelings, they often show insight and understanding of their parents. They tended to see how they were like their parents, even in negative ways, and showed little evidence of self-deception.

In her research of pregnant women, Arietta Slade found that those classified as secure using Main's interview were more open psychologically to becoming mothers. They had a balanced view of what motherhood would require of them, and they had already begun a relationship with their unborn babies, giving them nicknames and imagining what they were like. The majority of children of secure adults tested as securely attached to them.

One reason a parent who can comfortably reflect on herself is better able to provide a secure base for her child might be because she can take herself out of a situation and see it from her child's viewpoint. That enables her to empathize with the infant's emotions and thus respond to the child's signals with caring behavior that meets the infant's need for comforting. An insecure parent, in contrast, seems to teach her child the very defensive strategies she employs. One mother, for example, who laughingly disowned any troubles in her childhood, later vigorously tried to get her crying infant to laugh after a separation, rather than first trying to comfort the child.

Following up on Main's work, other researchers found that being able to reflect clearly in this way wasn't related to personality, self-esteem, intelligence, education or other social, economic or demographic factors. What distinguishes the autonomous adults is that they understand themselves and others and can relate a coherent narrative about their pasts.

Most significant, and reassuring, for under-mothered women is that not all the secure adults had secure childhoods. Main and her colleagues demonstrated that the way in which a parent presents her life narrative, regardless of its content, predicts caregiving behavior in highly specific ways. Parents do not *necessarily* repeat the parenting they remember. As Main has said: "The study of attachment would be dull indeed if we found only that secure infants tend to become secure children, who tend then to become secure adults."

Reading about Mary Main's work with adult attachment, I was struck by how my adulthood has been characterized by both the dismissing and preoccupied responses to my past. I carried into my twenties the avoidant or dismissing attitude of my childhood. If asked, I would have said that it was *fine* that I seldom saw my father. Although years often went by with minimal contact between us, that was okay. After all, I had my grandparents, and look at all they had done for me. Truly, I would have said, everything is just fine. As for my mother, well, she's been gone a long time. I'm used to it, and isn't it remarkable how well I've done considering my childhood?

In my thirties, the barrier to my past that I had propped up began to grow too heavy, and I now see that I shifted to a preoccupied stance, holding close the hurt, anger and resentment from the distant past. Phone calls from my father, always unpredictable and disconcerting, increased, as did my discomfort with them. He'd joined Alcoholics Anonymous after decades of drinking and was working on step nine of the twelve-step program, which asks the alcoholic to make "direct amends" to those harmed. In his effort, my father became more attentive than he'd ever been during my childhood. One day I came home from work to find a heavy cardboard box of books about alcoholism he'd sent across the country from his home in Seattle to mine in New York. Opening the carton triggered feelings I could neither identify nor tolerate. With my foot, I shoved the box to the back of a closet and dreaded his next phone call. He wanted my forgiveness, but to forgive him meant I had to take a look at the wrong he had done. Meanwhile, my relationship with my grandmother grew more bewildering. My grandfather had died by then and she was living alone. I frequently called and sent her gifts for no special occasion. I flew from New York to Colorado for holidays, though the celebrations were uncomfortable and unsettling, and I couldn't hold back my tears when saying good-bye.

A pivotal episode from one of those Christmases abides in my memory. My first husband and I had traveled from our Greenwich Village one-bedroom apartment to my grandmother's living room and sat opening gifts on Christmas Day. With a pleased smile, she indicated that the huge package under the tree was for us. I opened it to find a set of four TV trays. As a child, living with my grandparents in our old house—the one they built when they married, the one where they lived when my mother was born, the one around the corner from the house in which she died, the one my brother and I moved into when our parents were gone—I would sit in the living room to eat spaghetti on a TV tray and watch Dorothy Collins on *The Hit Parade*.

I awkwardly thanked her. Later, in private with my husband, I rolled my eyes and made jokes. But these were guises to hide the meaning of the utterly inappropriate gift. My grandmother had not given that gift to *me*—a childless magazine editor who lived in an apartment a long airplane ride away, who far preferred reading to TV watching. It was for the granddaughter—or, no, the daughter—she didn't have. The one who lived around the corner and cooked suppers for her family, the one she must have pined for every day of her life. Somehow, the hurt of that gift, one example in decades of blatant missteps between me and my grandmother, penetrated deeply. It showed me that, despite all my wooing of her, my grandmother couldn't see me. She couldn't value who I was because she didn't know me.

I don't know what kind of mother I would have been had I had children in my twenties, but in that dismissing mode I suppose I would have repeated the distant mothering of my experience. Later in my thirties when I was enmeshed in my anger and pain, I suspect I would have reacted to my past, maybe insisting that I would do *nothing* the way my grandmother had and most likely tying my children to me with my compelling need for their dependence and love. I don't really know. It took me all the way to my forties to learn my history and to make some sense of it, and I can only think that it's a good thing I waited until then to have children.

In my interviews I encountered mothers who have gained enough insight into their childhoods and distance from their mothers to enable them to achieve the balanced characteristics of secure adults. One such woman, Leanne, grew up with a mother she describes as "uncomfortable with herself, not an engaging person you'd want to talk to, an inward rather than outward person." Leanne's mother provided "the nuts and bolts" of mothering, Leanne said. "She wasn't able to be emotionally available, but she did the rest of the job." Because Leanne has a broad view of her mother's care, hard-won through years of trying to get to know her mother and herself, she can say, "There are pieces of her that I respect and admire and I hope I do emulate those.

"I want to be as committed as she was to whatever activities my kids are involved in. I want to get them to their soccer practices and make sure they have Easter cookies like she did. In my own mothering, though, I'm also trying to make the emotional connection and to help my children talk about their feelings. I want them to know it's okay to be angry and to admit to being wrong about something."

Susan Wiseman has developed a no-nonsense, sharp view of her past and her own imperfect mothering. She's the woman whose mother and father would lock their bedroom door each night and not allow any of their children in. As the youngest, Susan especially suffered times of being frightened and alone.

"I get mad about it to this day," she says. "Yet if my kids come up to our room not feeling well or having had a bad dream, I'm not happy. I'll take care of them, but it's a little begrudgingly."

Susan's mother also seldom allowed her children to stay home sick from school. Susan and I laughed a little at this, speculating that with nine children, a mother would have had to be a bit draconian to ever get them all out of the house at once. Conveying both exasperation and amusement, Susan elaborated, saying, "We had to be bleeding or very, very sick. You couldn't just be throwing up, you also had to have a fever.

"And I have to admit that it pisses me off when my kids want to stay home sick. I would love to turn into Florence Nightingale when my beloved offspring become ill, but I can't. I can't even avoid sarcasm just talking about it!

"When either of my kids is really sick, and my youngest has had major health problems, I click in and feel that my absolute purpose in the world is to take care of these kids and really mother them. In the less dramatic situations, though, my default response is 'Oh, come on. How sick are you? Prove it.'"

Here she paused, smirking at her own hardheadedness and giving her hair a shake, then continued, "My comfort with my mothering skills goes up and down, and is frankly not terribly predictable. I love talking with my kids, make a point to try to be honest with them, and tell them I love them. I'm less afraid than my mother was about breaking down the power structure. I say to my kids, 'Hey, I may not always respond the way that makes you feel loved, but never forget that I think you're the most special thing on earth.' And I must say I have felt completely incapable of 'showing up' for my life as a mother without the help of a very loving God who just waits for me to ask for some help. I tell my children: 'I can't always do everything right for you, but God is an excellent back-up guy who helps out big-time.' "

Like Leanne and other adults who can reflect on and evaluate their lives, Susan shows little evidence of self-deception about her mother and her mothering.

On the Brink of Motherhood

By the time I was pregnant with my first child, I had passed forty and had spent two good years in therapy mourning my mother and my first marriage. I had moved back to the town of my birth to marry a man I had known in childhood; together we would create a home and a family. By then, I had given up my childhood hope that someday it wouldn't matter that I didn't grow up with a mother. I had come to name the longings that haunted me. And yet, I arrived at pregnancy unprepared for the deluge of feeling for my mother that came as I made my transition from a motherless daughter to a motherless mother. I discovered new, unmined layers of grief around her as I carried and gave birth to the boy who would have been her first grandchild. I had stumbled through childhood and into adulthood without my guide and now I would have to make this trek without her as well. But within that bleakness also stirred a new connection to my mother; one that had been only potential now became reality: *We are both mothers.* I yearned to sit with her, to share with her the unbearable richness of life with my first baby. She was the ghost in my child's room but now the shadow she cast brought comfort, not a chill.

Beneath the decision, conscious or unconscious, to have children lies one's own childhood. A woman contemplating pregnancy or one who suddenly finds herself bearing a child will almost certainly be visited by thoughts of her own mother. Women who were abandoned by their mothers, as I was, may fear repeating the loss through the death of the child or themselves. Others associate childhood with vulnerability, powerlessness and a trusting dependency that wasn't honored, and they resist being around such helplessness again.

When I was twenty-seven I decided not to have children and asked my gynecologist to tie my tubes. Luckily, he refused. He thought I was too young to make that decision and that I might change my mind. He was right.

I viewed my mother as acting like a victim, and I didn't want that to be me. I also felt that I didn't want to bring a child into my life when I had so much work to do on myself.

I dreaded motherhood. In fact, I had decided that even if someone would pay me to do it, there wasn't enough money in the world. My own family was a mess. I've tried to explain it to myself over the years and only recently learned that my younger brother was probably bipolar as a child. Both of my parents just checked out emotionally, and I filled in the gaps. I entered my twenties feeling I had already raised a child and now it was my turn to have a life. I was also terrified that if I had a baby and it was a boy, my brother's problems would repeat themselves. But my husband desperately wanted a family, and his faith in the joy and love of family won me over. It's been a lot of work for me to get here, but I can say now that he was right.

Women have children for many reasons: to pass along their own genes, to please their husbands or mothers, to fulfill an idea they have about what constitutes a life or a family. They have children to fill a void or replace a loss in their own lives or to avoid the challenges of work or feelings of loneliness. The authors of *The Motherhood Report* found that although three of four women in their survey said that they wanted children in order to have someone to love, further questions often turned up not a desire to nurture as much as a desire to be nurtured. For many of the women, motherhood represented the possibility of renewal, a chance to start over again and relive their childhoods in a happier, more perfect way. Despite the wide range of motives behind bearing children, unconscious and conscious, those motives don't predict how a mother will eventually come to love and care for her children, according to psychologist Harriet Lerner.

Not until I was pregnant did I feel ready. I think it was the chaotic feeling I harbor from my own childhood that kept me from wanting to go ahead. It wasn't all that much fun for me being a kid. I was scared a lot and felt insecure.

It was a hard decision. We put it off for the first eight years of our marriage. We didn't feel like either of us had had a very stable home life, and although we knew we would do it, we just didn't know when would be a good time.

Until I met my husband I never wanted children at all. I think it was being emotionally strong and healthy enough to be in a strong and healthy relationship that made me change. In this relationship

I felt like I was home in a way I'd never felt before. With it came the realization that I would love to and even must have children with this man and that I could have a loving family around me, something I'd not admitted to myself that I wanted.

No matter why a woman becomes pregnant, her impending motherhood is likely to evoke her own childhood and the care she received. I heard the rumblings of remembered mothering and the desire for a maternal presence rising up in the soon-to-be mother when I interviewed Michelle Struthers, thirty-four, who was seven months pregnant with her first child. Michelle, a businesswoman, and I sat facing each other in her comfortable office chairs to talk. I admired her dark-haired good looks and she stroked her taut belly as she told me she'd been married for five years to a man who is her "soul mate for life." They had thought carefully about having a child.

The day I met her, Michelle glowed with the confidence of the healthy and athletic, so I was surprised when she said, "It's been a really, really difficult pregnancy." Not because of her health or the baby's health, which were both excellent, but "because of my mom. I cry all the time," she said, looking more ardent than weepy. "My friends saw a major change in me right after I got pregnant. I just began to crave my mother, but I kept thinking, 'Oh, my God, I don't have a mother.' "

Though Michelle feels motherless, her mother is alive, is only fifty-seven and visits Michelle often. "My mother once was my best friend," she said. Although her mother had divorced twice by the time Michelle was twelve, the two had remained very close. After the second divorce, however, her mother's life grew chaotic, and Michelle and her brother eventually moved away to live with their father. For many years of adolescence and young adulthood, Michelle seldom saw her mother. Now, many years later, her once "energetic and beautiful" mother has been transformed into a "collapsed-looking" woman who slumps, has "no vigor, no strength in her body," who can no longer hold down a job or care adequately for herself.

"I don't really know who she is. She was like a friend to me, but I respected her and she was such a strong woman. I don't understand what happened." Michelle saw the question in my face and said, "Believe me, I'm as baffled by this as you are." Her mother has been diagnosed as depressed, and although she's on medication, she hasn't improved.

"I had been taking care of her and thinking, 'Well, this is how it is while she's healing.' But once I got pregnant I was just *praying* for a mom. Now I have these dreams of having her back like she used to be. But I don't think that's going to happen. I keep hoping. It's hard to give up on someone who's so young.

"Until I got pregnant, I hadn't faced how our roles had switched and I became sort of the mother to her. I've been sending her money, buying the plane tickets so she can come visit, and then when she comes I provide *completely* for her. I have to tell her what to wear, otherwise she'd go out for the evening in sweats and slippers. If I didn't cook or shop, she wouldn't do it. I think she lives on cereal and toast when I'm not around. It's exhausting to be with her. I feel like she needs me to do everything for her, and that's really, really depressing for me."

Only when Michelle got pregnant did this challenge with her mother take on greater significance. Being pregnant activated her own attachment need to be cared for and supported, as it does for many women and for any adult who is anxious or under stress.

"When you become pregnant," Michelle says, "you become maternal yourself, but you also want to be mothered. It would be so nice to be mothered right now." Her voice trailed off as she shifted position in her chair, and her animated face softened.

"It would be so nice," she repeated. "And I won't get that. I'll have to be in this role forever. It's a hard thing for me. I have a lot of friends whose mothers come out and take care of them when their babies are born. And the new grandmothers love their new role.

"And I've been thinking about what kind of grandmother she'll be for my unborn daughter. It's a scary feeling. It makes me feel lonely. I don't relate to my husband's mother at all, especially as a role model. I am it. And I'm going to bring my daughter into the world with just the strength of myself and the support of myself and my husband and this is still really hard for me to face."

Michelle knows how she wants her mother to be toward her and her baby. She desires the symmetry of grandmother-mother-child. The good years that Michelle had with her mother as a child don't prevent her from needing her mother now, at this critical juncture in her life. She longs to be the mother in the middle, both protected and protector. "I've been depressed through my whole pregnancy," she told me, "though it's getting better now that I can feel the baby move a lot. I'm beginning to get excited. And I'm really happy it's a girl. I welcome that connection."

Becoming pregnant, giving birth and mothering a child all cause women to reconnect with their mothers and to reexamine that relationship, regardless of the quality or nature of those bonds. Kit Bishop, the woman whose mother dreamt of flinging her grandchildren away from her, worked with a psychotherapist for years to heal the pain of not being nurtured, and still dislikes anything that identifies her with her mother. "It just freezes me," she says, "when someone mentions our physical resemblance, our red hair and petiteness, our noses, whatever! And this is true even though I'm feeling loving toward her now!"

During pregnancy, the connections to her mother were complex and confusing. "I just kept thinking, 'This is what my mother felt.' And that was repulsive to me. It wasn't what I imagined other women thought. I think others must say, 'Oh, my mother was like this. I'm like my mother,' and feel *good* about that.

"When my daughter was three she asked me how I knew that girls can have babies. I explained about sperm and eggs and gently stroked her tiny tummy with my fingertips saying, 'All those little eggs are already right in there.' Immediately I had an electrifying feeling as I thought of my own mother's eggs. I go to that mother, daughter, grandmother connection immediately. I'm never very far from that intense awareness. In spite of everything difficult between us, there is also this primitive, powerful connection."

The Shadow Grandmother

What Kit, Michelle and I experienced is something psychiatrist Stern explains as a triangle. For all children, the triangle of mother-father-child plays an important role in forming their personalities. When we become parents we assume an adult role in that triangle. At the same time, the new mother also becomes one in a triangle of herself, her baby and her mother. "Quite surprising to new mothers," Stern says, "is the hold this triangle has on their inner psychological landscapes." If a new mother is to free herself from the past and get on with the tasks before her, she must meet the psychological demands this triangle makes on her attention.

Entangled with the psychological chores are practical concerns in the relationship between the new mother and the grandmother. A woman grows curious about her mother as she was years ago, and may care little about her mother's life now as a wife or woman. New mothers want to know whether they were breast-fed or had colic, when they started walking or teething and what their mothers felt about it all. The minutiae of infant care that fascinates many a new mother extends to the specifics of her own babyhood and her mother's motherhood. For under-mothered women, this knowledge is often lost. When one in the triangle is a ghost—either truly gone or simply unwilling or unable to be present—there's no satisfaction of the longing to know.

When I got pregnant I not only became acutely aware that I didn't have a mother to share this with, but there was so much I wanted to know. I wanted to ask my mother questions about childbirth, about what I was like as a baby and what her pregnancies were like, all that comparative information. My children are almost grown and that gap is still there. I often make comments to my daughters about things they did in their early youth. But for me, I don't have all those little pieces of information about myself.

When the triangle evokes positive and enriching memories, the woman and her mother may forge a deeper bond with the coming of the next generation, as one woman who has always been close to her mother did. "My motherhood deepened our relationship," she said. "She was there for me, through all twenty-four hours of labor. She attended some Lamaze classes so she could give my husband breaks. She was the first one to hold our first child, and she came to visit us every day for the first few weeks. She did housework, and we did things together with the baby. It was really touching. I remember being a little afraid when that time ended. And when she died suddenly and I lost her and our three children lost her, I found that I was more dependent on her than I ever realized. I wouldn't change that. It was really beautiful, but it makes it hard. I depended on her and she depended on me."

Some women I interviewed who had uneasy alliances with their mothers experienced a kind of truce or grace period during pregnancy, when despite earlier difficulties, their mothers were able to take a maternal role toward their pregnant daughters. Sometimes this allows for repairs in the old relationship or a deepening of an already good relationship, but the sad truth is that usually it doesn't.

She spent a lot of time with me when I had to be on bed rest with my second pregnancy. I appreciated it, and although she couldn't say it, I felt her love and caring. But now, though we live in the same town, she keeps her distance. I've said to her, "Don't miss out on your grandchildren," but she only comes by every three weeks to measure their growth and get a story to tell her friends. She doesn't really experience them, and our relationship hasn't changed.

When my twins were newborns my mother came to visit twice a week for the first three months and kept me company, and that was nice and comfortable. I didn't ask her advice. She mostly marveled at what a "good mother" I was and what a surprise that was to her. It didn't lead to any more in our relationship, though. My expectations were pretty low, so while it wasn't disappointing when she stopped coming, I did realize somewhat sadly that the little space of time we'd had together was over.

Becoming a mother renewed for me the loss of extended family I've felt since childhood. Although I'd adjusted to the scarcity of intimate relatives in my life, I found a new ache in seeing my children grow up without their grandmothers. My mother and my husband's mother are, to our children, nothing more than young women in photographs, smiling from the wall of remembrance we've created on the landing of our stairway. The faces of those women, framed in light brown permed curls, captured at happy moments in young adulthood, are background to our everyday lives. My husband and I have few stories to pass on, but we want our children to know, at least, our mothers' faces. We want them someday to see in their own faces—in the arch of an eyebrow, the shyness of a smile, the strength of a chin—the glimmers of their grandmothers that we see and hold dear. And in this nominal way I help to bring my mother into the triangle of grandmother-mother-child. I don't know whether my children will one day miss having had their grandmothers, but I'm aware of what they lack.

Many under-mothered women, often those whose mothers

are still alive, also spoke of that acute desire I've felt to complete the triangle. For some women, as for me, the fact that their mothers have not been able or willing to be the grandmothers their daughters hoped for is a profound disappointment.

My mother is attached to my children, but she doesn't see them a lot. She comes around to get the goodies and then she goes. She loves it when my children fawn over her. I remember once when he was a toddler my son was in her lap, stroking her face and kissing her, and she closed her eyes and soaked it up. I could tell she needed it desperately.

Once I had kids I thought, "Oh, she'll be better now. She wasn't a mom to me but she'll be a grandmother to them." That was my perception of how things would work out, but it didn't really happen that way. She never asks to see them.

Women are sometimes surprised and chagrined by a maternal figure's inability to make the transition to grandmother, as was a woman I interviewed named May Hung. Now a public health nurse in California and mother to two teenagers, May went to live with an aunt and uncle and cousins at thirteen when she lost both her parents. She adored her aunt, with whom she had a "fantastic relationship," and May came to love her cousins as siblings. Her aunt, May says, "filled the mother role without the baggage of a natural mother and daughter relationship. She had no preconceived ideas about who I should turn out to be. She wasn't in my face about the decisions I made and didn't badger me with unsolicited advice." As loving and supportive as this bond with her aunt was, however, May experienced fresh grief over the loss of her mother when she had her first child.

"My relationship with my aunt was wonderful, but I'm not her blood and these were not her grandchildren. By nature she's a clannish person and just couldn't open her heart to my children. They didn't get that total adoration of grandparent for grandchild from her. I know that lots of people didn't get that from parents who are alive, but I'm not talking about reality here. I'm talking about what I wanted."

The Portuguese have a word, *saudade,* to describe a state of longing and absence, but living well with that feeling. *Saudade* describes a missing that hurts and comforts at once, which is how I've come to think of my mother. Though she's but a ghost, I've come to see that my motherhood has linked us and that she is tied to my children, too, though there is a wall of silence between her and us. I've tried to bridge that distance by moving back to the town where my mother and I spent our girlhoods and where she is buried. Here, in the neighborhood of her childhood and mine, I have moored myself and my children. Beneath the mountains that rise above her grave and my home, I am rearing her grandchildren. As for many other women, the missing grandmother in my triangle exerts tremendous power.

Many factors in a woman's life have an impact on what kind of mother she becomes, including such circumstances of chance or intention as her economic and marital status, her age and physical health, the support of a social group or lack of one. The psychological terrain she covers in mothering her children is also affected by an assemblage of forces and factors in her past and present life. And although the mother she had doesn't necessarily determine the mother she becomes, the mother she had is always there.

CHAPTER FIVE

Exceptions

❦

There are those destroyed by unfairness and those who are not.

—Michael Ondaatje

It was in my junior year of high school, in psychology class, that I first heard Freud's ideas about how a child's unconscious and conscious experiences with her parents have a decisive influence on later relationships and life. That dry instruction on a drowsy spring afternoon snapped me to attention. At sixteen I didn't know that the past could leak into the present. I didn't know that each human is the sum of her experiences. I had wrapped the turbulence of my childhood tightly and put it away, but the teacher was suggesting that my efforts were futile. I remember hurrying out after the bell, disoriented by the jumble of unfamiliar emotion this slice of Freud had aroused. And there, in the crowded hallway of my high school, I leaned against my locker and cried. I wept, I now think, more out of confusion than sadness, though surely the loss of my mother was part of the babel in my head. What I most remember, though, was a feeling of fear stirred by the thought that I was damaged and could never be right—some version of normal—because of my childhood. Interestingly, there was also a faint undertone of excitement, a sense of being exceptional and unique that came, I think, from this rare into-the-self glimpse. I was at once mortified by my tears but also hoping to be noticed. I wanted—and badly needed, I see now—to talk to someone who could help me make sense of these new thoughts. For a fleeting moment I tried to think of someone I might turn to, but I could imagine no safe place to go. So I retreated to the stance I had assumed when my mother died. I steadied my face and jammed shame and hurt back to that place I had shoved it long ago, and headed down the hallway to class.

For the next twenty years, despite powerful tugs from within, I managed to steer wide of meaningful introspection and therapists. Then, when I was thirty-seven, my first husband and I left New York City for San Francisco so he could transfer jobs. That leave-taking drastically changed the shape of my life, in ways I could never have guessed as I boarded an airplane to fly west. The time had come for me to reinvent myself, and the move to the opposite coast provided the prod I needed.

The move dislodged me from a demanding full-time job as a magazine editor, a career I had pursued in the decade following graduate school. I began to work as a freelance writer. For the first time in my adult life, my days weren't subject to the dictates of a workplace or school. I had no regular office hours and a commute no longer than a flight of stairs to my home office. At first, I had but one friend in the city, a former colleague who had made the same transfer a few years earlier. I was married to a man who was deeply involved in his job. All that added up to give me more time to think and reflect than I had ever had.

Those circumstances converged with others, most notably heart surgery for my father, to finally break down the walls I had built around my past. I hadn't seen my father in more than a decade, but the prospect that he might die sent me into cold sweats. My first summer in San Francisco also coincided with my twentieth high school reunion. I had gone "home" many times before, but this time I went without my husband. Being there, socializing with childhood friends, being more aware than ever of how stiff and dishonest the dance I did with my grandmother was, added to my escalating turmoil. Every aspect of my life was suddenly up for inspection, and none of it any longer made sense. Why was I living in San Francisco? What was I doing in a marriage that precluded children? Where was my mother and where were my babies? The questions, doubts and confusions were overwhelming.

It was 1987. The self-help movement was in full flower, and I was a prime candidate for an overhaul. I asked my only local friend who her psychotherapist was and made an appointment. For the first twenty minutes or so of that initial session, I told the therapist my story, not providing detail, but stepping blandly through the years from birth, focusing on geography. Born in Colorado, moved to Arizona where mother got sick. Back to Colorado to live with grandparents. Dad and paralyzed mother come back for a while. Mother dies. More living with mother's parents in Colorado. Father reappears with a new wife and stepson midway through my third-grade year. They take my brother and me to live in Seattle. Midway through sixth grade, stepmother puts me, my brother and her son in the station wagon to drive to Colorado. She drops brother and me at our grandparents' house, and she and her son are never seen again. Dad stays in Seattle. High school, college, early marriage in Colorado. Graduate school in Kansas. Career in New York. Move to San Francisco. The story to date—brief, skeletal, with no interpretation, but it was all there.

I had never heard that story before. I had never told it. Fragments of memory—seeing my stepmother chase my father through our house with a fireplace poker, getting into the limo to go to my mother's funeral—would occasionally surface, but never had the whole tale been laid out before me. I understood then, without even the first pointed comments and questions from the woman who was to become my steady guide through the next two thorny years of therapy, that now I had to face and wrestle with the fact I had only caught a glimpse of at sixteen in psychology class. I *had* been seriously damaged in childhood. *How in the world,* I remember thinking, *have I been putting one foot in front of the other all these years?* Unlike that high school day, though, I had no inkling of excitement at discovering my uniqueness, only a sobering, leaden awareness that a hard road lay ahead.

On a cold, dry March day, I talked at length with Jeanne Beauvais, the woman who came to believe her mother truly hated her. She spoke of her mother's narcissism (a term Jeanne's counselor had used) and of how her mother couldn't look beyond her own needs to see someone else. Jeanne described being reared in a family that started out well, but began to deteriorate when Jeanne was about twelve and her father's business failed. Her parents' alcoholism escalated during her junior high and high school years, a time she recalls as "the clouded part." Her parents urged her out of their home when she turned eighteen and refused to pay for a college education.

Jeanne started working full-time while taking a few college classes, and then married her high school boyfriend. The two of them, over the next twenty years, achieved a standard of living that far outstripped that of either of their families. Jeanne's husband rose steadily through the ranks of a resort real estate company in New Mexico; he now owns the company and Jeanne is also employed. Her clothing on the afternoon we talked—jeans, a tightly woven white cotton shirt and a cropped, buttery suede jacket—along with the perfection of her teeth and nails, quietly reflected her affluence. She seemed younger than the forty-something she is, but by the time we finished talking, she looked tired and sad, worn down by the hours we spent going over her history. She studied her hands, which were resting in her lap, and then looked intently at me, saying: "How bad does your childhood have to be before you can't come out of it? I don't know many women who aren't wounded in some way." I nodded, and she went on: "What makes the wounds less severe? Was I lucky? What instilled in me the wish to change before I perpetuated the problems of my past with my daughters? That's what I want to know."

I was hesitant to explore with her what were then only the rudiments of what I was finding in my research and what I was beginning to put together myself. With Jeanne that day I only agreed that hers were significant questions. I might have told her that I'd long wondered about the same issues regarding my own life. And I might have told her that hers were the questions social scientists began addressing in the 1980s. Before that, it was well known what "risk factors" alone or, more dangerously, in combination made it likely a child would fail to thrive or would become an adult living a damaged life. The risks include: low family income, large family size, parental criminality, low intelligence, poor child-rearing techniques, parental mental illness or alcoholism, divorce, perinatal distress, and being male. Children from troubled families, whether they be marked by absent parents, violence, addiction, incest or poverty, are overrepresented among the delinquent, addicted and mentally ill. Jeanne didn't know all this as well-researched fact, but she knew she had avoided the path her childhood had pointed her down, and she wondered why. She wanted to know what it was about her or her circumstances that had saved her. It's a question social scientists wanted an answer to as well.

Exceptions to the Rule

In the 1980s researchers began to look at risk factors and their effects on children in a different way. They began to study the children, like Jeanne, who had *not* succumbed, who had bucked the conventional wisdom that says adversity always damages rather than challenges. This shift in focus toward individual strengths gave rise to a whole new field of psychological study called resiliency research. A pioneer in the field, Emmy Werner, at the University of California at Davis, studied 698 men and women born in 1955 in Kauai, Hawaii, whose lives were then followed from birth to ages one, two, ten, eighteen and thirty-two years. She found that two-thirds of the more than 200 children who were designated as high-risk—because they had encountered four or more specific risk factors by age two—developed serious learning problems by age ten and became teens with delinquency records, mental health problems and pregnancies. The other one-third, however, didn't take the predictable turn for the worse; instead, they grew into competent, well-adjusted adults who succeeded in school, managed home and social lives well and expressed strong desires to take advantage of whatever opportunities came their way. Their accomplishments not only equaled those of the low-risk group but sometimes surpassed them. As one psychiatrist said: "Problems don't predict how people will do. Something else does." Only about 15 percent of Vietnam combat veterans, for instance, developed chronic post-traumatic stress disorder. Clearly, something in the individual can get in the way of cause and its predictable effect.

That something is resiliency, a concept widely recognized in the field of human development but one that remains hard to define. One expert in the field refers to "the self-righting tendencies of young children." Another calls resilience being able to fall down seven times and get up eight. Yet another says resilience is "being able to recover your previous shape after you've been stretched psychologically." Resilience isn't a discrete, fixed quality that one either possesses or doesn't. Children are more or less resilient at different points in their lives depending on the mix of circumstantial and individual factors. No child is invincible and few are "so robust, so completely lacking in small as well as moderate or major handicaps as to be totally free from some zone of vulnerability," according to psychiatrist E. James Anthony, a resilience authority.

Resilience is not just another word for determination, stoicism or self-reliance, and yet temperament does play a part. Emmy Werner's analysis of data collected from her study of Kauai's children showed that resilient babies had outgoing, engaging personalities that made it easy for adults to connect with them. Their mothers described them as cuddly and good-natured. Tests showed they had at least average intelligence and, at all ages, more girls than boys overcame the odds.

When working with warehoused Romanian orphans in the 1980s, Daniel Stern saw something similar. The heartbreaking truth was that most of the institutionalized, traumatized orphans quickly deteriorated mentally and physically. After three years, 80 percent of those who hadn't died were sent to mental hospitals to spend the rest of their lives. But always, one or two children had what Stern called "star quality." They were able to draw members of the staff into relationships with them. These children seemed to have a special kind of intelligence, a social genius, that allowed them to process and react to others' cues. Some babies, by the age of two or three months, were already expressing sunny dispositions with smiles and noises. Protective factors such as this star quality work to mitigate risk in children's lives by promoting self-esteem or self-efficacy or by drawing adults to them who can reduce the child's exposure to a risk. Emmy Werner saw in her self-reliant subjects that the positive aspects multiplied through life as the children became more adept at finding nurturing teachers, coaches and other adults to take an interest in them.

Clinicians can't easily explain the ability of some children not only to cope with obvious stresses but to thrive. Some say that these children are able to extract from their environments what they need, even if the environment seems to have no redeeming factors. As Emmy Werner said, "they picked their own niches."

As a teen I realized I was stuck in a situation that I wasn't happy with, but that later I would be able to escape. There was a fighter inside of me that was willing to say, "Hold on, the real you is going to come out."

I heard hints of this elusive quality in Jeanne, as well, when she said: "I wanted it to be that I could hate my whole family, say they were bad people who didn't give me a good life. But it wasn't all bad, and it's not right to say it was. I've always known in the back of my mind that I'm responsible for me. I have to make something happen for myself. I can't say I'm handicapped because of them, and leave it at that."

Most of the resilient children in Emmy Werner's study didn't display any particular talents, but they did take pleasure in interests and hobbies that brought them solace when their home lives fell apart. Like many of the women I interviewed, they were able to nurture their self-esteem by taking on responsible positions such as part-time work or caring for younger siblings.

A complex, interactive network of inner and outer factors combine uniquely in each individual to create resiliency. Every life includes both risks and assets, but when the risks are high the resilient manage to create for themselves, as one researcher said, lives that "reveal a clear pattern of recovery, restoration, and gradual mastery." In the resilient person, relationships and experiences join with individual qualities to fortify the person, helping her find steadfastness and hope.

Listening to Jeanne's story, I could hear that she had traced a route for herself to "gradual mastery," despite her mother's efforts to hold her back. Jeanne left home when she graduated from high school, took a job and enrolled in night school. After struggling financially for more than two years and earning very few college credits, she asked her parents whether she could move home again so she could go to school full-time. Her mother's reply: "No. You're no longer a tax deduction." At this point a less resilient person might have stagnated, and Jeanne did struggle; but eventually she married and moved away from her hometown. Although she and her husband began their life together with few resources other than their personal strengths, they expanded their world, literally by traveling widely, but also by coming to see, as Jeanne said, that there was "much more to life than I ever knew and it's there for everyone. You don't have to be special or have a lot of money—your own personal ability to make it happen is all it takes." Eight years into their marriage they began having children, and Jeanne launched into motherhood determined not to perpetuate her mother's mistakes.

Just as some children from troubled backgrounds thrive, some from privilege don't. Not everyone with a high IQ, physical attractiveness, social skills, caring parents, a good neighborhood and a solid socioeconomic background (all significant assets in building a healthy life) turns out well. I think of several members of the Kennedy clan and any number of celebrities, as well as a girl I knew in high school who seemed to have it all but died in young adulthood of a drug overdose. Some people have assets but don't use them, while others with few assets use them well, as did James McBride and his many siblings.

What accounts for these differences and imbalances? One researcher involved in a longitudinal study of resilience concluded that one explanation is human will. "Resilience appears to be a lot of work, struggle, and pain," she said. She looked at adults who experienced adversity in childhood and adolescence and, in the course of her study, she "began to see that human agency—the will to do or to be something—has a major role in the resilience process." Emmy Werner also found that a feeling of confidence and hopefulness that odds can be surmounted was the central component in the lives of resilient individuals. The earlier this sense developed, the better, but many of the children she studied got their second chances later in life. And they did it through encounters with people who opened up opportunities for them and helped give meaning to their lives.

Strength from Others

Every resilience researcher makes this point: No one is resilient in isolation. No matter what an individual's personal characteristics or environmental risks, the resilient are always buttressed by positive, encouraging relationships with others. Perhaps that's where a child finds the will, confidence and hope that allow her to persist.

Emmy Werner found that few resilient children in her study experienced prolonged separations from their primary caregivers during the first year of life; many were oldest children; none had a sibling born before they were age two; and all developed a close early bond with at least one caregiver, sometimes someone in the extended family. Ideally, of course, a child is nurtured by a pair of loving, responsible parents who have a harmonious relationship with each other. But when that fails, other people, in and out of the family, can step in to encourage the child, to foster positive values and to model positive behavior.

My paternal grandmother loved me dearly and was my champion for many years. She'd kiss me and hug me and pat me and sit down next to me to snuggle on the couch. She treated me like a person. She asked me what I wanted to eat and where I wanted to go and listened when I answered. She couldn't cook worth beans, but when I said I wanted chicken for dinner one night she cooked chicken. It didn't taste good, but she tried because that was what I wanted.

I had an attentive and loving father. He was clueless about what was going on between me and my mother, but he was gentle and cared a lot about me. I was his favorite.

Teachers were my lifelines to sanity and hope. I soaked up their approval and generic concern as if it were all directed toward me. An alternative high school program provided me with the group experience of "family" when my own was disintegrating. When I went to school each day, I was going to the only safe place I had.

Having a twin cushioned the lack of intimacy with my mother. My sister and I had each other emotionally and physically. It's still a tight bond that no one can take away.

These positive relationships can have a more powerful impact on the direction a person's life takes than do specific risk factors. Having caring adults outside the immediate family circle has the added benefit of lessening or buffering the child's exposure to a strained or unhealthy home life.

I stayed with my grandparents for three summers while I was in high school. They live by a lake and I worked there and hung out at the lake after work. Boy, was that the life! My parents came up on the weekends, but it was a nice break away. My grandparents were parental figures to me and to this day I can talk to them more than to my parents.

My father's sister often took me with her when she traveled. She influenced my love of art and my sense of style. She was a single career woman, so I learned about work from watching her successes and mistakes. She showed me the larger world in a way my mother, with four children, no husband and a limited income, could not.

The child who finds supportive adults within the extended family is fortunate, for they're most likely to stay throughout a lifetime and more inclined to accept the child unconditionally. Sometimes the child's mother helps foster those alternative relationships, within or without the family. One study of mentally ill mothers showed that the children who did best were the ones whose mothers were the least selfish or possessive in their relationships and would allow or even encourage their children to develop connections with other helpful adults. Susan Wiseman's mother promoted such helpful outside relationships by encouraging Susan to enter an alternative, residential high school. Susan ended up there after she'd run away from home, and her mother offered the school as a solution. "There," Susan says, "they poured on the love and saved my life.

"And then I spent my nineteenth and twentieth years plunked at my godmother's kitchen table over countless cups of coffee, being what felt like 'reworked' and taught different ways to look at myself and life." As an adult, Susan has received other "excellent shoring up" from her priest and from twelve-step groups. "It's always helped," she said, "to get perspective, to get more accurate reads on life as opposed to the view my mom seemed to have."

On that pellucid winter morning when I spoke to Hannah Frank, the woman whose mother ran off with a lover when Hannah was five, it was clear that she had thought a lot about the adults who had helped fill the gaps for her. "I always found substitutes," she said. "I was an outgoing and affectionate little girl. I became a people pleaser to attract affection to me." Seeing how personable and lively Hannah is now, I found it easy to imagine her as a child possessing that "star quality" Stern identified, which draws in helpful adults. Hannah also had her father, a "flamboyant, cheerful, optimistic" man whom she idealized and to whom she remained connected throughout her life. Just speaking of her now dead father brought a catch to her voice. Hannah had found comfort in his love, though he had often been absent, chasing after work during the Depression; but she also sought mothering and affection from three very different women who brought their individual forms of nurturing to her.

"One was Aunt Mar. She wasn't really my aunt, but that's

what I called her. She was kind of an unofficial foster mother. She was a reserved Swedish woman who was never physically affectionate, but she imposed order on my life, and I needed that. She taught me how to sew, bake and cook, do laundry, milk a cow. She taught me so many things, and the teaching felt like a form of love.

"Another important figure for me was a nun, the piano teacher at the boarding school where I went after Aunt Mar. We shared a love of music and would play piano sometimes four or five hours a day. She encouraged me, talked to me, would put an arm around me.

"And my mother's mother was very important to me, even though I never saw her again after my mother left. I think she might have been my savior in those very early years. I remember her washing my hands. I remember feeling the softness of her hands on mine.

"Those early years are so important," Hannah said, echoing the wisdom of attachment research, "because that's when your basic needs are met, when you become a person."

Throughout her childhood Hannah had been able to draw to herself people who nourished her when her mother could not. Listening to her I could again hear that journey of the resilient from recovery to restoration to mastery.

In my interviews, women identified helpful adults of all sorts—grandmothers, housekeepers, aunts, fathers, teachers—who made a difference for them. But not all women had encountered supportive adults. One woman told me she grew up in an intact family but never felt cherished by or close to her mother. Her overall impression of her childhood and young adulthood was of being alone.

"I always think there must have been someone who mothered me as a child. How could I have gotten along without mothering? But, really," she said, "I can't think of anyone who cared for me regularly in ways I now associate with mothering."

Because so many other under-mothered women had been able to point to a special someone, I was surprised to hear this woman express the gap I also experienced. She told me she could remember a few specific times someone had paid special attention to her, but none of those relationships had lasted.

"I feel a certain amount of shame," she confessed, "having to admit that no one really took up the charge of mothering me. It's like never having been chosen for the team."

I've felt that also and have blamed myself, irrationally, for not seeking out and encouraging potentially helpful adults in my life. I've rummaged through my memories for someone who showed particular, consistent concern for me. What I found instead were many individual incidents of kindness: the neighbor who trusted me to baby-sit at a young age; my great-aunt who held me on her lap and talked of my mother long after her death; the nun who tenderly brushed my hair on the mornings I went to school dazed by my family's destruction; the nurse who carried me in her arms to my dead mother's bedside and let me say good-bye; my godmother who all through my life related affectionate stories of my girlhood; my taciturn grandfather who took me out for root beer floats; the high school English teacher who singled me out and encouraged me; the mother of a friend who explained menstruation to me and another who simply seemed to enjoy my company. And, of course, there was my grandmother, on whose physical presence I could rely and who never faltered in her homemaking. No matter how angry she was with me, she still made meals and ironed my blouses.

I've come to see that these attentive adults created a path of uneven stepping-stones for me to travel on. I would have preferred a tree-lined boulevard on the journey to maturity, but I'm touched when I remember those who laid that cobbled route. Somehow, with their help, like many other women, I eventually ventured forward and found for myself something more enduring than passing kindnesses.

* * *

Among the women I interviewed were many who showed themselves to be resilient, but one who stood out is Alexandra Reed, the young mother who saw herself as a baby-sitter. She related the complex tangle of her past, a childhood of shifts from mother to stepfather, back to mother, then to stay with a friend's family because her own was so mixed up and unsteady. She talked of the puzzle of her insouciant mother who lived in a beautiful home and yet seemed to have no source of income. Did she deal in drugs? When she disappeared for days, where did she go? When Alexandra lived with her mother as a young child, she told me, "life was just a big road trip." She never went to the same school for more than a few months. On her own from the age of fifteen, she endured true loneliness and isolation.

I needed a timeline and a diagram to keep up with her family, not because she couldn't explain it, but because it was so convoluted. Entirely poised and straightforward, she listed her siblings: a half brother from her mother, three half brothers from the man she calls her father but is actually a stepfather who adopted her, and a stepsister from somewhere else, whom she only recently learned about. All the time we talked, she remained collected, even when telling me that her mother, barely forty, is dying of a rare disease.

"I despised her when I was growing up," Alexandra said, "but not anymore. I've come to see her as a good person, just not a good mom. She thinks she was a good mom. Her illusions won't let her hear me when I tell her she wasn't." In the midst of telling her story, however, she stopped to say, without a trace of bitterness: "I don't know how I turned out the way I did. Maybe because I set goals for myself. I had high expectations of myself."

Tucking her neat brown hair behind her ear and shooting an eye toward her daughter in the next room, she resumed the recounting of her history, saying she had been, on the surface, "everybody's ideal kid." For a long time, she says, "I kept myself good" by keeping up grades and not going out at night. But eventually, in high school, she faltered.

"One night my mother's boyfriend came home drunk and started throwing things around, so I left and went to a friend's house down the street. My mom said it was okay if I wanted to live with them, and so I did. But they didn't do much more than give me shelter, and it only lasted so long. My mom didn't like it that I was still around. I think it was becoming an issue with the police and child services. But I went to live with some kids I barely knew, guys who were eighteen and nineteen in a studio apartment. They worked and I went to school and kept house, but every night there was a party there and everybody smoked marijuana, including me. I kept up at school, even though it was getting harder and harder.

"But then one day I went to school and the principal called me in to ask why I kept attending when my mother had withdrawn me. Here I am thinking I have a volleyball game that night and instead I don't even have a school to go to! After that, I moved to another town to live with a friend's family and went to high school there."

Little wonder, I thought as I listened, that she seems so much older than twenty-one. Today she shoulders full responsibility for herself and her child, refusing financial help from willing relatives. "Sometimes I feel like I can't take it anymore. I've had days when I've just felt I can't be a mom. I'm all by myself. I need to go back to school, to do something for myself."

I laid Alexandra's story next to what Emmy Werner had observed when she followed up with the children of Kauai in their thirties, trying to see how she fit the pattern. Werner found that the resilient ones shared these qualities: personal competence and determination, support from a spouse or mate, and reliance on faith and prayer. I thought about what other researchers, particularly those who have studied the intergenerational cycle of child abuse, have found about those who succeed: They're significantly more likely to have had an emotionally supportive relationship with an adult in addition to the abusing one early in childhood, to have participated in psychotherapy sometime in their lives and to have had a stable and satisfying relationship with a mate in adulthood.

Through all her trials, however, Alexandra's had few of the expected supports. She had some counseling in high school with a professional who did some tests and defined her life as "very dysfunctional with calm periods," and the state required a series of home visits from a social worker after she had her baby. But all Alexandra will say about therapy is that "it was nice to be able to talk about it at the time, but none of the people were even remotely helpful." She's never been in sustained therapy; she's never had a consistent, close mate, but she did have an early and ongoing good relationship with her adoptive father, along with a series of supportive friends. "Luckily I had some friends," she says. "They helped me a lot. I wouldn't be mentally sound without them." And she clearly has been aided by her personal strengths of determination and a sense of responsibility. "I have a good job," she says. "I make good money for my age. I just want for my daughter and me to be happy—that's my goal. I'm trying to be happy with what I have."

Somehow, the nearly invisible props around Alexandra—her own inner qualities, her adoptive father, her friends, her success at work—have combined to help her live differently from the way her mother did and the way her history might have predicted. Like all resilient people, Alexandra is both uniquely herself and part of a pattern. She falls into that exceptional one-third who face high risk but are able to find a successful path when fate tugs hard in the opposite direction.

Banishing the Ghosts

From Bowlby comes the good news and the bad news for those of us who were under-mothered. At the very beginning of his formation of attachment theory, he said: "What is believed to be essential for mental health is that the infant and young child should experience a warm, intimate and continuous relationship with his mother (or permanent mother-substitute) in which both find satisfaction and enjoyment." When I read that with my own childhood in mind, I hear the bad news; I recycle that regretful thought: "Why didn't I get a simple, uncomplicated childhood?" But when I read Bowlby's statement thinking of my own children, I'm encouraged and hear the good news in his words. My children are enjoying a "warm, intimate and continuous relationship" with both my husband and me daily. When our first child was born we joked, with the dark humor that can only be shared with someone who knows exactly how bad it was, saying, "All we have to do is stay alive and we'll do a better job!"

Although there's no magic key for those of us who didn't get that simple, direct route to stability, there are, as Bowlby went on to say later, other, well-established pathways to good mental health besides a peaceful, love-filled childhood. One, demonstrated in the ghost stories of Selma Fraiberg's research, lies in the way the mothers remembered the emotions of childhood. Women who repressed painful feelings were, in that odd, tangled manner of the human psyche, more likely to identify with the adults who had inflicted the pain, which made them likely to treat their children as they had been treated. Women who could still remember and feel the pain of their childhoods were unlikely to perpetuate the problems with their children. They could remember the feelings and were able to think or say, "I don't want my children to go through what I went through." In remembering, Fraiberg says, "they are saved from the blind repetition of that morbid past." In remembering, they identify with the injured child, whom they want to protect. The parent who can say "I remember what it was like when . . ." or "I remember how afraid I was when my mother . . ." or "I remember how I cried when . . ." is least likely to inflict that pain on her own children. The mystery remains, however, exactly why some people can do this and others cannot.

Kit Bishop is one of those who can and, therefore, she's been able to transcend the mothering of her childhood. She talked with a sagacious passion about her deliberate attempts not to let her mother's ways guide her in her dealings with her children. Criticism was her mother's primary parenting tool, and misbehavior, by accident or otherwise, was dealt with swiftly and harshly.

The experiences of her childhood engendered in Kit not the self-focused brusqueness of her mother, but considerable patience, empathy and compassion. Kit remembers what it was to be the injured child. When she brushes her six-year-old daughter's hair before school each morning, she enjoys taking care not to tug at her sensitive scalp, choosing to be late rather than treat her hair roughly and accuse her of being a "baby" the way her mother did to her. As we talked, Kit remembered a story that illustrated for her perfectly the contrast between her mothering and the mothering she received as a child. Sitting in an overstuffed chair, her legs tucked under her, Kit concentrated as she told of the day she took her children to a coffee shop to get them hot chocolate.

"Luke's hot chocolate spilled. My heart went out to him. Here he is, this three-year-old little boy dying to have this treat and bitterly disappointed at losing it. I wiped up the mess and made jokes about the chocolate flood, and then I got him a fresh, full cup.

"I was very aware as I was doing it, as I often am, that I was acting differently from the way my mother would have. She wouldn't have been kind, and she would *not* have replaced the drink. She would have wanted to 'teach him a lesson.' But I loved taking care of him in this little instance, knowing I wouldn't have received such care as a child.

"Two weeks later, my mother happened to take the children to the same coffee house for hot chocolate, and the same thing happened—Luke's hot chocolate got spilled! But my mother made him get up from his chair and apologize to the proprietor, and she didn't get him a new one.

"I didn't hear about this until sometime later when one of the workers at the coffee house, which I go to often, related the incident. He reassured me that he had given Luke high fives, told him he didn't care about the mess and presented him a piece of candy. But I was *enraged.*"

Here Kit paused, struggling to control her voice and the tears that were coming. She placed her hand over her heart, as if to comfort herself, and her eyes glistened. "Her lack of understanding of a three-year-old with this prize thing was unconscionable."

She paused again. "I see myself as that poor child, a poor little girl. Oh, my God, what did my mother do to her?"

Kit's ability to reach back into the emotions of her own childhood have helped her escape her legacy. Like many other women, she became an exception to the rule, a mother who doesn't "pass on the bad stuff," as one said.

Sometimes I get to feeling really rigid and I'll tell my husband: "I feel my mom coming out in me." I'll want to go into my son's room and put every Matchbox car in order. I'll want to push everyone aside and go straighten my closet or clean the refrigerator. Sometimes I walk in after a stressful day at work and look for what's out of place. I don't want to do that. Then I miss seeing my husband and son creating a volcano on the porch. I see only the mess, and not that they are having a great time together.

After Dad died, Mom was in a lot of ways a rock for us kids, but she also was unable to express or meet any of her own needs, which would eventually make her angry and then she'd lash out at us with snide remarks and yelling. I now do the same thing sometimes. But it helps to be aware that I'm repeating my mother's pattern. It makes me search for ways to avoid it.

I didn't grow up seeing a lot of mistakes made, and I was afraid of making them as a child. I felt really bad about myself when I did. I don't want that to be so for my children so I try to keep them aware of when any of us messes up, so I can say, "See? No big deal."

My tendency is to let loose with anger, just as she did. So when my teenager blindsides me with something, I really try to remember to say, "I need time to think about that. I'll get back to you later." Otherwise, what pops out of my mouth is going to be some snide thing my mother would have said.

The Examined Life

The pull to repeat is so powerful that it's almost impossible to resist without considerable self-awareness. Some women deny or dismiss the importance of their relationships with their mothers, either not thinking about it at all or refusing to see it as playing an important role in how they relate to their children. And yet, keeping emotional distance from childhood experiences also keeps a woman from self-reflection and increases her chances of repeating family patterns.

One woman told me that when her first child was born she blindly started down the path of repeating the toneless, undemonstrative model her mother had provided. Like her mother, she avoided reflection and intimacy, keeping her focus on the outside world. But she soon learned, as she said, that "you can't straighten up the house enough to make you happy. I was always looking for something on the outside—the stock market, my job, my husband—to fill me up because I didn't have enough inside." Mostly, she sought alcohol and drugs. "The powerful maternal feelings I had when my first child was born frightened me," she says. "They reminded me on some level of the lack of intimacy I had with my mother. I doubt I had any infant nurturing and cuddling from her."

The experience of her second child has been different. "I've been able to be more present with him. I can stop what I'm doing and really look this child in the eye." In the six years between her children's births, she became sober with the help of Alcoholics Anonymous and entered intensive experiential psychotherapy, which helped her release the anger and grief that built up in childhood over her mother's emotional abandonment. Her efforts to become self-aware are paying off in her daily mothering. She now can recognize, some of the time, when she's lapsing into rigidity and emotional distance—when, as she says, "I'm doing the same things I hated in her"—and can stop it.

The key to the stability of healthy adults, those secure-autonomous adults of Mary Main's research, is *not* that they had secure attachments to their parents, but that they had an open and coherent way of *reflecting on* their parents. Some researchers use the term *earned-secure* to refer to those who are autonomous in adulthood despite childhood experiences that would suggest an insecure state of mind. The earned-secure behave as sensitively and responsively to their children as those who had smooth, positive early attachment experiences. They have earned a healthy stance by working through the wounds inflicted by their parents and by integrating positive experiences with earlier unhappiness and rejection. However such a woman may accomplish it, in the words of Bowlby, she's thus "no less able to respond to her child's attachment behavior so that he develops a secure attachment to her than a woman whose childhood was a happy one."

Many of the women I interviewed were proudly in the earned-secure category, though none would use that term. These were the women, such as Kit Bishop, Susan Wiseman and Hannah Frank, who were aware of the shortcomings of their childhoods and yet also aware of their ability to prevail.

I feel good and solid about myself as a mother. Not that it doesn't challenge me. It does.

I think I do a good job. I love doing it, although I often complain. My children are old enough now to give me signs that they've gotten good parenting.

I never wanted my children to feel what I felt growing up. Over time I've come to see I'm giving my kids a good foundation.

Though these women may tell their stories with tears, they're fluent and coherent, not cut off from feelings or overwhelmed by them. And they may have worked hard to get to that point.

Those wounded in childhood can get caught up in the struggle, as Alice Miller says, to ward off something that cannot happen any longer, because it *already* happened, at the "beginning of our lives while we were completely dependent." Avoiding the pain of our past experiences takes a great deal of effort in carefully wrought denials and illusions. For decades, I lived in deep fear of the future and tried to keep myself safe from loss. And yet I had already suffered the loss a child fears most—my mother had disappeared. I couldn't face the emotional experience of my mother's death, so I worked hard to deny it. I called my grandmother "Mom," which I now see as blatant and poignant evidence of my confusion about who we were to one another. And, of course, it further obscured the truth about the woman who truly was "Mom."

For some people, freedom from the struggle to ward off the wound that has already occurred comes from willing listeners at the kitchen table. Others of us find that healing the wound is better accomplished with formal help, from social workers, psychologists, psychiatrists or other professionals. Someone like me, whose parents discouraged or even forbade noticing, remembering and discussing painful events, may have a very hard time reaching back without professional help. She may need help in order to revisit unhappy memories so she can reprocess them and bring them into her story.

My therapist had a small, round sticker on the back of the door leading out of her office that read: "Life is what it is." It took me many weeks to notice it, but once I did, I responded with roiling anger. I interpreted it as meaning life was immutable, and I didn't want to be told that I was stuck with my past and present circumstances. For months thereafter, no matter in what state my therapy hour had left me, once I headed out the door and spotted that sticker I took a nosedive into fury, muttering in my head: *But I don't want to be the woman whose mother died, whose father was feckless. . . . I don't want to be thirty-eight, childless, divorcing and completely baffled about how to carve out a meaningful future for myself. . . . I don't want my life to be what it is.* My arguments against that simple sentence were elaborately foolish. But with time, as I spent week after week sitting across from my therapist grappling with my childhood losses and my fears about the future, the sticker no longer bothered me. I could glance at it and move on. I had finally admitted defeat in my struggle to change history; I had come to tolerate who I was and where I stood in my life. In time, the sticker made me smile. Because I no longer felt helpless before my own past and present, I no longer saw the message as a taunt, but rather as a simple fact. And I could begin to think, *Okay, that happened. Now what?*

Under-mothered women need, from a therapist or other nurturing person, a new model for an intimate relationship. They need new ways to reflect on feelings and events and new behaviors to try. Sometimes what's most needed is a safe haven where painful and difficult emotions can be aired.

Counseling has been shown to change the course of mothers and children attached anxiously and help them become securely attached. Mothers who have been abused as children are able to break the cycle of abuse with therapy, which helps them to gain new perspectives on their parents and to recognize the effects abuse had on them, as well as its potential effects on their children.

When Selma Fraiberg titled her study of impaired mother–child relationships "Ghosts in the Nursery," she may have been evoking this much earlier pronouncement from Freud: "A thing which has not been understood inevitably reappears; like an unlaid ghost, it cannot rest until the mystery has been resolved and the spell broken." Fraiberg demonstrated that even women who had harrowing childhoods could break the spell of the past with sufficient aid. She and her colleagues came upon one severely depressed mother who had been neglected and abandoned as a child and was well on her way toward emotionally abandoning her own infant. The mother's face would take on a dazed, distant, self-absorbed expression as her baby screamed and cried. And the child, only five months old, had already learned that seeking comfort from mother was futile. But in four months of intensive psychotherapy the mother learned to croon to, hold and nurture her daughter, and the child caught up with her peers in development and appeared happy, even joyful. Another year of therapy helped the mother further sort out her past and separate her own experiences from those of her baby.

Motherhood itself can provide the trigger that leads a woman to seek help. May Hung, the woman who lost both her parents at thirteen and went to live with an aunt and uncle and cousins, found herself facing a profound psychological hurdle when her first child, a daughter, was four. The girl did something—May can't remember what it was—that triggered an episode of rage in May. "I screamed at her," she said, "and walked away." Then a thought came to her that's typical of people who've suffered early, deep loss: "What if in the next sixty seconds she dies and this is our last interaction?" Her next thought—"Tough shit"—jolted her into seeing that the anger she felt toward her daughter was inappropriate and misdirected. "Nothing a four-year-old could do could make me feel that much anger," she recalled. Soon after, May, a thin, delicate woman with a girlish voice, entered therapy to expose the fury that was rooted in her parents' deaths. Although change becomes more difficult as we age, we all retain throughout life a vulnerability to both adversity and positive influences. It is, as Bowlby said, "this persisting potential for change that gives opportunity for effective therapy."

How much help and what kind a woman needs, of course, vary greatly depending on who she is, what resources were and are available in her life and how her childhood wounds affect her now.

I went to a counselor for about a year and a half to try to learn to deal with my mother. Finally I came to a place where I didn't want to keep saying, "Guess what she did this week." My counselor suggested ways I could alleviate the tension I feel when my mother makes jealous and competitive comments that make me tight in my spine. She helped me with those times when I'm talking to my mother and think, "Oh, there it is, that feeling I can't stand."

Today Kit Bishop is a mother who's easy to admire; she's confident of her ability to nurture; she clearly takes pleasure in her children and thinks carefully about what they need from her. What has brought her here, she says, is long-term psychotherapy that allowed her to free herself from the matrix of her mother and maternal grandmother. She started therapy in her mid-twenties and stayed eight long years. In that time, she says, she came to feel the love, security and nurturing she had not had from her mother. Kit now thinks she learned from her therapist how a good mother figure treats children. Her connection to her therapist was profound and in that relationship Kit's desire for children awakened.

The therapy Kit experienced went beyond diagnosis— unending examination of the problem and who's to blame—to true treatment that made way for change. In the relationship with her therapist, she experienced a fulfillment of those unmet needs from her childhood for safety, love and esteem, and thereby gained the courage and means to transform her world-view. She was able to break the pattern of anxious attachment to become that earned-secure adult who can relate a coherent life narrative. Therapists and analysts since Freud have claimed this as a desired outcome of successful therapy. The ability to tell an organized life story is linked to mental health because doing so requires rational thought and emotional maturity. Being emotionally mature—that is, having stable moods, being free of chronic anxiety and depression, controlling emotional outbursts—isn't possible if one is hiding from the past.

Clinical psychologist and attachment researcher Arietta Slade calls it a fantasy when people say, as most do, that they're going to parent differently and not repeat the past. "And I think most people don't exactly repeat the past and they do certainly do things differently," she says. "But to really deal with these emotions requires a consciousness, and that means you have to give up the fantasy that you are really going to do a *completely* different job." Gaining a big-picture view, whether through counseling or other avenues of healing, can give a woman an awareness of what she tends to repeat and give her some choice in the matter.

The Price of Resilience

As anyone who has survived a trying childhood can attest, "resilient" doesn't mean "perfect" or "impervious." Successes attained later in life may come at a cost. Though some "fortunate exceptions," as Bowlby wrote, "manage to struggle through," the toll on their emotional lives may be much greater "than meets the undiscerning eye." They may not feel as carefree as other people or may not easily bend and flow with life's setbacks. And stress-related health problems can show up. Adults who have had to maintain distance from troubled family members, for instance, might carry a certain aloofness into all their personal relationships. Few of the resilient adults in Emmy

Werner's study of the children of Kauai emerged unscathed, but that special one-third who rose from childhoods marked by difficulty to become adults who "loved well, worked well, played well, and expected well" had managed to build up enough buffers to weather the effects of their childhoods. By age thirty they had begun to have many positive experiences that served to reinforce hope and confidence. If we could revisit young Alexandra Reed, now twenty-one, in ten years we might find that she, too, has continued on an upward spiral. She may feel and appear even more resilient than she does now.

Each of us rests on our own unique spot in the continuum of harmful childhood experiences, determined by the particulars of our parents' and our lives and personalities. Because every human being is unique, there is no definitive answer to that question Jeanne Beauvais posed: "How bad does your childhood have to be before you can't come out of it?" Some people, though resilient, may be able to do no more than grasp the edge of that earned-secure perch. Others are able to climb fully aboard. Although repair is sometimes possible even for people who have had extreme experiences in childhood, that never excuses adults in responsible positions from their duties and obligations to children. As Bowlby said, "the fact that some heavy smokers survive is no argument for tobacco."

Most women don't experience childhood trauma as extreme as mine or that of Alexandra Reed, and most are not "coming from a mighty long way back," as one woman whose father committed suicide described it, in their journeys toward stability and toward becoming "ordinary devoted mothers." Many more are like Susan Wiseman, Jeanne Beauvais and Kit Bishop, who grew up in and are rearing their children in conventional families, complete with husbands, fathers, permanent addresses and family outings. Their mothers were far less obviously damaging, the deprivations were far more subtle and the scars less visible, and yet the suffering is there, too. Always, the interface of a particular mother with each of her children is unique. One child may be able to tolerate a mother's shortcomings but another may not.

Long ago, in emphasizing the important job mothers perform, Bowlby said this: "One cannot ever really give back to a child the love and attention he needed and did not receive when he was small. With understanding and affection, and perhaps skilled help, one can go a long way toward it, sometimes a very long way, but it will never be quite the same." To me, this seems only a statement of simple common sense, yet it remains one of his many controversial opinions. Experts in the field like to parse this pronouncement and argue about how much more flexible human beings are than lower animals and about to what extent we can make up our losses. But that's academic. Having been a child whose critical needs to feel secure at home, to be honored for my singular self and to be loved without agenda were not met, I know that Bowlby is right. Having now interviewed many other women who were under-mothered, I know that my situation, though unique in its particulars, is not uncommon. Healing from a wound is not the same as never having been wounded. Nonetheless, the resilient can and do transform the wounds into lessons and wisdom that go on nourishing them and their children. Just as "one can enjoy a rainbow without necessarily forgetting the forces that made it," as Mark Twain said, one can take pleasure, even joy, in finding meaning and purpose in the present without forgetting the past. And it's not just a matter of remembering that makes way for fulfillment. Rather, it's the circling back to embrace the past and the strides one has made toward restoration that strengthen the happier present. Wrestling with our ghosts and reflecting on our young selves and the kind of care we received, along with giving ourselves credit for the efforts we make to heal ourselves, may be exactly what allows us to stand in the sunshine with our children and experience true happiness.

CHAPTER SIX

Reclamations

Sometimes we do not know we are waiting until the awaited thing arrives.

—Barry Unsworth

Newly married and first-time parents-to-be at age forty-one, my husband and I were firmly in the "old parents" category. Others assumed we were set in our ways, and most of our peers already had parenting experience to share. That meant we heard plenty of that standard new-parent warning: "You won't *believe* how your life is going to change!" They were right, and they were right in suggesting that some of those shifts would be arduous. But what I didn't expect, and no one mentioned, was how radically *I* would change.

From the other side of motherhood I could predict the upcoming restrictions on my work time, on my freedom to come and go, and on my opportunities to be with my husband. But I had no way to predict the seismic ramifications for my emotional life. I couldn't have seen from the other side that becoming a mother would be the second major defining event in my life. Until then, my life was split between the time before and the time after my mother's death. The birth of my first child became the new line of demarcation. Both the great divides of my life have involved mother: the loss of her and the rediscovery of her and myself in coming to my own mothering.

Most women, including those who have difficult or distant relationships with their own mothers, hold within an important identity as a daughter, even when they're autonomous and deep into career or marriage and other aspects of adult life. That identity holds a central spot until a woman crosses over and begins to see the world through a mother's eyes. Being entirely responsible for the survival of another human being changed me, as it does nearly every new mother. It was as if I put on "mother glasses" when my child was born, through which I now view everything that passes in front of me, both significant and trivial. I read the newspaper and imagine the mothers and children affected by world events. I walk out of the movie *Little Women* and notice that to me it's no longer the story of a girl who wants to grow up to be a writer, but the story of a mother rearing her children in difficult times.

Before my "new divide," I had never identified with being a nurturer or caretaker. I had gone so long never expecting to be a mother, so long without one, that "mothering" was a language I'd never learned. I never guessed I had a capacity to be as undefended, as focused on another being, as *adult* as motherhood has asked and expected me to be.

The women I interviewed also spoke of the sometimes surprising changes in identity that motherhood brought.

I was more intellectual and detached before having a child. I never got angry about anything. And then I got married and had a kid and suddenly all my buttons were being pushed. I hadn't known how much people suffer, how much difficulty and joy there could be in life.

Being pregnant scared me because I hadn't thought about having children. It opened up a part of me I didn't know existed, a part that's so human and base. I was at my best being a mother when my children were very, very young, and we had that whole connection

*with breast-feeding and being so nurturing. I didn't know I had
that in me.*

*When I was pregnant for the first time I had a twelve-year-old step-
daughter who just adored the whole thing. She couldn't wait for the
baby to be born, and she thought I was the queen. She said to me,
"I see you as a mother now. You were just a stepmother, but now
you're a real mother." And I began to see myself that way, too.*

The Motherhood Constellation

After decades of studying mothers and infants, Daniel Stern
concluded that motherhood presents a particular psychic orientation. A mother, he says, "is a woman in a unique period of her
own life, playing a unique cultural role and fulfilling a unique
and essential role in the survival of the species." He developed a
concept he termed "the motherhood constellation," referring to
the special nature of most mothers' disposition to think, feel and
act in certain ways. This constellation becomes the dominant
organizing factor in a mother's psyche and can last for months
or years; and even when it fades to the background in a woman's
life, it almost always can be evoked again. "It is a unique, independent construct in its own right," says Stern, "of great magni-
tude in the life of most mothers, and entirely normal."

A key part of that constellation is a powerful reshaping of
the woman's identity. Once a woman becomes a parent, says
Stern, every aspect of her self is opened to reinterpretation:
"woman, mother, wife, career-person, friend, daughter, granddaughter; her role in society; her place in her family of origin; . . .
herself as the person with cardinal responsibility for the life and
growth of someone else; as the possessor of a different body; as a
person 'on call' 24 hours a day; as an adventurer in life, a creator,
a player in evolution's grand scheme, and so on. . . . All these
networks are thrown by events into the postpartum crucible,

potentially to be reforged." This reshaping happens with each new child, but most powerfully with the first.

Part of what's going on in a new mother's shifting psyche is the completion of her girlhood, as she moves from being a daughter first to being a mother. Michelle Struthers, the young dark-haired businesswoman whose pregnancy ignited deep sadness over the physical and mental changes in her own mother, said, "I always thought of myself as a girl. I never liked being called a woman. I feel young, I feel attractive, but being pregnant has been such an ego confrontation. Men don't look at me." For many women, part of facing the end of girlhood is releasing whatever fantasies they might have had about repairing or redoing their childhoods. This necessary letting go can cause a profound sense of loss beneath whatever excitement or happiness the woman is feeling. Some clinicians have suggested that this sadness may, in some cases, contribute to postpartum blues. Michelle voiced this struggle to let go with her repeated statements about "knowing" her mother won't change, but "wishing" it could be different. "I'd give anything to have my mother back the way she was," she said, no doubt thinking of the vibrant, energetic woman Michelle had adored as a young girl. "I have dreams of her coming here to live with us and our baby and being the mom she was for me."

Parenting is often viewed as the culmination of an individual's psychosexual development; marriage, sexual intercourse, childbearing and child-rearing make up the final stage of sexual development. Just as important, however, may be the role of parenting in the formation of the self. "Since, in becoming mothers, women return via their babies to the stage where it all began," explains psychotherapist Joyce Block, "they may be temporarily *more* vulnerable or to put it more positively, more receptive, to the unconscious and unarticulated. Doors shut tightly years before are opened, and old and new experiences rush into conscious awareness." Parenting encourages growth in part because of the personal investment parents have in their children. Our stake in their very survival creates demands that have never been made before.

While caring for her own child, a woman's memories of having been cared for herself are called forth, either consciously or not. Opening to the baby's emotional needs evokes memories and emotions of having once been a baby. If a woman's parents were withholding and unable to nurture her, then remembering babyhood can be, as psychologist Robert Karen says, a painful reenactment of "being totally dependent and desperately in love and yet being shut out" from the one who matters most. Most often, these memories have lain dormant, hidden because they have not had what psychologists call a "present remembering context." But on becoming a mother, a woman's daily acts of care constantly evoke memories of her own infancy and of the mothering she received. The interaction with a baby, especially the first child, is a very specific "remembering context" that a woman has not experienced before. Women find themselves inexplicably experiencing both pleasant and uncomfortable emotions and engaging in new behaviors, such as spontaneously singing songs they haven't thought of since they were children, rocking their infants and humming, seeking out arousing baby smells. "The flow of evoked memories, triggered by this new remembering context," says Stern, "is the raw material for an important part of the mother's reorganization of her identity as daughter and as mother. And in this remembering context, the old schemas of being-with-mother will tumble out and pervade the new mother's experience."

Motherhood can be a labyrinth of change that leads women to enrich and refine the self. As one woman I interviewed said, "I found out that motherhood, as my sister likes to point out, is the project you can't put back into the closet unfinished." The emotional challenges of parenthood can, if we are open to them and stick with them, heal old wounds and transform the self.

A New View of Mother

The potential transformation presented by parenthood includes the opportunity for a woman to gain a new perspective of her own mother. For some, like Kit Bishop, becoming a mother allows them to draw closer to their mothers, if not permanently, then at least for a time. Kit's relationship with her mother had only deteriorated as Kit grew into adulthood, despite efforts on both sides.

"Then," Kit said, "I began trying to get pregnant and couldn't. I was shocked to find myself infertile. My marriage was good and I wanted children so much and the disappointment I felt in my body and in not being pregnant was terrible. I was grieving and that triggered something in my mother.

"She really got into my trying to get pregnant and called often and went with me to appointments with fertility doctors. She was being protective and caring and helpful. She was being very *motherly*, in a way I'd never experienced with her before.

"During that long time I was trying to get pregnant, she made a crib quilt. I love patchwork quilts and she knows that. It took her a whole year. A whole year of my struggling with infertility, she hand stitched this beautiful quilt. For some reason, it bridged a gap between us. She put so much work into it. And she *stayed* with the baby idea. She didn't give up and turn it into a pillowcase. She put time in for me, which really helped. It was an act of faith. I still wasn't pregnant, but she was making a crib quilt.

"For the first time ever we were in sync. She wanted for me to get pregnant and I wanted for me to get pregnant."

Kit became energized as she related this "good time" in her relationship with her mother. She remembered that they had latched onto visualization as a way of encouraging those sperm and eggs to find each other.

"One day, I was lying in bed after an in vitro session, and I was trying it; I was trying to visualize becoming pregnant, and my mother called and said, 'Are you doing it? I am.'

"We were *sharing* something," Kit said, leaning forward to emphasize the significance of this. She was silent for a moment as she seemed to turn the memory over in her mind, and then suddenly she laughed, saying, "I forgot for a second that that's what mothers and daughters do!

"Once I did get pregnant I was just awestruck. And my mother was so excited. I think she saw it as a sign that I was finally doing something right, something other women do.

"And I think my joy and excitement, and my mother's good care of me, helped insulate me from all the old, bad feelings I had about her. Before, I'd felt repelled when she tried to be comforting about anything. Any closeness with her brings on fear of humiliation and hurt, because she hurt me so many times as a child. She never did anything you could call out the child services for, but her refusal to be motherly when I was a child took a terrible toll on me. She rejected my efforts to be close to her so often when I was a child that I became afraid of her, and as I got older I felt repulsed by her and her inability to be intimate and nurturing.

"But this time I didn't have a chance to fight the care she was offering—I needed her. And that really helped.

"One day she took me to a doctor's appointment and there I found out I had toxemia and had to be hospitalized. She took me to the hospital and wheeled me into a room with tears rolling down her face. She sat at the end of the bed for days, and one day said, 'I feel like I'm mothering you.' I didn't say anything, but I was thinking, 'And I need it.'

"I had a C-section and my husband was with me and afterward the doctor said, 'Your whole family is out there. Is there anyone you want to come in?' And I said, 'My mother.' When she came in I could see that she was really moved by the whole thing. She was very attentive and stayed that way for a while. It's shifted since—and she's still my screwed-up mother—but we've never gone back to being as tense with each other as we were before."

Entering into that triangle of grandmother-mother-child demands a realignment of a woman's stance toward her mother. Whether or not the relationship is rich and right, whether or not change is provoked in the grandmother, the new mother is likely to experience change. "Of all the people in your personal matrix," Stern emphasizes, "none will affect you with more emotional force than your own mother. For this reason, whether your relationship has been good or bad, it will require some of your time, attention, and, perhaps most of all, reflection."

For some women, motherhood brings a more positive view of their mothers, and the relationship moves forward.

In the first few days after my son was born, both my mother and mother-in-law came to visit and I was in a dilemma about whether to feed him or not. To my amazement my mother showed a lot of appropriate detachment. "You're the mother," she said, and she didn't try to take over and tell me what to do.

Soon after my twins were born I was struck by the fact that someone had done all this for me, the bathing, the diaper changing, the feeding, the not sleeping. While I knew it wasn't done the way I would do it, still, I had not been physically neglected as a baby, and that was a touching, comforting revelation to me. I hadn't been given much in the mothering department, but this little scrap of knowledge was something I did have. I actually felt honored and required to do for my babies what I finally understood had been done for me. It was a link to my own mother I'd never seen before.

For other women, parenting becomes a daily reminder of what they didn't receive as children, and it can add to the disquiet a woman feels about her mother's behavior.

Being a mother changed me in little ways almost every day, as I remembered bits of my childhood. I was increasingly horrified to realize that things my mother had done—or more often not done— that I had assumed were normal were actually neglectful and hurtful. As a mother, I couldn't imagine never cuddling my children or saying "I love you" or running my hands through their hair or being at the school play to watch them.

I developed more appreciation for her and understanding of her behaviors. It isn't easy being a mom and I can understand the frustration she must have been feeling at times. On the other hand, I also found myself wondering why she acted the way she did. Why couldn't she have some empathy? I got more confused, too.

For still others, mothering validates what they experienced as children, and they gain a clearer, though not a positive, view of their mothers.

When my second child was in the hospital at three months old and our first child was only two and my husband was struggling to pay the medical bills, my mom didn't even come to the hospital to visit, much less help me. That was a real turning point for me. I saw her for the first time as she really is.

I didn't become a mother until thirty-six, and it was only then that I began to see my mother's role in my dad's abusiveness. If my husband hurt my son in the way my father hurt me and my sister, I never would tolerate it. I saw that my mother put her needs and fears in front of ours and I found that unacceptable.

My children have told me that their appreciation for me grew as they got older, but the opposite happened for me. When I became a mother and took on those responsibilities it became very, very easy to see where she had failed. When I saw what being a mother entailed, I had insight into how badly she had mothered.

Mother's Story

When we become mothers we are presented a unique and valuable opportunity to see our mothers with fresh eyes. Seizing the opportunities for reflection and insight that the moods, memories and emotions of mothering provoke helps us avoid mindlessly following or mindlessly rebelling or getting tangled in unconsciously confusing ourselves with our mothers or children. Avoiding those stumbling blocks is a key ingredient in mothering well.

Many of the women I interviewed revealed keen perception of their mothers' personalities and experiences, gained through quizzing their mothers and others about their mothers' lives. Trying to puzzle through the reasons why her mother had always been inaccessible, self-focused and unyielding, one woman looked into the story she had heard about her mother long ago relinquishing a child, a half brother to the woman I interviewed. She found that her mother had become pregnant at fifteen and, although she married her teenage boyfriend and had the baby, her strict Catholic family disowned her and her husband's large extended family treated her poorly, blaming her for the unplanned pregnancy. When the child was nine, the young mother abandoned him to his father's family and fled, never again accepting her role as his mother. Later she married again, bearing three children, including the woman I interviewed, who said, "It's not surprising that someone so betrayed and so wounded would have a hard time doing anything but protecting herself. The compassion her sad life inspires in me not only helps me to understand why she treated me as she did, but also helps me be more compassionate toward others. You never know what secret troubles people might have suffered."

A woman's relationship to her mother doesn't have to change as much as it needs to be understood differently if the woman is to rise above her childhood experiences and create something new with her own children. For an under-mothered woman, an important part of being able to structure a coherent, fluent narrative of her own past—the key characteristic of the earned-secure—is incorporating into her story a true understanding of her mother's history. Knowing under what circumstances she carried out her mothering, what supports she had and didn't have and keeping in mind a kind of psychological resume of her mother can spare a woman from being detached from or entangled in her past. Thus, it can help her create a secure attachment with her own child. "A woman who is able to reconstruct the story of her relationship with her mother with openness and perspective will have set herself free of the past," says Stern.

I knew this intuitively when about fifteen years ago I began investigating my mother's life. I sought out her high school classmates, interviewed relatives, including my grandmother, and read old, out-of-print memoirs written by people who had had polio. We lived in Phoenix when she fell ill, and by hunting through local newspapers of the time I learned that she'd been transferred in an iron lung onto a military troop transport plane that flew her to a rehabilitation center in Seattle. I even tracked down the U.S. Air Force physician who accompanied her on the flight to ask what he remembered.

When I began my research into her life I knew so little that every fragment seemed significant. A handful of letters and early photographs my grandmother had saved told me my mother had ironed, baked cookies, made jokes, worn halter tops and cultivated a tan. But in the end what I found wasn't enough. I wanted to know her the way you know someone who has sat at the breakfast table with you for years. I wanted to look in her cupboards, listen to her talk to my father in the dark, see her smile, hear her voice, know what mattered most to her and what she regretted. I searched for all that, suspecting that what I found would hold clues to my own identity as well as hers. What I wasn't looking for but found instead were insights into my grandmother and how the events of my mother's life had shaped her. Both becoming a mother myself and searching into my mother's life allowed me to catch sight of what my grandmother suffered as a mother who lost her only child. I've come to believe that my mother's death must have been for my grandmother, besides all else it was, an indelible failure. That haunting, fundamental concern of all mothers—*keep the child alive*—throbbed for my grandmother, I think, until her own death forty-two years later.

This central psychic theme of being responsible for another's life is unique within the human life cycle. "What is at stake here," says Stern, "is whether the mother will succeed as a human animal. Is she an adequate, naturally endowed animal? If she is, as measured in terms of the baby's life and growth, she can take her place in the evolution of the species, the culture, and her family. If not, she will fall irreversibly out of these natural currents of human evolution, perhaps forever. I am overdramatizing the situation for emphasis, but the power of this theme is enormous and long-lasting." For my grandmother, it was, I believe, everlasting. No matter how irrational it might be, I think my grandmother felt responsible for her daughter's death. The most poignant moment for me when I interviewed her about those last years of my mother's life was when my grandmother confessed, almost in a whisper, that she, the champion worrier, had never thought to worry about polio, as if her dread held magical protective powers.

Only after I had my own children did I begin to understand that my grandmother's anger at me was real, not simply a guise for her sorrow. For many years I couldn't understand why she didn't—wouldn't—take me in her arms and say, "Isn't it awful what happened to us? Isn't it awful that we lost Virginia? But at least we have each other." Now I think she couldn't do that because, in an unexplored part of each of our hearts, we deeply resented each other for not *being* Virginia—my mother, her daughter. Grandmothers and granddaughters are expendable. Mothers and children are not. The woman who stood between us, in life and in death, kept us apart.

I understand better now the anguish that led my grandmother to tear into tiny pieces every photo of my sick, paralyzed mother after her death and to refuse to speak of her. I understand better her refusal to open to me. Understanding doesn't change my childhood experience, of course, but it does help me soften toward my grandmother. As another woman said about her mother, "Although I recognize her pain, that doesn't negate mine." Understanding not only can provide insight, but can affect how we mother. Learning more about my grandmother, for example, teaches me that I want to show my children that they're worth whatever heartache might come for us. What we learn about our mothers and their substitutes doesn't change them, but it can change us.

I appreciate what my mother did to raise three of us as a single mother in a town where there weren't many divorced women and where she had to deal with my father, who wouldn't take time for us. As a mother of three kids myself I have a great appreciation for how meaningful it is to have a husband who is a good father. When he's out of town I sometimes wonder how single mothers manage at all.

I tried to have more intimacy with my mother when I had my children, but she just couldn't reciprocate. She couldn't physically write a letter, but I wrote lots of letters to her telling her all about the girls as they grew and later she gave them back to me in a scrapbook, which was all cattywampus and disorganized. She couldn't even tape a letter in straight. But I saw this as a sign that she did care and had cared all those years.

Often the most difficult aspect of seeing our mothers clearly is recognizing the resemblances to ourselves. Many women I interviewed insisted they were nothing like their mothers. Others, like Kit Bishop, acknowledged similarities, but also spoke of how painful it was to see herself being like her mother in any respect, even physically. Most difficult of all is seeing our mothers' worst traits in us. Jungians like therapist Naomi Ruth Lowinsky speak of this in terms of the "shadow," the unknown side of the self held in darkness by our fears, values, temperament and cultural prejudices. Often the very traits we most dislike in others, particularly our parents, are parts of our shadow selves, the traits we deny and repress. But if we can face those traits of our mothers that are in us, especially the ones we most dislike, we move toward knowing ourselves more fully.

Mother would always tell a friend how well one of us girls did, but would never tell us directly. I don't know what that's about, but I know I'm the same way. I'm better with my kids, but I have a hard time telling my friends and my husband when they've done something great. It doesn't come naturally to me.

I had lunch one day in a downtown Seattle cafe with a woman named Cathy Patterson, an interior designer who also teaches in the field. She slung her black tote over her chair, sat down and snapped her napkin onto her lap. We made brisk small talk, ordered our food, and then she looked at me expectantly with her dark eyes shining from behind black-framed glasses. I plunged in, skipping the warm-up questions. I could see she was someone who appreciated efficiency. Before long, Cathy was telling me, between bites of salad, about that disconcerting experience of seeing her mother's worst traits in herself.

"I remember years of what I thought was unbearable bitchiness from her," she said. "She was cranky and moody, and always denied it. Then when my kids were teenagers I hit menopause and lost all emotional balance myself. Suddenly I found myself behaving the same way. I who once had a sunny disposition was ready to *kill*!

"My husband confronted me one day, saying he had over-heard our children talking about how icky I was. I made a doctor's appointment right then. If I was the bad apple in the family, I was going to take care of it. I wasn't going to make them capitulate to me the way my mother had in our family.

"I tried to talk to my mother about menopause, but she dismissed it, saying she never even noticed going through 'the change.' But now that I've been there I'm convinced it's a good explanation for all those years my mother's snappish behavior escalated.

"When I was a teenager I tried to get out of my mom's way—I'd just leave the room—before she could say something belittling or insulting. And I know I have a tendency to act the same way with my kids, because they tell me. But I like that they aren't afraid of me and know they have a right to say what they think and a right to be treated politely."

For those of us who were under-mothered, seeing ourselves clearly, which also means seeing our mothers clearly, may be an essential step in becoming free of the past. It's easier to skate through life cushioned by the security provided by our defenses, particularly denial, as Cathy's mother seemed to be trying to do, than it is to face the fears that cast a shadow of anxiety over our lives. Our children, however, will be the beneficiaries of our efforts to face those fears.

The desire and concern of parents at all social levels to do well by their children, says Robert Karen, is evident in the millions of books, magazine articles, TV shows, videocassettes and more on child care consumed each year. "Parents learn," he writes, "how the baby is likely to behave during each new week or month, what it needs to eat, what the variations are in physical and cognitive development, how to sleep train it, how to toilet train it, what its emotional needs are, and so on down to the last detail. But, as useful as this is, none of it will help potentially anxious parents do the one thing they most need to do—gain a deeper understanding of their own motivations, conflicts and inner needs."

Getting to know myself has helped me to be available to my children. When you're not so busy with figuring out your own self and your own life, you can pay more attention to your children.

Without motherhood I would have had a longer time to slop around in my own mess. Becoming a mother and taking that position seriously and not wanting to miss out on it prompted me to move quickly to find out what was wrong with me and to get sober.

Sipping a cup of coffee, Cathy Patterson said that motherhood had given her many opportunities for learning about herself. "Most of all," she said, "it has made me much more patient with people who don't think or talk as fast as I do. My teaching changed. I'm much more sympathetic to students who don't get it, who aren't motivated. I don't give them good grades, but I'm more sympathetic. I'm more accepting of people doing things different from me."

As for me, I resisted change and self-reflection well into adulthood. And now, after traveling far afield both emotionally and physically, I've come home. I still don't want TV trays, but I live a life—and *want* a life—more like my mother's and grandmother's than I ever imagined. I fled my hometown to avoid repeating their lives, and yet I now live in our old neighborhood and my children go to the same schools I attended. I feel my grandmother's hand in all my domestic pleasures. I bake cookies and put them in the cookie jar that once sat on her kitchen counter. I fold my sons' clean laundry and put it back in their rooms, just as she did for me. I lean gratefully on the homemaking model my grandmother provided. I now know that I don't have to avoid being like her in all respects in order to avoid being like her in how I show my children love.

Forgiveness

Coming to know and understand their own and their mothers' stories can, for many women, open the door to forgiveness for childhood wounds. Not every under-mothered woman unearths a defining event that explains her mother's behavior and switches on a light of understanding. For most, understanding and forgiving come slowly and gradually lead to a letting go of the past. And often it is motherhood that opens the door, as it did for Kit Bishop.

A woman named Dionne, who was an only child and now has an only child, found that changes between her and her mother inched along after Dionne's daughter was born.

"I've never asked anyone in my family about my mother so almost everything I know about her comes filtered through her. I don't really know why or how she came to be the mother she was to me," she said. "I know she was the middle child between two 'star' children who could do no wrong and that she never had much in the way of parental love. But that's all stuff she says, not something I see in my grandparents and aunt and uncle now.

"She's a strong personality, so she overshadows others. She had this way, for example, of blaming my father for things that pertained to me, claiming her own innocence and pretending that she wasn't the one who felt that way or thought that. She always told me that he was really disappointed that I wasn't a boy. I wish I had gotten up the nerve to ask him questions before he died.

"What little I know about her past hasn't been especially helpful in leading me to forgive her for the way she doles out love and approval in meager, grudging doses. But something that has helped is that she finally admitted that she was a bad parent. I've gotten a lot of validation and satisfaction in showing my mother, through the way I treat my daughter, how a loving mother behaves.

"My pregnancy was very difficult and I worried throughout about *everything*. I worried about whether I'd live long enough to see my baby. Then I worried about the baby's health and if there would be birth defects. Then I worried about SIDS and childhood illnesses. Beneath it all, though, I think what I feared most was that I'd never get the chance to raise my baby the way I wish I'd been raised. And I hate to admit it, but part of me wanted to rub my mother's nose in the fact that things could have been different between us."

Dionne's mother admitted that she was "too selfish" to want to be around children much and over the years "has tried to make up for it." Dionne says she and her mother now get along pretty well, though their emotional involvement is minimal.

"I'm still a disappointment to her," she said. "I'm quite over-weight and that embarrasses her. And I'm never quite good enough no matter what I do or accomplish. The thing is, though, that on an intellectual level we get along quite well, and I really enjoy the weekly phone conversations we've had ever since my father died. I think she loves me, especially now that I'm an adult and she doesn't have to take care of me."

I asked Dionne what else has helped her let go of her anger toward her mother.

"My husband. He gives me the unfettered love I didn't get from my mother. And I went through therapy to help me realize that I didn't have to *be* my mother."

Therapy, of course, has helped many women walk out from under their mothers' shadows, and one of the many reasons that's so is that therapy helps women tell their stories. Once a story becomes familiar, it loses the power to ambush and to create fear. Through the stories of her life experiences a woman can become alive to and comfortable with who she is and who her mother is or was. She's then much closer to being able to behave in ways that say, "I may not be the child you wanted and you may not be the mother I wanted, but here we are."

Another woman in her mid-forties, mother of a teenager, calls herself "the therapy poster child" for having been in therapy longer than any one she knows, twenty-two years and counting. "It has helped me be able to feel, much of the time, great joy in the simple facts of my life: where I live, who my family is, what I do in my day-to-day life.

"Another crucial result is that I now understand what my mother went through and can forgive some of the most damaging behavior on her part. I have a relationship with her now that wasn't possible when I was growing up. I'm now generally not afraid to be different from most people in the choices I make in order to be true to myself."

A secure adult knows those signal events in her life that mark the points of change or that explain behavior and emotions. And she can tell her stories with honesty and clarity, even when the stories are ugly or painful. Dionne, for example, told me about what for her is an unforgettable memory of being three years old and wetting her bed.

"My mother was *furious*—more work for her, you see—and the next night she made me wear a diaper, though I had been out of them for some time. Not only that, she humiliated me by making me go into the dining room where my adored father was working and tell him that I had wet the bed so I had to wear a diaper like a baby. She stood there holding my hand and saying, 'Tell him! Tell him!' I was so ashamed. That memory has stayed with me because it's the first time I remember hating her."

Dionne can never forget this incident, but she also can say matter-of-factly, "If you want some more horrid examples, just let me know. I have plenty of them." Those "horrid" memories of her mother's cruelty may still sting, but they no longer define Dionne to herself. With the emotional maturity gained through effort over years, Dionne can now see those stories as revealing of her mother, rather than as revealing herself as the daughter unworthy of love. She's no longer the girl who could do no right by her mother. She's a conscientious, loving mother herself. And she's come to this place with help not only from her husband and therapy, but from a mother's group and her grandmother.

Many women find that the simple passage of time also helps create an easing of a difficult relationship. One woman in her late forties said that she surprised herself recently by inviting her mother to come for a visit, something she had done only rarely in the past and only out of obligation. This time, her invitation was sincere. What changed, she told me, was that she had come to see that "what I once thought was intolerable—having a relationship without speaking my mind and without pushing her into figuring her life out—is no longer intolerable. She's just old and awful now. She wants a nothing daughter, a facade daughter, which is what she always wanted. I couldn't do that when I was young and figuring myself out, but now I can give her what she wants. I can do this 'being nothing' for her at no cost to me."

Since that invitation this woman has seen her mother several times and has found it easier to be with her with each visit. "I can sit and talk about the weather with her," she said, "and, in fact, I've even come to see that I can do for her and I *want* to do for her."

I went to a therapist hoping to find peace and acceptance, and most of all to forgive my mother. It's hard to say whether I'm there yet. My therapist was soothing and affirming and it was good to talk about my feelings, but I can't say I've been completely successful in forgiving her, though I now accept that she loved me, and that her intent was to do a good job raising me.

Over time, I've come to feel a lot of compassion for my mother. It sounds trite, but I really think she did the best she knew how to do in her circumstances. She did as she was told and taught by her mother. I just wish that she could finally find some joy in her life.

I was never close to my stepmother and never made it easy for her, especially when I was a teenager. But becoming a mother myself gave me some perspective on how hard it is. I'm glad I've lived long enough to be able to apologize to her.

A few women, like Susan Wiseman, find that the only bridge across the fissure between them and their mothers is death.

"The fact of her dying," Susan said, "brought on an amazing switch. For years I prayed, did therapy, worked the twelve steps, and forgiveness didn't come. But with her dying came a rush of understanding. I think it had something to do with not having to struggle any longer against her, not having to work to be independent of her.

"One day, during those last awful months of her dying, a hospice worker called me to come to my mother's bedside. She said, 'She's frightened and needs comfort.'

"I went there and sat on her bed rubbing her hand with my thumb, just like she had done for me so long ago, when we'd watch TV, all squeezed together into a chair. I can't explain it, but that small act stirred such a deep tenderness in me and changed how I felt toward her."

The question of whether we're going to blame our mothers for our suffering lies at the heart of forgiveness. Resisting blame requires that an under-mothered woman strive for a full picture of her mother and how she mothered and requires an effort to understand without passing judgment. Jungian Lowinsky suggests that we all share a "collective fantasy" about "the perfectibility of childhood." She argues that we rage at mothers "for all the negative things that befall us. But no mother sets out to hurt her children. She has her own limitations, those the culture imposes, and she has her fate." Assuming that mothers exist for the sole purpose of supporting their children's healthy development, she continues, leads to forgetting "that mothers are people with their own lives, who are profoundly affected by the experience of having children."

Lowinsky sides with mothers, but I think an under-mothered woman is best served by reaching for a delicate balance. In one hand, she holds her awareness of where her mother fell short in filling her childhood needs so that she can understand the effects of those failures on her own life, personality and mental health. In the other, she holds the knowledge that her mother is a human being with shortcomings and unfulfilled needs of her own. The danger lies in tipping too far, either toward blaming her mother or toward dismissing her own suffering. An important task of a wounded daughter is to see the mother-child relationship from *both* sides. She knows what a child—every child, including herself and her mother—needs and lays it alongside the truth that it's impossible for any mother, including herself, to fulfill those needs perfectly. Without absolving mothers of accountability, we can let go of the maternal ideal, that myth of oneness and the "naive egoism" described by Alice Balint. It was she who said that the "ideal mother has no interests of her own," not to validate that position or to suggest that mothers ought *not* have interests of their own, but to illuminate the *child's view* of mother, a view she says many adults cling to all their lives.

I would say my mother did the best she could with what she had, including the children and husband she got. She was emotionally ill-prepared to handle the challenges she faced. Her ideas about mothering had more to do with controlling than teaching, nurturing and preparing children for independent lives. And she was beaten down by my brother's serious problems. But she also had mo-

*ments when she was a wonderful mother. She is very bright, creative
and curious, and when things were okay, she could relax and just
enjoy us.*

By recognizing her mother's flaws without condemning her,
by giving up the hope that the past can somehow be reshaped in
a more perfect way, a woman not only is freed from bitterness
but, most important to her as a mother, she is freer to build a relationship with her own children that is not lashed to the past.
Though many of our mothers may have been unable to forge
intimate emotional ties to us, we *can* do so with our children.
For each mother, the path to that healthy relationship is different, but it always involves some measure of acceptance, some
letting go of blame, some version of embracing the idea that
"life is what it is."

The nature-nurture debate—the question of whether human
beings are products of their biology or the world around them
(the answer is, of course, both)—holds as a subtext the blaming
and defending of mothers. On the nature side are theories about
infants with difficult temperaments, about a "poor fit" between
mother and infant, along with genetic research that has found
genes for some traits. These theories help take the onus off parents by using the child's biology to explain difficult relationships
between parents and children. On the nurture side is the field of
attachment research, where little data supports the idea that a
child's temperament, which is formed by hereditary factors in
the child, shapes the child's attachment to his or her parents. In
fact, research strongly suggests that adult-child attachment flows
from the parent. For example, some infants are securely attached
to one parent and insecurely attached to the other. Also, infants
who are insecurely attached to their mothers at twelve months
are highly likely to become securely attached to them at eighteen
months if there are favorable changes in the mothers' life circumstances. And, finally, mothers can and do respond sensitively to

"difficult" infants. Handicapped, sick and otherwise more challenging infants are as likely as low-risk infants to be securely attached to their mothers. Attachment theorists insist that the primary caregiver does not necessarily have to be the biological mother, a position Bowlby repeatedly stressed, but they have not been eager to let mothers, or caregivers in general, "off the hook," says Robert Karen.

Bowlby thought it important to look at the amount of emotional support a mother had as well as the mothering she received as a child. Once these factors are examined, he said, "the idea of blaming parents evaporates." What then becomes important is providing help and support in the effort to repair and change. What's needed is the broad view, that of the secure adult who can see her parents' defects without the veil of anger and blame or without the unreal, banal insistence on never speaking ill (even when it's the truth) of one's parents.

One woman told me she spent three years in therapy before she could turn the corner toward something positive with her mother. The change came, she said, when she began to look at her family as a whole, not just at her mother's failure to protect her from her emotionally abusive father. "I had been so busy blaming my mother," she said, "that I hadn't been paying attention to my role."

Another woman expressed that balance saying this: "My own spiritual journey started with going into my past and finding that I could take power away from my mother. She was a great disconnecter and a lot of my therapy has been facing the terror of being the child who wasn't safe with her. But she didn't make me who I am, and when I claim the choices I've made I feel my own power.

"If I give my mother all the blame then I'm afraid of my children, because I'm thinking, 'I have so much power I'm going to mess them up.' Then I mother from fear. My aim is to mother from love, not from a fear of messing up."

Balance is essential if women are to see themselves as a bridge between the generations behind and those to come and as the agents of change, the ones who avoid passing on the wounds. I heard this again and again in my interviews and research and was not surprised to find this truth expressed, as well, in my reading of fiction. In her novel *Breath, Eyes, Memory*, Edwidge Danticat's character Sophie attends a sexual abuse group where a ritual is performed of writing the names of their abusers on paper and then setting them aflame. "I felt broken at the end of the meeting," Sophie said, "but a little closer to being free. I didn't feel guilty about burning my mother's name anymore. I knew my hurt and hers were links in a long chain and if she hurt me, it was because she was hurt, too.

"It was up to me to avoid my turn in the fire. It was up to me to make sure that my daughter never slept with ghosts, never lived with nightmares, and never had *her* name burnt in the flames."

Like Sophie, we can't change the mother we had in childhood, but we can speak the truth about what we experienced under her care. Penetrating the nature and scope of the mothering we received, however, doesn't absolve us of responsibility as adults for our own lives. As Robert Karen says, "Eventually, one must separate, in the positive sense of becoming one's own person, which means not just letting go of the [anxious] tie to the parent, but letting go of the wound that perversely sanctifies that tie and letting go of ways in which one's own behavior with others (including one's children) replicates it."

Seeing how I was mothered compared to how I mother my children has helped me to further understand my own childhood and myself. The fact that I didn't have the mothering I needed has often made me feel that I must be somehow defective, to have made my mother unable to be a mother to me. Now I see that, of course, it wasn't my responsibility to make my mother love me, or perhaps more accurately, to make her behave like a mother. Her narcissism governs the way she is with everyone, not just with me.

It took me longer than many people to reach the point where I could risk moving forward, toward growth. I dared do no more than tread water for years; but, like some other women who have known deprivation, I've found both renewal and the healing of childhood pain in the experience of bringing a child into the world. I heard this theme of purgation from many, but not all, of the women I interviewed. One, who has two grown children and a new grandchild, said she's surprised at how joyful mothering has been, even though she experienced abuse in childhood and divorced just months after her second child was born and reared her children entirely alone.

She looks back on her mothering with deep satisfaction, saying, "I feel great." She expressed what may be the ultimate in mothering contentment when she said that she is the kind of mother and grandmother she wishes she had had. She can ask herself, "Would you want to be the child of a mother like you?" and answer, "Yes."

As for many of us, much of her healing has come through love for and from her children. Of her own mother she says: "She's eighty-six and continues to explore her life and I admire her. I have respect for my mother, but I have never felt any love for her. I wish I had felt toward her what my daughter feels toward me. She sent me a card recently and wrote in it: 'I love you more than you will know—even though we drive each other crazy sometimes. I hope I will be lucky enough to have my daughter love me as much as I love you."

Although the sadness that she didn't experience those feelings about her own mother remains, the satisfaction and fulfillment of her own motherhood overpowers it. "The love I have known in my life has come through my children," she said. "I feel quite blessed." Not every mother, of course, has such a positive experience. One woman said to me, as we finished our interview, "I have not had serious regrets about having these children," but she couldn't muster more enthusiasm than that. Child-rearing is simply too complex, chaotic, maddening, demanding, irksome and diverse to shoot every mother out the other end feeling satisfied.

Therese Benedek, who was interested in the connection between the biology and psychology of motherhood, once wrote: "We are all but a link in the chain of generations." For me, the hardest times in my life have been when I felt stranded and apart from that chain, especially in my thirties when I was acutely aware of the generational gaps on each side of me: no mother, no children. A larger linking of human beings exists also, one my then-seven-year-old son once reminded me of in that out-of-the-blue way children do. "We're all related, aren't we?" he said. When I asked what he meant, he tried to articulate a thought that had come to him about how, if we go way, way back into the generations, we'll find that somebody's great-great-great-grandmother married somebody else's great-great-great-grandfather. I listened as he, charming and quasi-articulate, stumbled his way through ideas about the Native American web of life, about six degrees of separation, about spiritual bonds. I, too, have glimpsed that sense of being connected to everything, but my own psychobiology seemed to require a more tangible connection, which my children have given me.

More than a decade ago, I sat on my grandmother's back patio, holding my baby in my arms, shading him from the low autumn sun. There with my mother's mother, who was forty-eight years older than I, holding my firstborn son who is forty-one years younger, I thought about those missing generations: my absent mother and the children I didn't dare have with my first husband, the children I wasn't brave enough to love and risk losing. I spent too much of my life afraid of the future, waiting for the other shoe to drop after my mother died, frozen, bereft, fearing miseries that might lie ahead. My children have connected me not only to them but to an imaginable future. I feel myself in the flow of the stream of humanity. Nietzsche, whose father died when he was young, came to believe that each of us must embrace our fate entirely if we are to be happy. He thought that when life's traumas lead to bitterness and anger, when a person feels cheated and deprived, then life is not appreciated for what it is but despised for what it is not. The antidote against letting resentment act like a cancer on one's spirit, he said, is to love one's fate, all of it, not just the joys and pleasures but the pain as well. I think he was right, and I think he expressed the hardest task of life. But I have glimmers of it when I acknowledge that I would not be who I am today—married to my husband, mother to my children—had not every other piece that came before been in place.

Jung expressed this same idea when he said that a complete life isn't a theoretical or ideal completeness, but an acceptance, without reservation, of "the particular tissue in which one finds oneself embedded, and that one tries to make sense of it or to create a cosmos from the chaotic mess into which one is born." Therapist Lowinsky says that idealizing childhood and thinking that if "our mothers were only not so dense, or crazy, or limited, such a childhood could have been ours," is a defense against confronting the tragic, imperfect nature of life. Only by letting go of the wish that we, our mothers, and our childhoods had been better do we begin to see our mothers' humanity and our own. Only by letting go can we move wholeheartedly into the fullness of our own lives.

Children as Healers

For me as for many other women who came to motherhood trailing ghosts, my children have been teachers and agents of change. Our children come to us as a mystery. They come not only loaded with potential and hope, but also with the possibility, even the likelihood, that they will reveal our most humbling faults.

Like good therapy, parenting can provide an experience of being in the world and of relating to others in a new way. And, like therapy, it's not necessarily easy or comfortable. Our children bring out both the worst and the best aspects of ourselves, not once but again and again. Along the way, we can't help but be confronted with our own conflicts. As we mother our children and help them grow and develop, we, too, mature and change. Much of this goes on unconsciously and over time.

I feel strongly that in mothering my infants, I was re-mothering myself in many ways, and thereby teaching myself to be a good mother. It's no accident that I have so many children, and it may even be no accident that I was given twins to begin with. There was a big hole to fill! I wanted, needed, to be totally immersed in mothering. I was fascinated by the concept that people mothered and made conscious decisions and choices about how they raised their children. That's why home birth, and that whole natural mothering trend, was so important to me. It was all based on making your own decisions given who you, and your children, are.

My children have helped me to slow down and to shift my focus from worldly achievement to a more general appreciation of life. Most of all, work is no longer the center of my life. It's more like one of the rings in a multi-ringed circus of family, community, church and work.

I had this concept of mother power as being ineffective and circuitous, and I'm slowly learning to see how my image of my mother created that. She dispersed her power as a response to my father's power. That was my model and I've had to find a new one. My son has been a great help by letting me see how using a male approach with him, being confrontational and powerful, leads to deadlock. Being with him has helped me see that female energy, what I see as moving with the other person instead of confronting him, really works. I can trust that female energy.

Having children has taught me to regulate my life and keep on schedule and be focused. I can't dwell on a slight or a setback or a disappointment like I did in my single, indulgent days. We just keep marching on.

Among the many women who spoke to me of the healing effects of having children was May Hung, who lost both her parents as a teenager and whose angry outburst at her four-year-old sent her to seek help. As a young girl she had assumed she'd have children when she grew up, but she lost interest during college as she got caught up in the women's movement in the 1960s and developed, as she said, "an attitude about kids." She wasn't drawn to them, not even babies, and came to see herself as "too cool" for motherhood. "Being a doting mother didn't appeal to me," she said. "I wanted a career, a whole life and maybe kids in child care. I wanted to be a 'modern woman.'" Before she was thirty, however, she had fallen in love with an intense, energetic man whose hands reminded her of her father's. She met him on a blind date. Later they married and had their first child—and May lost her attitude.

Her children are young adults now, and May looks back with amazement at herself. "I would never have expected myself to be the mother I came to be. I didn't intend it, but my kids became the center of my universe," she says. She had the career she wanted, in public health, and a satisfying, long-term marriage as well, but motherhood has been the capstone of her life.

"The moment I became a mother and lay there looking at my newborn, I felt this was the most fabulous thing in the world. The piece that blew me away—and no one knows it until you're there—is the experience of unconditional love. As deep as my relationship with my husband is, there are parameters he could cross that would end the feeling and the relationship. But with children, there's nothing they could do that would make me withdraw my love from them. I know not every parent feels this, but it was loud and exceptional for me, and still is."

May doesn't think that having children offset the lost mothering of her childhood; instead, the healing for her has come from experiencing mother love from the mother side. "Being available to my children," she says, "was my response to the loss of my parents. And being aware of the miracle of raising these people and having them in my life has been the reward. I missed out on a lot of the child side of the mother-child relationship, but I've gotten the mother side in a profound and huge way."

Hannah Frank, the woman who has seven children and stepchildren, expressed a similar thought, saying, "When you give to other people, you give to yourself. That's why making my children the focal point of my life has been healing. Doing something for someone else made me feel good. It increased my self-esteem to know I was important to someone else."

One young woman went into therapy when her two children were two and four to try to make sense of her anxiety and of what she called "the frightening times when whole aspects of me that were not allowed to surface as a child would explode and scare me." She worried about being sad and upset around her young children as she struggled with seeing her parents and her own childhood in a new light.

"My therapist told me that children want to know their mothers. 'It's okay,' he told me, 'if they see you having a hard time. What scares them is when you fake being okay. They need to know you as a whole woman. Kids respond well when adults are honest.' That has really helped me sink into my being and let my children experience me as I am. It helps me be really present with them. And it's exactly what didn't happen for me as a child. I couldn't be myself and be accepted by my family."

For those of us with wounds from the past, our children make it imperative that we heal, that we let whatever craziness and difficulties our parents showered on us end with us. Living our own lives as well as we can, being our truest, most healthy selves, may be the best we can do for our children. Winnicott is among the many thinkers through the ages who has considered what it means to be a healthy individual. He first divided the world of people into two categories: those who were not "let down" as babies and are candidates for "the enjoyment of life and of living," and those who suffered some sort of trauma as a result of "environmental letdown" and are candidates for lives of storm and stress and perhaps illness.

Some people in that second category go through life rigidly or in denial, but others follow the human tendency toward healthy development and "make good." Those are the resilient ones. Winnicott decided that the meaning of mental health must extend beyond those who are healthy from the beginning to cover those who "carry a germ of ill health and yet manage to 'make it' in the sense of reaching in the end a state of health that did not come easily or naturally." These he called "healthy by hook or by crook."

Healthy people, said Winnicott, live three lives: inside ourselves where we each have our own psychical or personal reality, in community with others and in cultural experiences. The last category begins with child's play and leads to art, history, philosophy, mathematics, religion, humor and more. "In some anxious, restless people," he wrote, "it has practically no representation, whereas in others this is the most important part of human existence." I find in Winnicott's discussion of a healthy individual threads of Maslow's concept of self-actualization, and have come to see that one of the surest ways to put my children on the road toward fulfilling that highest need is to strive for it myself.

Self-actualization is that last of the universal human needs, coming after physical care, safety, love and esteem. Maslow contended that the healthiest of humans, those who reveal the best of human nature, are those who can be described as self-actualized, which implies satisfaction of basic emotional needs and of cognitive needs for knowledge and understanding. In his study of subjects deemed to have achieved this, he said that they all felt safe and unanxious, accepted, loved and loving, worthy of respect and respected; and that they had worked out their values and their philosophical or religious bearings.

It seems to me that motherhood, though it dwells in the mundane, can provide for some women opportunities for self-actualization, for touching on peak experiences of beauty and truth. In fact, as I studied Maslow's list of characteristics of the self-actualized, I saw much that helps define a good mother: having a clear perception of reality, not threatened or frightened by the unknown, accepting of self and others, having some mission in life outside the self, being capable of deep interpersonal relationships, seeing humankind as a single family, being strongly ethical, possessing an ability to appreciate or even be awed by various basic experiences of life, such as nature, music and children. Motherhood offers opportunities to enter a transcendent state. One woman I interviewed expressed it this way: "I remember clearly bringing my first child home from the hospital and feeling I was walking into a whole new life—a wonderful life. I loved my life before, but to me being pregnant and then giving birth was such a spiritual experience. It was a clear experience of God for me. I had a clear, profound feeling that my husband and I didn't do this by ourselves."

All the work we do to lay to rest troubles from the past, to become objective and balanced about our mothers, to heal old wounds, to put ourselves on the path toward self-actualization, allows us to be clearheaded, perceptive and evenhanded in our treatment of our children. As psychologist Harriet Lerner says, our children "are the major benefactors of the work we do on our own selves." But in all this, it's crucial to bear in mind that we need not be perfect.

The measure of healing for me is not getting over having lost my mother, but abandoning the effort to fill the hole she left and turning my attention instead to my children and to the future of our family. Having a secure place in my family of husband and children, loving them and being loved in return, has driven out the yearning that marked my life before them. My past remains unchanged, but my present is rich and full. It took years of psychotherapy for me to see the experiences of my childhood in a new way and to reach the acceptance that allowed me to turn away from the past. I'm fond of a cartoon in *The New Yorker* depicting one mother saying to another as they sit on a park bench with their babies: "I like to think that each generation will need a little less therapy than the generation before." I like to think so, too. Just as surely as dysfunction can reverberate through generations to come, I believe the positive changes we make will live on. Someday we'll be the mothers, grandmothers, great-grandmothers whose photos hang in the hallway. Maybe the stories told of us, one day, will be delivered with good humor, affection and even love.

CHAPTER SEVEN

Mother Lore, Mother Love

Come forth, and bring with you a heart that watches and receives.

—William Wordsworth

During pregnancy and my children's infancies I didn't think much about where motherliness comes from. I may have been too overwhelmed with caring for two young children close together in age to have any real time to think, or perhaps I unconsciously relied on my mother's sub rosa example. As my children grew past the age of four, however—the age I was when she disappeared into hospitals—I began to wonder whether mothering is passed down in a mysterious, cellular way from our mothers and grandmothers. I wanted to know what being a mother without a solid model to follow would mean to me and to my children. Where do women learn to mother?

In my own mothering I found it easy to come by advice and instruction on how to fill the lowest of a child's needs. Diapering, feeding, tending to the myriad childhood illnesses and all the rest, as any mother of young children knows, kept me well occupied. But how does a mother help a child feel safe, valued, capable and beloved? Was the ferment of love, tenderness and protectiveness that stirred in me leading me to do and be what my children needed? Where were the guidelines for nurturing and loving a child? I felt like the woman who had told me in an interview, "I always imagined that by the time I was thirty someone would hand me the rule book on life." Like so many other women, I wanted the handbook on mothering, something that would tell me I was doing it "right."

At first, I hoped to find that the rules for mothering came in the form of elemental knowledge, so basic and so deeply embedded in biology that if I didn't get it from the mothers before me, then instinct would take over to guide my hand and heart. Some "meta-natural" way would overpower any "unnatural" impulses that my own experiences had taught me. Under-mothered women I interviewed sometimes spoke of their faith in this unwritten guide. When I asked them where they learned how to mother, I often heard such replies as "There's got to be instinct involved" or "Mothering came naturally to me" or "I've always been nurturing."

My mother wasn't cut out to be a mother, but I've always felt I had some innate thing inside me that has kept me going with my children.

Most of what I know about being a mother has been instinct. But I've also learned from reading and talking to friends. Of course, I learned many things from my mother but lots of those are not my mothering style.

Biological instinct, which implies inherited behavior that steers each member of a species to behave in a preprogrammed way, is seldom ascribed to humans by scientists. Specifically, the notion of "maternal instinct" as an innate drive *all* mothers have to love and nurture *all* their children has been laid to rest, buried under mountains of evidence from the animal and human worlds of infant abandonment and infanticide by mothers. Biologists have found ample evidence that species from beetles and spiders to mice, prairie dogs, wolves, hippopotami and lions cull their litters and abandon or cannibalize their young under a wide range of conditions. Among humans, few mothers directly commit infanticide. Instead, they abandon infants in whom they are unwilling or unable to invest the considerable resources needed to rear them to independence. Research tells us, for example, that in the first three centuries of the Common Era in Rome, as many as 40 percent of children were abandoned to uncertain fates. And maternal instinct as a biological impulse that leads all women, with the implication of all "natural" and hence "good" women, to want to have children and thus to be transformed into their full feminine selves holds no credence either.

Still, the notion of instinct remains comforting to undermothered women, and we're not entirely without help from human biology. Although mothers are not biologically "hardwired to bond to their infants," as anthropologist Meredith Small explains, there must be some "primal urge to act a certain way toward infants" because "it would be odd if evolution did not, in some way, ensure that parents and infants 'hook up.'" This hooking up is easy to see, again, at the lowest levels of an infant's needs. Most likely, however, the *baby's* instincts are in the driver's seat, bringing mother along. "Nothing blank about this slate: human infants are predisposed to seek out a familiar, feminine, person: a person likely to be its mother," says anthropologist Sarah Blaffer Hrdy. No one needs to teach babies to cry, grasp, nuzzle, suck and otherwise act in ways that signal their needs and vulnerability. In addition, babies come equipped with physical features that mothers are primed to adore: round heads, chubby cheeks and big eyes. Human infants have evolved, in the words of Hrdy, to be "activists and salesmen, agents negotiating their own survival." What makes a woman maternal and makes her the likely, but not only, candidate to be the primary caregiver, Hrdy explains, is not some magical "essence of mother," but the fact that she's invariably the one who's there at birth, "hormonally primed, sensitive to infant signals, and related to the baby."

A mother responds to her infant's vulnerability by keeping her child warm, fed and protected from physical injury, which not only drastically increases the child's chances for survival but sets the stage for attachment. At the root of attachment theory is that mewling infant seeking not only milk but relationship from his primary caregiver, like the piteous little monkeys clinging to their cloth mothers. Bowlby was the first to link evolutionary theory and infant development, as he strove to explain "the desperation, rage, and despair" he'd seen experienced by infants when their attachments to caregivers were ruptured. Bowlby is unequivocal on this point, saying, "Human infants, we can safely conclude, like infants of other species, are preprogrammed to develop in a socially cooperative way; whether they do so or not turns in high degree on how they are treated." A baby's need to be protected from predators, ingrained in the ancient past of humans, is the spark that ignites attachment behavior.

Other ideas, like the minute interactions between mothers and babies, revealed on Stern's slow-motion films, elaborate on the ways mothers know, without being taught, how to fall into step with children. In particular, the first year with a baby is loaded with focused moments of interactions, as when a baby gets excited by a toy, reaches for it and lets out an exuberant noise. We act, without thinking, by matching the baby's excitement with our bodies and voices, showing the child we understand and share in the experience. We do this, too, with babies we spot around town, riding in backpacks and grocery carts. An infant's eyes meet ours, and, feature for feature, we mimic his open mouth, wide-eyed delight or puckered concern.

Even when a mother-infant pair begins out of sync, they can make adjustments that enable them to realign. An animated woman who's controlling, intrusive and in need of a high level of stimulating interaction approaches her new baby with such intensity that over the first weeks, the child becomes withdrawn and expressionless. Mother looms over her baby, wanting to play chase and dodge, but the child avoids her eyes and turns his face away. Engaging with her is too dangerous, she's too ominous; the child is learning to avoid social interaction, not just with her but with everyone. Then, for reasons not known, the two begin to accommodate one another. Maybe the child becomes better able to tolerate high levels of stimulation. Maybe the mother sees her child retreating and lightens her behavior to bring him back. She learns not to overshoot quite so far; he risks looking her in the eye. Something balancing in the mother-child relationship pulls them back from the edge of catastrophe for the child and into the broad swatch of normal. Out-of-step infant-mother pairs, of course, can't always save themselves from the brink, as insecure attachment attests, but often they do.

Monica's Experiment

A battle between the imperative of the past (a mother's "ghosts") and the self-righting tendency of many human children ("mother nature") can be seen in the mothering experiences and behavior of a singular woman known in human development research as "Monica." Beginning in 1953, when she was a year old, she was under uninterrupted study until well into adulthood as she became a mother herself to four daughters. Monica's unique start in life provided observers with an opportunity to explore aspects of human development in an experiment that never could have been deliberately engineered.

When she was born, Monica's esophagus and stomach were not attached, requiring her to be fed directly into her belly through a surgically implanted tube for her first two years of life. During that time, Monica was not held or cradled while being fed because a caregiver needed both hands, one to hold the funnel that attached to the tube that protruded from her stomach, the other to pour the formula into it. Nurses did this in the hospital for two weeks and then sent Monica home with her mother, who continued the practice, laying Monica either across her lap or on a crib or sofa. The tubing, covered in gauze and jutting from Monica's stomach, also limited how closely she could be held even when not being fed. Because of these peculiar circumstances, she did not chew or swallow food in those first two years, and she never related sucking, tasting, swallowing and the cycles of hunger and satiation with the person feeding her. Unlike other babies, Monica had no control over when she was fed. It could be done at her mother's convenience, even when Monica was sleeping or fussing or crying. She spent much of her time those first two years alone, on her back, and her physical development was so retarded that she couldn't stand until age three. By then, additional surgery had corrected the congenital disorder and, in time, the tube-feeding of her early years faded to nothing more than a scar on Monica's stomach.

Monica came to live a typical childhood of home and school, all the while she and her family (parents, four siblings and sometimes grandmother) were periodically observed and their activities recorded on film, audiotape and, later, videotape. They were captured while engaged in spontaneous behavior as well as during interviews and psychological testing. Over the years, her researchers came to see that Monica provided a unique opportunity for a cross-generational study of maternal behavior. Among the questions she has helped answer is one no one would have predicted in those early years of observation: How will a mother who had no experience as an infant with face-to-face, skin-to-skin nuzzling and suckling feed her babies?

Monica married at nineteen, and when she had her first child, Adele, at twenty, she was visited by her researchers. "Our first view of Monica feeding Adele at 3 1/2 weeks in 1972 was stunning," one reported. She held her baby in the same awkward, distanced way she had been held while being tube-fed. The researchers remembered that as a girl she had held her dolls the same way. Her observers were so struck by Monica's lack of engagement with her infant during feeding that they went back to replay the films and verify their memories. And there she was as a little girl with her dolls laid across her lap or on the floor, never with them cuddled in her arms, to give them a bottle. As a new mother, she had no conscious memory of her first two tube-fed years. What she knew of that time was only what her mother had told her, and although she had seen photographs of herself as a baby, they don't show her tubes.

Monica eventually bore four girls and never considered breast-feeding any of them. Each was, in fact, fed the same way her first baby was, which replicated the feeding she had received. When she took her child in her lap, Monica would hold the bottle with one hand and use the other to gesture, smoke or take sips of coffee. She usually talked or watched television during feedings rather than pay attention to the baby. When her babies were as young as two weeks old she would leave them alone to suck from a bottle propped nearby. Once each child was able to hold the bottle herself, Monica rarely did the feeding. In other situations, however, such as diapering or bathing, Monica engaged with her children and made eye contact, but she didn't hold her babies close. The girls' father, however, gave them bottles in the conventional cradled manner.

Many photos accompanied a journal article I read about Monica, and I studied them, saddened to see her tiny baby, arms and legs dangling loose, alone on a couch with a bottle propped nearby. I was finding Monica's story discouraging anyway, just more evidence of the power the past holds over us. Then I turned a page and saw a truly dismaying photo: Monica sat feeding her second daughter in her usual style, with the baby across her lap, and next to her was her first daughter, then about a year and a half old, feeding her doll in the same way. The intergenerational transfer of this aberrant behavior had begun; but it was not to last.

Although at very early ages Monica's daughters fed their dolls the way they had been fed by their mother and the way they saw Monica feed younger siblings, by age five all the girls were beginning to hold their dolls in their arms. Soon, they came to prefer the close-to-the-breast, face-to-face method, the way their father gave them bottles. The girls found their cuddling way more "comfortable" than Monica's method. They resisted both the experiences of their own infancies and Monica's direct insistence and instruction that she knew the best way to feed a baby. The pull of the practice favored by evolution to make breast-feeding possible (and to encourage tender connection) was stronger than their mother's model. Her researchers concluded that a deviant experience apparently must be thorough, consistent and enduring, as it was for Monica, to become ingrained. With no deliberate intervention, only the example provided by their father, the daughters tipped away from following their mother's path. Monica could not overcome the message of her own experience, but she also could not pass it on to her daughters.

No one has been able to find a direct link between a particular hormone and the urge to act maternally, despite considerable effort. Nature appears to provide mothers with help in caring for infants, as demonstrated by Monica's daughters, but the messages are broad, faint and based on a single tune: "Keep the baby close, otherwise the baby will die." The highly specific and individual quality of human mothering is so diverse and extended that any modern mother hoping for "nature" to lead the way will be sorely disappointed. In beings as intricate as humans, nature cannot be separated from nurture, especially when it comes to the complex behaviors and emotions involved in loving, cherishing and nourishing a child. Maternal commitment emerges in a piecemeal fashion and is "chronically sensitive to external cues," says Hrdy, especially the baby's signals. It's not as simple as innate versus acquired behavior or genetically predetermined versus environmentally produced practices. "Nurturing has to be teased out, reinforced, maintained," says Hrdy.

Cultural Influences

Just as biology exerts an influence on mothers, so does culture. The way we wear our hair, dress, dance, find our mates, worship and eat are molded by the culture we live in, and so are our ideas about parenting. "Every act by parents," says anthropologist Small, "every goal that molds that act, has a foundation in what is appropriate for that particular culture." Even ideas that seem inherently true—talking to the baby ensures that he will learn to speak, sleeping with the baby encourages emotional dependence—are merely cultural variables. Just because the culture promotes a notion about parenting, of course, doesn't mean it's necessarily good for children or mothers or appropriate for an individual mother or child.

In this country parenting is powerfully influenced by the pervasive American ideal of the independent, self-reliant individual who strives for personal achievement. Parents keep a close eye on the cognitive and motor skills of their babies, measuring them against developmental norms. Mothers are expected to be teachers who make sure their children are ready for each new level of schooling and later achievement in life. "Control over the baby is a major issue for most parents," Small contends. Our culture tells us that babies need to be trained and given a structure so that parents can be free of their manipulations. Parents fear "spoiling" their babies and resist "overindulgence." American babies spend a lot of time out of contact with their caregivers. They sleep alone; are pushed in strollers and propped up in backpacks, car seats and high chairs; their eating and sleeping schedules are separate from those of the rest of the family. Within this context of parent as teacher, child as unrealized potential and the overriding value of individual power, achievement and ambition, American mothers are subject to constantly changing prescriptions for how best to achieve these goals with their children.

A glance back at our history turns up what today is considered laughable advice. Around the time of World War I, our government urged mothers to combat babies' bad impulses. Thumb sucking, for instance, could be discouraged by pinning baby's sleeves to the bed. Theories about child-rearing have come thick and fast in the last thirty years, swinging back and forth between permissiveness and toughness. Since the 1970s, diverse theories have come and gone with the fickleness of hemlines. Parent Effectiveness Training came on the scene to persuade parents of the importance of allowing children to express themselves freely. Tough Love urged strict control by parents and cautioned against allowing children, especially teens, too much self-expression. Later neurobiological discoveries unleashed labels such as Attention Deficit Disorder and Pervasive Developmental Disorder that explained childhood difficulties in terms of physical causes and spawned numerous theories about how to deal with those children. Authoritarians jumped in to say that biology was a flimsy alibi for spoiled children and that parents needed to punish, with spanking if they wished, the transgressions of their children. These days, child-rearing theories don't last long enough for any of us to raise our children under a single one.

In my interviews, I found women who were able to cite specific authorities that have guided their mothering.

I read a lot of books about motherhood and parenting and child psychology and how to talk to children. Spock and Haim Ginott's books were most helpful, I found.

When I read Virginia Satir, I realized that the purpose of parenting was to make your children independent of you, rather than an extension of you. Then I could be a parent.

More often, however, women sought the voice of authority broadly from books and from their children's physicians and teachers. One said she had learned a great deal about mothering her son from her own therapist and the one who had treated her son after her husband's early death.

Extended and immediate families seem like a logical place for a mother to learn about mothering, but even well-mothered women often find little help there. In our culture the family is usually an isolated unit, not part of a wider network of kin, and parents alone are deemed responsible for the care of children. Few women today had opportunities as girls to practice mothering skills. Some women haven't even held an infant, much less tended one, before having children themselves. One woman who had grown up an only child told me she knew so little about childbirth that she went to the hospital to have her first baby, in the 1960s, carrying a paperback book and a pack of cigarettes. Once they become mothers, women are often isolated in their homes, away from the example of other mothers. Even women who had exemplary care by their own mothers are unlikely to have had their experiences reinforced by watching others nurture children over the years. This explains why so many women in Western society turn to authorities for help. "How odd it would be," muses Meredith Small, "to tell Ache [of Paraguay] or !Kung San [of Africa] women that in this country, we learn our parenting skills from books and from doctors (mostly male)." Here we call on pediatricians, trained to detect organic diseases, to answer questions about baby's sleeping, eating and crying. Under-mothered women, in particular, can be set adrift, without even their own mothers to rely on, with nothing but nearly mute instincts and ever-changing expert pronouncements to rely on.

Mothers Need Others

Whether mothers need expert advice to get along is debatable, but without question they need other pairs of hands besides

their own. As members of what anthropologists call a "cooperative breeding" species, women require help to mother. Those
ready assistants in other species have gone by such names as
"helper" and "aunt," but the term preferred by anthropologist
Hrdy is "allomother," from the Greek *allo-* meaning "other
than." An allomother can be male and is anyone other than the
mother who provides for the young. Among species that seek
parenting help, which include humans, allomothers are re-
cruited most often from the extended family. They're either
family members too young to be parents themselves or those
past reproductive age, specifically postmenopausal women. An
older woman from the family is the ideal allomother. She's most
likely to be dependable and hardworking and to have an investment in someone else's offspring. In other words, even the anthropologists and animal behaviorists tell us that our own mothers
are the ones we need most when we bear our children.

When a mother is surrounded by sisters, cousins, aunts and
her own mother and grandmothers, as she is and has been in
other cultures and other times, she receives not only practical
help in caring for more than one child, but companionship,
guidance and emotional support. Our foraging ancestors could
not possibly have fed and reared families by themselves, any
more than women today can. Those caring allomothers not only
provide practical care but sometimes become additional attachment figures who can help fill the higher love needs of children.
Caring for babies and young children, Bowlby said, "is no job
for a single person. If the job is to be well done and the child's
principal caregiver is not to be too exhausted, the caregiver herself (or himself) needs a great deal of assistance."

Beginning with giving birth, women are reminded that they
are social beings who need others for both emotional and practical support. Giving birth alone is difficult, thanks to our having
babies with big heads and the resulting demands on a mother's
energy to release her infant. (A sobering illustration in Hrdy's

book *Mother Nature,* an anthropological history of mothering, shows the comparative sizes of the pelvic outlets in humans and various apes. The neonate's head in drawings for the apes looks like the yolk in a hard-boiled egg. The human neonate's head fills the opening, save for tiny moon slivers on either side.) Once born, the baby's airways must be cleared, the umbilical cord cut, and the baby, who is utterly helpless, must be tended while the mother expels the placenta. Throughout human history, women have gathered around birthing mothers to aid, protect and nourish them and their infants. In nearly all cultures studied by anthropologists, someone, usually a woman, stays with a mother throughout labor and delivery and often into her first weeks of mothering. And the need for companionship and assistance carries on. Social isolation is not what we were made for.

Diane, a massage therapist and single mother, described several years of struggle as she sought to parent her daughter without the support of a community.

"My daughter was three when my ex-husband left the country and left us without a home or money. I didn't know what to do. I didn't want to go home to my parents. My mom was just so volatile and unreliable I didn't want to be around her, and my sisters aren't much better. The older one is a serious Type A, really rigid and driven, and the other one's just plain irresponsible.

"My daughter and I just kind of drifted around, looking for a place to be. I think I was looking for a spiritual home, too.

"I finally came to realize I had to grow up with my daughter, because I had never done it myself. I didn't have that inner parent that some people have guiding me. Getting married and becoming a mom gave me the realization that it's very easy to *think* you know how someone else should be behaving and be *very* wrong about that. There's a Buddhist saying: 'Choosing family life is like walking into a burning house.' That's been true for me.

"I had to figure out what it means to be a parent. And one of the realizations I had was that I needed other parents around. I befriended another single mother, and we moved in together with our kids. We're relying on each other, and we're creating a stable home life—keeping our kids in the same schools, getting involved with the neighborhood and developing a circle of supportive friends—that sort of thing.

"We help each other a lot. I've had to learn how to be a mom, and I need these friends to bounce ideas off, to give me reality checks."

In industrialized countries, women get little help from the larger culture in forming supportive social networks. Our mobility disperses families; the design of suburban housing developments and the reality of urban crime discourage neighborhood street life; our economy and standard of living demand ever higher incomes, pushing parents to work longer hours. Within this social climate that hinders community life, women patch together the help they need with varying degrees of success.

Sometimes women find support in their husbands, in part because Western men are encouraged to seek involvement in their children's lives, even infancy, and because their wives sometimes have few others to turn to.

I have an amazing husband. I've watched him be a very different father than what I had. We talk a lot about parenting, values and goal setting.

I learned most how to be a mother from my children's father, who now has full custody of them. He astounded me with his boundless patience, love and ability to give. In our relationship, he was the mother. I played the role of the father.

Once I met the man who became my husband I started thinking that maybe having children was something I could pull off. He was great with kids, especially little ones, and I began to see that he would be there to help me if I started screwing up.

A huge part of the energy I put into mothering is connecting with my husband. We work at allowing each other to be different types of parents. We share the same values, but we're different in our parenting styles, the way we play with the children and interact with them, and we have to allow each other the space to do it our own ways. We work at not belittling or disempowering each other. Sometimes one of us will have to step aside and let the other take over when something isn't working with the kids. We support each other.

As helpful as some men are to their wives and children, and as strong as some are in modeling good parenting, most men still put in only a fraction of the time and effort that mothers do in caring for their children and homes. Even in instances when men earn less money than their wives, they still spend less time, measured in hours, with their children and doing housework. Even an unemployed husband and father is unlikely to take on more than 30 percent of the child care and housework. The allomothers most Western women rely on are not fathers but paid nannies, babysitters and day care providers. Such trusted others as teachers, husbands and friends who are mothers can shore up the confidence of under-mothered women, though they don't necessarily care for the children. One mother said, "I don't question my nurturing at all," but told me she often needs to check in with others to test her judgment and decisions about practical matters such as, "How sick is too sick to go to school?"

The Role of Other Mothers

Many women don't live near extended family, even if they are the ones they'd choose as intimates and role models. Because women so urgently need others, most find or create a network through happenstance: the women met in childbirth preparation classes or at the playground, the women who live nearby or the parents of our children's friends and classmates, the women who've been friends all along and now include the sharing of motherhood to deepen the bond. Often, women seek other mothers who have more experience.

One friend of mine has a grandchild the same age as my son, and another has raised her own kids and now has stepchildren. I turn to them with problems, not to my mother. She would focus too much on the problems.

I have a friend who's ten years older and her kids are grown. She's been through her share of joys and disappointments and is always helpful to me when I go to her wanting to talk. Another friend is seventy-five, and she's always willing to elaborate on the problems she had when her kids were the ages of mine.

This search for a close circle of trusted women occupies a new mother deeply. The need to "create, permit, accept, and regulate a protecting, benign support network," says Daniel Stern, "is unavoidable, given the great demands that both the baby and society place on the mother, without providing her with the necessary preparation and means to accomplish them." Under-mothered women who don't want to or can't turn to their own mothers must find that maternal support elsewhere.

This matrix of other women helps a new mother make the shift in identity from daughter to mother, from one generation to the next. "If the mother is, indeed, going to alter her emotional investments, her allocation of time and energy, and her activities"—all part of the identity reorganization that must take place, says Stern—then she needs models. And her preoccupation with maternal figures in her life is likely to be intense.

Critically important is that the intimates a woman takes into her circle be encouraging and sympathetic. "One or more members of the supporting matrix can undermine, sabotage, or outcompete the mother in the mothering role, with the result that the mother fears the loss of the baby or the baby's love," says

Stern. This can happen with anyone—a nanny, a friend, a sister—but for an under-mothered woman it may be her own mother from whom she most needs to shield herself and her baby. For a woman who doesn't have a healthy relationship with her mother, the emotional stakes in turning to her for help can be too high. "The price is usually in terms of self-esteem, autonomy, independence or dignity," says Stern.

A solid social support, from within the family or without, helps the mother form a secure attachment to her child, especially when the infant is difficult in some way. The more opportunities mothers have to observe other sensitive, caring parents, the more opportunity they have to learn about the rewards, difficulties, mistakes and successes of parenting. This kind of observation, Bowlby contended, is worth "hundreds of instructional talks" by experts.

When my children were tiny I joined a group called Mothers and Babies. All of us were first-time moms and we shared a lot of information and emotional support. Later, I learned from watching other families at church. When I liked the looks of one, I made sure we became friends with them.

When my first child was three months old, I joined a women's group. I still belong to it these twenty-five years later. My group, along with my studio partner, helped me to be a good mother.

My relationships with other women are extremely important to me. What's worked for me is not finding women in play groups or mother groups, but meeting women on other levels and at other points of interest in my life and then sharing mothering.

A mother has important psychological needs that must be met: She needs to feel accomplished, validated, encouraged and valued. She needs to know she is not alone in her struggles, and she needs not to *be* alone in them. She can get this help, or some of it, from other mothers. Other mothers play an important part in reassuring us that our struggles, disappointments, experiences and emotions around caring for children are not unique. How many times do we hear the refrain, "Oh, I'm so glad to know I'm not the only one . . ."? All mothers, but especially those of us who weren't well mothered, can fall prey to assuming that everyone else is having an easier time because they know something we don't know. A network of women willing to share the truth about their own parenting provides an honest picture of maternity. In particular, other women both validate and temper such painful emotions as anger, boredom, self-doubt, frustration and even hate, which all mothers are subject to. If we're fortunate and have chosen a village of women well, they keep us from the misery of being alone with our worst selves, the deep, secret parts we never knew existed or else hoped would never be revealed: the impulse to smother an infant who is inconsolable in the night, the rage engendered by a four-year-old's tantrum or a teenager's belligerence that can barely—or not—be contained. These feelings need to be legitimized by others who also have experienced the confounding, inscrutable ways in which our children can shoot us back to being raging, slamming, stomping toddlers ourselves.

British psychotherapist Roszika Parker contends that all mothers experience ambivalence and that it's normal. In psycho-analytic thought, ambivalence is not mixed feelings but "contradictory impulses and emotions towards the same person," says Parker. Problems can arise in how mothers deal with the guilt and anxiety ambivalence provokes. Parents who can tolerate these feelings, rather than banish them to a place where they will later explode in actual (rather than fantasized) emotional or physical abuse, are good mothers, not the idealized parent who never raises a voice or feels anything but perfect love for her offspring. Mothers need other mothers to help us know this, and to take the children off our hands when tolerance feels impossible. In a !Kung San village, like other hunter-gatherer societies, many adults are readily at hand to share the tedium and frustration of child care. The lack of privacy in a village with grass-walled huts providing the only separation between people protects everyone from violence. Today, our village women, though they likely don't live mere steps away, keep us from the isolation that can be destructive to us and our children.

I just assumed that because I wanted children and think of myself as nurturing it would be easy to be a good mother, but that's not been quite true. Thank heavens, I choose my friends well and watch what they do. One particular friend, Lydia, brings a gentleness of spirit to parenting what must be the three most difficult children ever, who have severe mental and physical problems. When I feel myself responding to my son with echoes of my mother's treatment of me, I stop and think about what Lydia would say or do.

I watch other mothers I know for clues about how to handle difficult situations, and I ask myself, "What would a nice *mother do here? Or a* sane *one?"*

One study of forty mothers of infants revealed that the women found their relationships with peers as important as, or more important than, their relationships with their parents in solidifying their priorities. As one mother in the study said: "You sort of *compare* yourself." Sometimes the comparisons led mothers to want to emulate others, but sometimes it helped them clarify their own assumptions, beliefs and values by making them think, "I wouldn't do it *that* way." Overall, however, the relationships with other women helped the mothers in the study gain confidence, deal with their ambivalence and maintain high morale.

Particularly significant for the under-mothered is the role their village women play in giving them the experience of being mothered. When mothering brings on that need and urge not only to care for the child but to be supported and nourished ourselves, other women can help alleviate the neediness and helplessness that arise. Under-mothered women may, in fact, be more likely than others to deliberately create a community of women to rely on. They know *someone* must fill the grandmother position in the triangle.

When I had my first child, my grandmother was eighty-nine. Although she still lived alone and cared for herself and her home, she was incapable of providing any practical or physical care of me or my child, even if that had been her inclination. I would have been grateful, however, to learn whatever she might have remembered from mothering my mother those many decades ago, but the separation between us was far more profound than age. Because of our lack of intimacy through the years, I wouldn't have known how to talk to her of something as vital to me as mothering. Friends filled the role instead. They listened to details of my pregnancies from the very beginnings. They offered reassurance and information, and they cared about my concerns, questions, worries and joys.

Early in my first pregnancy, a friend with grown children gave me a piece of advice I've used repeatedly in my mothering. It came when we were having lunch one day, and I was expressing my anxiety about prenatal testing—again. She had listened patiently over the previous weeks as I gathered information and agonized over the pros and cons, risks and benefits. She supported me as I made the decision to undergo amniocentesis and booked an appointment. That day, I was going back over old territory, second-guessing myself. Had I made the right choice? Kindly and firmly, my friend said to me, "Embrace your decision." She soon moved away and we lost touch, but in the years since I've many times heard her voice reminding me to champion my well-considered decisions about my children.

Another friend attended the births of both my children, and she dropped by nearly every day in the first weeks and seldom left without having answered some critical, immediate concern I had about breast-feeding or diapering or bathing. One day she noticed the beginnings of a breast infection and sent me straight to bed with the baby to rest, to drink the jug of water she put on my bed table and to nurse. She also mobilized other women to bring meals in those early weeks. Faithfully, these village women came by, casseroles in hand, to break my isolation. They were my intimates, the props that supported me while I supported my baby.

Advising new mothers to think of pregnancy as a metaphor for motherhood, Elizabeth Bing, the woman who pioneered natural childbirth, said: "Just as the fetus cannot get a nutrient the mother does not consume, so an infant cannot receive emotional nutrition that the caregiver does not receive. To be able to feed your baby the emotional calories of love, you must consume 'nutritious' love yourself." Mothers who don't get enough nurturing, according to Bing, suffer fatigue, anxiety, frustration and depression. I wonder whether this sort of nourishment was just what was lacking in the lives of many of the mothers of women I interviewed. With too few "calories of love" themselves, they had little to spare for their daughters. Nonetheless, many of those daughters have found a store of emotional nutrition in other mothers who help them feel supported and held.

I've become accustomed to relying on my village women to do for me what I imagine mothers do for their grown daughters. When our children were toddlers, for instance, my husband wanted me to go away for a weekend with him, but I was reluctant, fearful of leaving our boys overnight in the care of someone else. A friend who is younger but whose children are older than mine must have heard my husband say something about it, because she came by one day, sat next to me and stroked my arm, telling me how important it is for mothers to nurture their marriages as well as their children. She reminded me that she, who lived nearby, and other good friends in our neighborhood would be there to help our babysitter with the kids. Another time when my children were very young, I fell suddenly ill with a cold that left me huddled on a couch, coughing and barely able to breathe. That night I was to receive an award, and I called a friend to ask her to take my children so I could get some sleep. She took them, brought over a bowl of soup, called my doctor for a prescription, called my husband to pick it up and, in the end, made it possible for me to appear at the award dinner.

These are women in whose care I can leave my children with confidence and trust. I've come to know, love and enjoy their children, just as they do mine. I carefully print their names onto the forms required at schools and camps that ask whom to call in an emergency if my husband and I are unreachable. Name. Phone number. Relationship: *friend.*

These women and their generous, loving, nourishing acts not only rescue me from difficult practical situations but tell me that, motherless though I am, I am not alone. I am not without kind, smart, nonjudgmental and maternal support. And when my village women sometimes ask me for help, advice or comfort, I give gladly and gratefully, all of which helps validate me not only as a friend but as a competent mother. And it tells me that we under-mothered women can participate, one way or another, in the fullness of mothering.

Lessons from Mother

In my interviews with mothers, a question that usually drew elaborate and enthusiastic response was this: "What aspects of your mother's care of you do you deliberately try to repeat or avoid with your children?" Women of all ages had thought about this question at length, and some had concluded, as one woman said, "My mother taught me how not to act."

I just want to be the kind of mother my mother wasn't! I want to be nurturing. I want to be there for my kids. My mother pretty much did what she wanted to do without thinking of my needs.

Women often spoke of very specific behaviors they cultivated in order not to repeat some quality of their mothers'.

I can act silly with my son, which I don't remember my parents ever doing. They were more formal than I am.

In my family a lot of things weren't talked about. We weren't told anything about money, including how to manage it, nor were we given an allowance. They never talked about sex, either. I talk about both with my children.

My parents presented a picture of perfection about their marriage. They rarely argued in front of us kids. My mother held things in. I try to be more real with my kids.

I deliberately try to be consistent and follow through with what I say. My mom was so bad at this!

As a small child, I worried about the phone bill, about everything, because Mother was always preaching, "The sky is falling." I want my children to feel safe.

I'm consciously aware of being very physically loving, hugging and touching a lot. And I'm open about my own feelings, to a point. My children don't have access to every nook and cranny of my life (even if it does feel that way sometimes), but I am genuine with them, revealing times when I made mistakes or struggled with decisions, as well as times when I came to a good conclusion.

Women, too, told of using childhood memories as a guide to alert them to what their children needed. They are doing, in essence, what they wish had been done for them as a child in that same situation. These are, again, the secure-autonomous women who can remember the feelings of childhood and who know their own stories.

What became clear as women answered my questions about where they learned their mothering was that their mothers, no matter who they were or what their shortcomings, were always teachers. Some women were able to take negative lessons from their own childhoods and re-craft them into positive behaviors and ideas used in living their lives and rearing their children. These women didn't blindly react, doing only "opposite" of mother, but deliberately wove lessons learned from childhood into their mothering. One woman, for example, has vivid memories of waiting to be picked up from some activity, as her mother had promised, and finally giving up and walking home. "It made me feel that neither I nor my time were valuable to her," she said. She learned from that to take schedules and promises seriously, not only with her children but with everyone.

Cathy Patterson, who recognized in her own menopausal surliness her mother's ill humor, wasn't permitted to speak her mind while growing up and learned from that to act differently with her children.

"My mother didn't allow for any feelings or reactions that ran counter to hers, which made me determined that no matter how much I didn't want to hear what my children had to say, they would always have the freedom to say what they thought.

"I'm Jewish and wasn't allowed to date outside my religion in high school. But I went away to college and met James, who's Episcopalian. I told my parents about him, but he was an abstraction to them. When I visited home during vacations they wouldn't ask about him, because one didn't talk about anything my mother didn't want to talk about.

"At the end of one of those visits, my mom was driving me to the airport and I screwed up the courage to say, 'I feel caught in the middle because I love you and I love him.' My mother snapped: 'Stop being so melodramatic.' That was it. End of conversation.

"I dated James for three years before my parents met him, six years in all before we got married.

"Now my son, who's also been reared Jewish, is dating a non-Jewish woman in college, and I'm deliberately handling things differently. I have no idea whether this will lead to marriage, but rather than lay guilt on him I've tried to be proactive and keep lines of communication open. When we talk on the phone I ask how she is and what they did this weekend. Silence is as powerful as being obnoxious."

Many women find, in time, that their mothers, even those who failed their daughters in many ways, did *something* appropriate and useful. When I asked one woman whether her mother did anything right, she said, "Okay, fair's fair," and launched into a short list of plusses. Cathy Patterson's relationship with her mother eventually led her to seek therapy, and there she achieved a broader, more objective view of her mother.

Just a few weeks into it, Cathy said, in her crisp, confident manner, "I was griping about my mother, and hit one of those turning points in life when my therapist said: 'Cathy, your mother had to have done something right. You're a kind person, you're conscientious, hardworking, responsible, self-sufficient. Your word means something. You have a good sense of humor. She couldn't have been *all* bad for you to turn out this way!'

"I had so focused on all the stuff that had hurt me that I had forgotten the good things. And one of the especially good aspects of my mother was her lifelong commitment to creating a good marriage with my father.

"I was on the phone one day recently with my son, and he mentioned a friend who 'hates her father,' and I said: 'Are you the only kid left who speaks to both his parents?' And he said, 'I'm the only kid I know whose parents are still married and still love each other.'

"I know that both my children appreciate being in a home

where their parents have worked on their marriage. And I know I got that from my mother. She always put her relationship with my father first."

Other women had similar awakenings.

Whenever I was sick, my mother would turn into the most wonderful mom in the world. I had lots of childhood illnesses, lots of tonsillitis, measles, flu, colds, an appendectomy, a tonsillectomy and pneumonia. Something about my being ill brought out the best in her and she would give her utmost. It's one of the reasons I couldn't flat out hate her. I knew she had it in her to love me.

I had defined much of my life by not being like my mother. She married young, I married older. In my first year of mothering I was overprotective because my mother neglected us. With the help of a lot of reading and therapy I came to see that I couldn't feel authentic if my whole identity was being "not her." I learned that I could relax and wouldn't suddenly turn into her. And I've come to see that in some ways she was wonderful, and I can hold on to those things, too.

Overcompensating

Among the women I talked with, particularly those whose children are grown or nearly so, were those who could look back and see where they had tried too hard to compensate for what was missing in their childhoods. Some women had focused on one particular trait or behavior or mistake as the key to not being like their mothers and then, in aiming to do the opposite, overshot the mark. The consequences might not be more than a memory, as was the case for one mother of two grown sons who looked back at her efforts to avoid any sign of neglect and said, "I didn't want them to go without the guidance that I felt I lacked, so I nagged them about getting things done and was the super organizer. I was accused by their teachers when they were in grade school of over-parenting."

Other mothers of grown children expressed deeper regret, as did one who, as the oldest of eight children, felt she had had to be too responsible too early and had been "robbed" of her childhood. "I worked so hard trying to allow my children to be children that perhaps I let the pendulum swing too much in the other direction. I don't think I had high enough expectations of them and didn't give them enough responsibility. My older son, now thirty-three, is particularly undisciplined and unfocused. I haven't really seen him follow through on anything."

I listened to her, wondering whether she was describing cause and effect, knowing that mothers are not the sculptors and children the clay, and then she said, "I often wonder how much of this has to do with the way I raised him."

I was frequently troubled by this struggle I saw in women to be clear about their roles in their children's lives. Mothers exert a powerful influence on their children, but they certainly aren't the only influence. What parts, women wondered, could or should they take credit or blame for? No one expressed this regret and conundrum more clearly and poignantly than Melinda Morales, the vivacious, dark-haired woman with seven sons.

One afternoon she regaled me with lively stories about rearing those boys whose antics, including shooting BB guns at the sliding glass doors of their Florida home, led to the cancellation of her homeowner's policy. She peppered her conversation with mothering maxims: "As long as you don't quit, there's hope for fixing it," and "Life is about family."

Throughout our conversation Melinda displayed an engaging but hard-edged, self-deprecating humor, especially about her mothering. She's fond, for example, of saying to her sons: "I may have done a bad job, but I did it clean and sober." When we first began talking, I thought her comments about Donna Reed and being the perfect mother were the usual kind in the vein of, "Oh, don't we all wish we were unfailingly patient, kind, cheerful and wise mothers who always feed their children nutritious breakfasts." For Melinda, however, an image of the ideal mother cut more deeply. Her own mother careened between being the child herself, who sobbed when overwhelmed, and being a volatile, compulsive person who flung the contents of drawers on the floor if they weren't ordered with precision. When Melinda was a shapely sixteen-year-old, she leaned against the kitchen counter one Saturday afternoon, thinking of her upcoming big night as homecoming queen. Her mother sailed through the kitchen and without a glance said, "If I were you I wouldn't eat a thing or we'll never get you into that dress."

Melinda's father was in the military and the family moved frequently, always living in the cinder-block houses built for enlisted men's families. Out of the upheaval and insecurity of her childhood, fueled by television images, Melinda concocted a picture of the ideal life and mother—rooms with canopy beds, houses with picket fences.

"I wanted it so passionately," she told me, "that it colored everything."

I asked how that desire showed up in her life.

"First of all, at eighteen I married the former high-school quarterback, then twenty, who, like me, was shot out of a dysfunctional family and ill equipped to be a husband and father. With him I set out to live a TV-perfect life. All I ever wanted was to create a family so I could be in it."

Once embarked on child-rearing, Melinda lived in the same house on a tree-lined street for twenty-two years, to give her children the stability she hadn't had, and eventually she went over the top trying to achieve her ideal.

When her twenty-year marriage ended, her youngest son was an infant and she worked full-time in the gas station she and her husband had owned and run together; but still Melinda volunteered to be room mother in an older son's classroom. Despite the pressures of being a working mother, she was determined to feed her children home-cooked meals nightly.

"I went to bed with cookbooks, got up at 3 a.m. to jog, make brownies for an after-school snack, do housework and then get my boys off to school before I went to work. For holidays, I'd invite twenty guests for a lavish meal. I took *fifteen* teenagers camping! That tells you something, doesn't it?

"And all along the way other women accused me of ruining my boys. 'They'll think all women are superwoman,' they told me. 'Those boys won't know how to do a single chore themselves.' Someone once told me I was rearing seven only children."

But no matter how often other women said, "Stop! You make the rest of us look bad," Melinda raced on toward the paragon she knew was lost the moment she and her husband divorced. How could she be the perfect mother without the perfect father in attendance? "I felt like such a failure after the divorce," she said. "After that, I couldn't win. I could only try to make up for what I had done wrong."

Like most women, Melinda went into motherhood harboring unrealistically positive fantasies about the road ahead; but Melinda's fantasies were especially strong for reasons revealed in *The Motherhood Report*. That survey found that the more a woman romanticized motherhood, the more likely it was that she had felt unaccepted by her mother. In her determination to do better for her children than was done for her, Melinda held herself to an impossible standard. She had no images of mother to draw on other than two extremes: her own mother and television sitcoms. She wanted to make up for the shortcomings of her mother and her own childhood by being perfect herself—as under-mothered women are wont to do—thinking, mistakenly, not only that perfection was possible but that there was one "right" picture of motherhood.

Articulating an undercurrent in the lives of many mothers, she said: "I never did as well as I wanted. I would get up in the morning and make mental lists of how I could improve. 'I'm going to hug everyone no matter what' or 'I'm going to say something nice to every one of them today.' If I was having a problem with a particular child, I was sure that if I were a better mother—more patient, more loving—the problem would be less severe."

This thought, driven by her fear of being found out as a fraud whose perfection was all pretense, along with her deep fear of failing her children, stalked and finally ambushed her a year ago when her oldest son, who had struggled all his life, died of a heroin overdose at age thirty-four.

"My first thoughts after being notified of his death were, 'Oh, my God, it's my fault. It proves I was a terrible parent. My mother was right, my grandmother was right, my ex-husband was right.' "

Images of those three important figures—whom Melinda calls "the three demons of my life"—descended, and deepened her grief. "After he died I wanted to collapse and behave as if the world had ended, because it felt like it had. But I had to show my other six kids that their lives matter, too. I didn't want them to think that all the good they do is overshadowed by the bad things he did."

With her first child, Melinda met one of the most formidable tasks of parenting. As an infant he was colicky, refused cuddling and struggled developmentally, but Melinda, a first-time mother at nineteen, didn't know enough about babies to recognize the signs of trouble in her child. Only much later in his life did doctors determine that the boy had probably sustained brain damage during his very difficult birth. According to psychiatrists Anna Ornstein and Paul Ornstein, caring for an impaired child can elicit extreme responses from parents, tipping them either to overprotectiveness and oversolicitousness or to covert (or overt) rejection. Particularly complicated for parents, they say, are the subtle, subliminal impairments, like those of Melinda's first son, that have no definitive diagnosis but inter-

fere with the child's daily functions. The infant might vomit after eating, be sensitive to noise, express general irritability or ex-
hibit poor motor coordination in speech and locomotion. For
all parents, a child's development affirms their effectiveness;
without that development, especially if there's no obvious clinical reason, parents can feel guilt, shame and frustration.

"The need for adequate mirroring of the parent by the child
continues throughout the parents' life," the Ornsteins wrote.
"Children, who, for whatever reasons, encounter difficulties in
the course of their lifetime, affect their parents' self-esteem to
various degrees." This was certainly true for Melinda. "When
you have a child with problems," she told me, "you always think
you held the magic key, and you just couldn't find it. If you had
just figured it out, it would have made it all better."

Though her children now live independently, Melinda continues to be involved in their lives, and slowly, now that she's
out of the daily fray, she's beginning to shift her view of her
mothering. "I realize that I could have made a lot worse mistakes," is how she puts it.

After we parted, long past the time we'd set aside for the interview, I thought about Melinda's resilience, determination,
honesty and self-awareness, and about how, throughout her ex-
traordinarily challenging life, a thread of loneliness ran. "I never
had a village," had been her parting comment. I couldn't help
but think that a group of caring women would have helped her
immensely with her child-rearing. Maybe those mothers who
kept trying to tell her to relax and slow down were trying to be
her village women. Maybe they were trying to help her see herself more clearly and less critically.

Benefits of Under-mothering

No matter what path a woman followed to become a motherless mother, having had a less-than-adequate maternal model
may, paradoxically, make her a better parent than those whose

resilience hasn't been tested, who haven't had to learn to be self-reliant and determined, who haven't been motivated to gather to themselves the resources and relationships they need. In striving to overcome childhood deprivations, large and small, women may become more self-conscious, less relaxed and free-flowing than other mothers. But that awareness also can make them thoughtful, devoted, deliberate and passionate mothers. Kit Bishop, the woman whose mother made a patchwork quilt and helped Kit visualize the sperm meeting the egg when Kit was trying to get pregnant, says she most certainly thinks about mothering more than other women do. That's because, she says, she has so thoroughly examined her childhood experiences with her own mother. "I'm constantly attracted to the mother relationship. In my worst state, I can't even see a pregnant robin in the spring without thinking, *'mother.'* I know other women worry and are involved in their children's lives, but I don't see them drawn to mothers and motherhood the way I am. Maybe they're interested in a normal way, but for me, it's a passion."

There may be a plus to having had a lousy mother. The slate is truly clean. There's no one for me to measure up to. By comparison, I could be a better mother with one hand tied behind my back!

I was never a priority in my mother's life. And I decided I would be different. No one would come before my daughter.

One young woman I interviewed expressed well both the wavering confidence and the heightened sensitivity to her mothering that I heard in many conversations. This mother of a three-year-old confessed that when she learned that one of her friends plays music all the time for her preschooler, her immediate thought was: "Oh, my God! I haven't taught my daughter show tunes!" She laughed at herself as she related this, but then said seriously, "I just have no sense of whether I'm hitting all the bases. I'm very careful."

I laughed, too, at the "show tunes" comment because I recognized myself in it. I've had similar thoughts and similar doubts about "hitting all the bases," especially when my children were very young and seemed to be all potential waiting to be shaped. When I get twinges of that "show tunes" panic, I recall that seemingly simple advice a friend gave me long ago: "Embrace your decisions." Through our children's elementary school years, my husband and I have chosen specific activities, mainly piano lessons and sports, over the wide range of other pursuits we could have put our time, effort and money into. When I hear of a child who plays the marimba or speaks fluent Spanish, I remind myself of the good, sound reasons we've chosen as we have for our boys, and I pay attention to the echo of my friend's advice.

For me, that "show tunes" panic comes from two sources. One stems from our culture of affluence that presses those of us with means to feel as if we ought to be giving our children as many "opportunities" as possible. The other source is more personal. It's the feeling that, given my history, I can't possibly know how to "hit all the bases." And so I remind myself of what I do know: There is no *right* way to mother. I know what the essentials are (remember Maslow and attachment). I look to my imperfect, thriving children and to the richness of our family life and know that my husband and I are doing well by our children.

In my interviews I heard how other under-mothered women are able to let their heightened sensitivity and carefulness translate into attentive parenting that honors the child's perspective and experience. They do this by keeping a line open to the mothering they received. Kit Bishop spoke repeatedly of her abiding desire to treat her children differently from the way she was treated. In the stories she told about her children, I heard again and again how she tries to imagine what they are experiencing, rather than focusing, as her mother did, on her own response to a particular situation. She told me, for example, of a day she was running late to pick up her son from preschool and take him to a play date.

"It had been an iffy type of spring morning," she said, "where I couldn't tell what the weather was going to do, and I had sent him off to school in shorts, but it had gotten chilly." Rather than taking him directly to his play date, where he'd be for the afternoon, Kit swung by home to get long pants for him and in doing so, made herself twenty minutes late for an appointment. "I went back to get the pants," she said, "because my mother wouldn't have. And, of course, I wanted his skinny little legs to be warm."

In my mothering I try to maintain the channel to my childhood memories and experiences by asking myself, "What am I teaching?" So much of what I learned from my grandmother was surely not the message she wanted to send, and so I try not to jump at the first, obvious answer, but to look beneath the surface for the underlying message—the lesson to a child, intended or not, inherent in an adult's actions. About that day, long ago, when my grandmother abandoned me in the department store, she probably would have said she was teaching me that children shouldn't wander off in public, which scares and inconveniences their parents. What I learned, of course, was far different and indelible. I learned that I couldn't trust her to look out for me. I try to remember that with my own children. Once, for example, my eight-year-old son wanted to sign up to play basketball with a YMCA team. Fine, we said. He usually plays whatever sport is in season, though he hadn't yet tried basketball. He loved the practices, which we later found out was exactly what he wanted from basketball: a few kids in a school gym with a friendly dad. The games, however, were in a regulation-size gym with two contests going at once on either side of a curtain, with referees blowing whistles, crowds cheering and parents ringing cowbells. To make matters worse, another boy accidently landed an elbow on our son's head in the first game, nearly knocking him unconscious. He toughed out a few more weeks and then pleaded with us to quit. Before answering him, my husband and I talked about what we would teach him if we let him quit and what we would teach him if we insisted he finish the season. I think many people would have advised us to make him continue, so he would learn to commit to and stick with projects and to be a team player. But we knew he had lots of opportunities for learning that in school and in other sports. We also knew that, in other ways, we were helping him to learn that sometimes the activities that bring us deep satisfaction—such as mastering a difficult song on the piano—involve long stretches of hard work and tedium. What I wanted to tell him instead was that his father and I listen to him and respect his feelings and won't push him in a direction in which he doesn't want to go. So we let him quit.

What I heard in my interviews coincided with what the authors of *The Motherhood Report* found in their survey of mothers who reflect the general population. "To our amazement," they wrote, "we found that women who felt *less* accepted by their own mothers were often better mothers than women who felt more accepted! . . . Women who felt they could not confide in their mothers, or felt that their mothers preferred one of their siblings, or who were otherwise rejected by their mothers . . . tended to bend over backwards to make sure they did not recreate the same negative pattern with their own children." The reason this is so lies, I think, in the earned-secure research, which tells us that people who have worked through the wounds of childhood can be as sensitive and responsive to their children as those who had secure early attachments. Women who know the shortcomings of the care they received in childhood, who know their mothers' stories, who can remember what being a child felt like, can use all that knowledge and experience to help themselves be "ordinary devoted mothers."

Under-mothered women can bring their children lessons

learned about self-reliance, truthfulness and determination; about being sensitive to the suffering and needs of others; about living an authentic life. They can carry to mothering the knowledge that despite the apathetic or even severe mothering they received, they've not only survived, but perhaps built a fulfilling life. Earned-secure mothers may bring to their child-rearing a well-tuned appreciation for what children need and feel. Awareness of the shortcomings of their family lives as children, whatever they may have been, can allow these women to cherish, enjoy and appreciate their children in ways they were not. They may gain, most of all, the deep satisfaction of knowing they've broken the cycle of inadequate mothering.

CHAPTER EIGHT

The Mother Within

The nature of this work can give you a nervous breakdown—or teach you how to take life by the smallest detail and do it well. If you can do that, you've got it.

—Liza Lou

If my life with its accompanying emotions were charted on a graph, anyone who took a look would demand, "What happened *here,* at the point marked San Francisco?" In those three fleeting years the trajectory altered, abruptly shoved by forces that set my path at a new angle, one that couldn't have been predicted a year, let alone twenty years, before. In San Francisco, my first marriage ended. I found an apartment and lived alone for the first time in my life. I was thirty-seven. I entered psychotherapy, also for the first time. I began to ask of my father and grandmother the questions I had wanted answers to all my life. What happened to my mother? What happened to our family? Who are you and who am I?

I went over and over my history, like making a brass rubbing, allowing more and more emotional and factual detail to show itself. I let myself feel again what it was to be that little girl whose mother slipped out of reach. Between therapy appointments I practiced yoga, brooded in coffeehouses, ran along the bay to the base of the Golden Gate Bridge, explored the city, started going to church after a twenty-year absence and worked with an intensity I wouldn't have mustered had I still had a husband to supplement my income. I renewed old friendships and made new ones. In San Francisco I broke into pieces and began to put myself back together in a new, truer way.

During those years, I now know, I laid the groundwork that made it possible for me to become a mother, or rather, to become the individual mother that I am today. Each bitter, vexing, hard-fought battle with my ex-husband or my father, and in therapy, each painful new insight that came about my mother, grandmother and me, all the cracking open of my past allowed me to stand where I had so long feared to be: alone in the world. I discovered my own rhythms, appetites and strengths after living all my adult life as half of a twosome.

I now miss the city and my friends there and hold treasured memories of those days, but unlike so many earlier periods of my life, I can look on that time without regret. The difference is simply this: While I was there I was alive in a way I'd never been before, more aware of my internal and external life than ever before. I squeezed just about every bit of living I could from my San Francisco juncture. And I've come to think that someday I want to look back at these years of mothering my growing children with the same thought: *It was demanding, but it was good, and I remember because I was there.*

Already I experience some nostalgia about long-gone phases with my children. Running across photos of my boys as toddlers, with their starfish hands and earnest faces, I melt. But I don't want to be there any more than I want to be back in the life I had in San Francisco, before this marriage and these children. I do want, however, to live in a way that will allow me someday to remember these years I'm living now and know that for each confounding, raw and lush phase with my children, I was present with my eyes and heart and ears open.

Mothering goes on so long into our lives and the lives of our children that we have nearly endless opportunities to choose, again or anew, how we mother. And no one knows better than under-mothered women how very important to the child are the choices a mother makes about the life and relationship she builds and shares with her children. Though how mothers relate to their offspring may be powerfully influenced by culture, biology, the past, friends and family, each mother decides, consciously and unconsciously, what she's able and willing to give to each child. Daniel Stern, who like Winnicott understood well the tie of mother to child, wrote of the "first relationship" as a "creative venture" that, like all creative endeavors, is improvisational and highly personal. And like all creative efforts, it now and again comes to "that lonely place where both the path that has been taken and everything you are now doing is questioned." Every good mother, he wrote, "is out on her own limb." For some, this is exhilarating; for many others, it's frightening.

Each mother, but particularly those who arrive at parenthood without a positive role model, needs to summon her will and self-knowledge. She needs to gather the wisdom and insight gained in exploring her origins and her mother's identity. She needs to embrace it all and let it help her define for herself what kind of mother she wants to and can be. Creating the mother within with care and ingenuity becomes part of the journey toward becoming whole, becoming completely who each of us is.

Unfolding myself as a woman is part of my work as a mother. I understand now that my mother couldn't offer to me what she had never offered to herself. She wasn't willing to open those spiritual and emotional places inside herself, so she couldn't open them to us. So now, for me, I know that my work as a woman is my work as a mother.

I've looked to my friends, therapist, books, my daughter's teachers, my stepmother for help. But I've also tried to develop in myself a sort of internal good mother figure. I ask myself, "What would that kind, loving mother do in this situation?"

Among women I interviewed were those who spoke of a careful exploration and testing to find their way toward the mother self.

I collected information like a journalist. Then I made my decisions based on what I knew about myself and what I saw in my babies. I wasn't a disciple of those I collected information from. I felt I was developing my own hybrid version of mothering.

Conventional wisdom said you shouldn't pick babies up every time they cried or you'd "spoil" them. Well, I was constitutionally unable to do that and through the La Leche League I learned that conventional wisdom is anything but wise. My inability to let my daughter cry was my good maternal instinct kicking in. A baby's cry is her communication, and I'm glad I fought off the "let her cry" crowd, including my parents and friends. But if I hadn't had the support of La Leche, I probably would have caved in. With their help I learned to trust myself and trust my child. I think she and I still benefit from that now that she's seventeen.

I never felt I was the right person to be the ideal mother, the cookie-baking, house-fixing, garden-tending kind. But I was certain that spending time with my children as they grew up was something I cared about and that I had to do myself. So I structured my life with time to work as well as look after my children, and I paid someone else to do the housekeeping.

Every mother may be out on her own limb, but if she's done the work of coming to know herself and if she's gathered a circle of trusted others who can reflect the universal in her individual trials and efforts, she's out there with sturdy resources. Two other important supports can help an under-mothered woman become Winnicott's "ordinary devoted mother." They are strong values and a clear knowledge of her individual children. Both can help filter the conflicting theories and advice, can drown out the chorus of "conventional wisdom" and can lead to finding her own mothering path. My hope, and that of many other under-mothered women I've spoken with, is that with those reinforcements I can thoughtfully consider what each of my children needs from me, what kind of mother I am capable of being, and what is possible for us given where I've come from.

What Matters Most

My grandmother served fried trout on Fridays, went to Mass every week, said the rosary at night and in this way told me she valued her religious practice, though she never spoke of God or her beliefs. She cared deeply about what outsiders thought of us, which she demonstrated repeatedly, as when I experimented with smoking and she gave me this unsurprising advice: "Never walk with a cigarette. It looks terrible when a girl does that." Watching her, I learned that she valued her home because that's where she put her time and energy. She avoided challenge and risk-taking and encouraged me to do the same. When I was looking for a part-time job in college, I told her I applied to be a bookkeeper at a bike shop. "You don't know anything about accounting," she said, implying that I shouldn't try anything new. About my grandfather, she said nothing, but I could see her loyalty and the tenacity of her bond to him. They shared an intimacy by proximity, as best I could tell, rather than one based on self-disclosure. My grandmother created a life framed by order and routine and taught me to value that, too. The overriding lesson I took from her, however, was that life was to be survived rather than enjoyed, that the world was a dangerous place and our mission was to keep safe.

I sometimes wonder what she meant to teach me, what I might have missed and whether this nonverbal modeling of values is what she intended. My guess is that, like many other parents, she didn't think much about what she conveyed to my brother and me about how to live our lives. Her values, I suspect, were mostly unconscious, ingrained, acted upon rather than considered. But, like every parent, my grandmother revealed what mattered most to her.

A woman I interviewed expressed a deep sadness about a gap in the parenting she experienced growing up. She said that as a mother herself, she often wanted to be able to quote poets and philosophers, to provide a life lesson at just the right moment. "But I didn't have the background," she said. I think what she was getting at was less a failure in her academic education than in her moral education. Her parents hadn't provided a moral compass for her. As a mother herself, she knew intuitively that passing on and instilling values was something she wanted to do, but she felt unprepared.

All families, consciously or not, teach children what to value in life. In some families, children learn to seek the satisfactions that come from outside themselves, in entertainment, stimulation or distraction. Other families teach children the importance of service to others. Some show children that nothing is more significant than television and work. Other families measure themselves and others by their possessions, and some seek God in all matters. Others teach that nothing counts more than feeling good.

In my interviews I found that women who had defined what they value and desire for themselves and their children and who deliberately model and teach those standards are more confident in their mothering. Their values—firm, known and grounded in morality—were the navigational stars by which their lives and the lives of their children could be directed.

Especially important to me is exposing my kids to a loving community of people who help each other and are caring in their outreach to people in the larger community who have less.

Religion is at the center of my life. It's what has enabled me to cope with all the challenges I've faced in mothering. It's like the fountain, the oasis I dip into again and again. And it's important as a shared family belief system, as well as a set of shared and defining practices. In that way I'm very like my mother. I just do it in a different church.

Today drugs and violence are so pervasive that children need to be solid inside to survive. If I raise emotionally empty children, they'll search for something to fill that emptiness, the way I did, and they'll become addicts, the way I did.

We live in a very wealthy community where kids are given too much and lack appreciation for anything. This is where we live, but it's not what I want my children to see as the real world. My husband and I try to counter those values by taking our kids on hikes, by making sure our friendships include the guy who cuts our hair, not just the rich neighbors. We try to help our children enjoy the simple things. We sit down often and talk about what we believe and whether we're getting there. Kindness is number one, which means treating people the way you want to be treated and knowing that we can give and receive from everyone we meet. Honesty, integrity, love without agenda. This is what we want our children to know.

I've tried to teach my daughter to love and respect other human beings because all humans have a spark of God and deserve respect. Most of all, I want her to know she has a higher power, and I am not it!

When a mother knows what she values and what she wants to teach her children, she helps them form their own strong ethical core. Ron Taffel, a clinical psychotherapist in New York, strongly urges parents to take a moral position, to stand for something in the lives of their children. Otherwise, he says, the voice of "moral relativism," the attitude of "the second family," which is "the kiddie culture of peers and media," comes to over-power the influence of a child's parents and siblings. That "second family culture" teaches children to expect instant gratification, to find fulfillment in material possessions, to feel entitled rather than grateful, to expect more and to lose touch with the concept of *enough.* In his conversations with children about their lives, Taffel has heard repeatedly the anger of children whose parents fail to set rules, who have lost their own moral direction, who don't know what shapes their own lives. One eleven-year-old girl said: "If adults don't know what's going on, it all turns to chaos." And into this chaos, into the "psychic void" that family used to fill, rushes "the great, roaring hurricane of the mass media culture— particularly the culture of celebrity."

Mary Pipher, the psychologist from Nebraska who wrote *Reviving Ophelia,* sums up the destiny of rudderless families this way: "It's become clearer and clearer to me that if families just let the culture happen to them, they end up fat, addicted, broke, with a house full of junk and no time." However, the parents who can keep their goals and objectives in mind even while children rebel or protest, who track their stars and keep themselves and their children on course, are less afraid to say "No" to their children, to speak their minds, to be the adults in the relationship.

Modeling and teaching values goes a long way toward filling children's needs, as defined by Maslow. Children who know their parents as decent beings can feel secure and valued themselves. And parenting is certainly easier when those navigational stars are kept in sight, guiding parents as they carry out the minutiae of child-rearing with its never-ending decisions and choices. Much more difficult is facing every crossroad without a destination in mind. The mindful parent knows the truth, as Thomas Merton said, that "Your life is shaped by the end you live for. You are made in the image of what you desire." Knowing that, the aware mother helps guide her children to the desires that can lead them to a meaningful life.

Cathy Patterson, whose college-age son is dating a non-Jewish young woman, is not only trying to keep lines of communication on the subject open with him (in contrast to what her mother did with her when she dated outside her religion), she's making sure she reinforces her values. In her conversations with her son about his girlfriend, she has repeated what she had told him and his sister all along about dating outside their religion: "One reason for finding a mate who's the same religion is that marriage is difficult and there are many differences no matter what, so the more common ground you have from the beginning the easier it will be. But if you know what you value, you can work things out, just as your dad and I did."

Judaism is very important to Cathy, and she's been steadfast in ensuring that her children receive strong, consistent instruction in their religion and many opportunities to nourish their faith. "My religion helps me be a better person," she says. "I see it as my way of filling the void left by unanswerable questions." She shares her faith and ideas about life with her children and encourages them to talk to her. Now that they're nearly grown, she's found that she cherishes these relationships "where secrets aren't necessary."

Being conscious of what she's teaching her children allows a mother to be deliberate and to seize the moment to reinforce values. One mother I know always seems able to help her children place their behavior in a larger context and judge it against their values. When her son began getting poor grades in middle school and developed a reputation as the class goof-off, the one the other kids could count on to say something funny, disruptive or outrageous, she said to him: "Is this who you want to be? Right now, you're making choices that help define who you are and what kind of man you become. Are you making the right choices for you?" He decided he wasn't, but he has gone on needing her to help him stay the course.

In my interviews, the most self-assured, comfortable mothers seemed to come to the task mindfully, asking themselves good questions and posing them to their children. Some had arrived at the end of their day-in, day-out mothering knowing they'd made choices whose outcomes weren't necessarily positive or predictable. If, however, they'd made those choices carefully and thoughtfully, women seemed less likely to be regretful or to feel guilty.

Much of mothering is learned by doing, which is why so many mothers say they approached their second and later children differently from the first. I look back at my own early anxieties about doing it all "right", and I see now that I was frightened by the unknown. I didn't realize that as each year passed, I'd gain assurance and competence. As Winnicott said, a mother "grows in the job." He also reminds us that good parents don't wish to be worshiped by their children. They're able to "endure the extremes of being idealized and hated" by their children, "hoping that eventually their children will see them as the ordinary human beings they certainly are." He urges parents to remember that the rewards come indirectly, "and, of course, you know you will not be thanked."

My second child receives more hugs and smiles from me than my first did. I was scared to death I'd do something wrong with my first, so I was very reserved. I'm more relaxed now and have learned to be much, much more patient.

It was many years before I believed I truly was a good mother. For a long time, I was sure my kids were so great because they had such a good father, not because of anything I did! However, I did have flashes of feeling I was a good mother in at least a limited sense, early on. When I nursed my babies I knew I was, body and soul, do-

ing the very best I could do for them. I was certain that there was
nothing more and nothing else I could be doing that would be bet-
ter. Now that my kids are older, I realize how very rare are those in-
stances of absolute certainty.

Who Is This Child?

Good mothering doesn't yield to formula or prescription. Each
individual mother forms a unique relationship with each of her
children. And yet, there is this essential: A mother must know
her child. We under-mothered women especially need to know
our children in ways our mothers did not know us. If we can
see our children, truly listen to them, assess what they need from
us right now, in this situation, and give to them what we're capable of giving, we'll surely do better than was done for us.

"I always watched my mother," a woman told me, talking of
her girlhood, "trying to gauge her mood and her likely response
to me. I remember discovering in the fourth or fifth grade that if
I asked her a question about herself, about something I had seen
from watching her that was important to her, I had her full attention." As unfortunate as this inverted circumstance was for
this woman growing up, from it she learned to be an astute ob-
server of people, a skill that serves her well as a mother.

"As the years have gone by," she told me, "I've come to appreciate the value of watching my kids to see who they are and
have made it a conscious trait. It sums up a million examples of
me trying to do differently for my children than was done for
me: I try to step back and see my child as he or she is, to keep
from intruding myself into his or her experience, to see the big
picture and judge what that child needs now from me."

What this woman was describing is a vital task of parenting.
Sometimes called attunement, at other times empathy or the
ability to see a child's point of view, it is essential to responding
appropriately to an individual child, and it's more difficult and

complicated than is generally acknowledged. Psychiatrists Anna Ornstein and Paul Ornstein say the reason attunement is so difficult is that it requires the parent to immerse herself in the inner life of a child without that threatening her own sense of separateness and "without the parent injecting his or her own needs into the interaction with the child." They say that with each child, the parent's empathic capacities are tested anew.

The empathic parent responds to her child not out of her own needs or in keeping with "rules" she might have learned about parenting. Instead her responses are determined by the needs of the particular child at a particular moment in the child's life. From the very beginning of caring for an infant, a mother relies on her ability to empathize—to distinguish, for example, between her baby's cries that signal hunger and those that mean general discomfort—and the need for this capacity carries on through the child's growing years. This ability to see the child's point of view characterizes the secure-autonomous adults of Mary Main's research.

Being able to tune into the child's needs and experience, the Ornsteins contend, is central to parenting and inextricably linked to the parents' self-development. Only an adult who has well-developed psychic functions, such as humor, wisdom, self-esteem and an ability to regulate tensions, is able to do this. A woman must have maturity and self-awareness to see her child clearly. Many of the women I interviewed experienced "empathic hunger" in childhood, a failure of intimacy, because their mothers didn't have those well-developed psychic functions.

Psychiatrist Norman Paul contends that everyone has a need for empathy, but children often don't get it, in part because parents don't know themselves well enough and aren't mature enough to provide it. He describes typical situations that provide opportunities for empathy but that are often bypassed by parents. A child, for example, preparing for her first day of school hears from her parents, "Won't this be exciting!" and "You're a big girl now!" Maybe the parents can't remember what it was to be six and heading off to all-day school; maybe they remember the anxiety but are afraid that expressing it will make the child afraid. So they say nothing of this, but the girl goes to school and experiences a whole range of emotions: fear, inadequacy, discomfort and a lack of freedom, along with some fun and excitement. Her parents, however, have let her know that they expect only "fun," so she keeps to herself all the other experiences. Her parents are relieved that all is going well. As the girl progresses through school, her parents respond to her transgressions or failures, such as skipping school or flunking a test, not with stories from their own youths, but with trips to the school counselor and punishment. Or, as was the case for a woman I interviewed, a girl who is not a popular child and is a late bloomer despairs at age sixteen when all her classmates and even her younger sister are wearing bras, but she remains as flat-chested as a little girl. Despondent, she talks to her mother, who cuts her off immediately by saying, "You don't need a bra and when you need one, I'll let you know."

"My mother couldn't see," that girl, now grown, told me, "that what I was asking for was to have a bra even if I didn't need it. But for her, getting me a bra didn't fit her guidelines: 'Need a bra, get a bra.' What I wanted was some reassurance, maybe a story from her own life. Did she get breasts late? Did she ever feel different and left out? But I got nothing like that from her."

As happens so often, that mother, instead of trying to see her child's point of view, imposed her own adult view on her child's feelings. "There's nothing to be afraid of," says the parent to a young child who wants a light left on, forgetting her own childhood fears and anxieties. "The child is viewed," says Paul, "not as a separate individual, entitled to his own emotional development, but as an extension of the parents' wisdom accumulated through the years." The empathic parent, on the other hand, both feels and shows her respect for the child, as the child grows as a separate person with a separate emotional life.

The Ideal Child

Just as our culture influences the way we mother, so, too, it helps shape how we see our children and what we expect from them. Deeply ingrained in each culture is an ideal child. In America, the well-functioning child is highly verbal, independent, emotionally controlled and self-reliant. Being smart and competitive are prized as well. But these traits don't begin to cover the wide range of personalities and strengths, weaknesses, challenges and quirks that characterize American children. Add to this ideal whatever an individual mother expects for her own conscious or unconscious, helpful or destructive reasons, and a vast number of children are left falling short of someone else's notion of who and how they should be.

Many of the women I interviewed told of growing up with the kind of mothering that asks the child to mold him- or herself to a preconceived form. Their mothers, reacting to their own histories, end up making the mistake that Lindsay, a spirited woman with a musical voice who is thirty-two and mother to two young girls, said her mother made:

"She raised us as she wished she were raised and didn't spend enough time or have enough emotional openness to know us and what we needed.

"My mother grew up a smart girl in a blue-collar family that didn't value cultural interests. She was really aware of what she missed out on and was determined to provide it to her kids.

"My parents were cutting-edge people, ahead of the curve on social and cultural movements, very visible people in the university town we lived in. And they knew exactly how they wanted to raise us kids. They were determined that we would have all the cultural opportunities my mom didn't have growing up.

"We traveled the world with them. They took us to art museums. I took violin, piano and ballet lessons. We went to academically challenging private schools. We ate health food and could never watch television.

"We simply weren't allowed to be kids, to be free-spirited, to be self-centered teenagers, none of it. Well into adulthood, though, I thought I'd had the perfect childhood. I had two parents and lots of family experiences that my peers were envious of, and I heard that from friends often."

As I listened to Lindsay, I couldn't help but think that too much intellectual and cultural opportunity didn't sound like a serious complaint against one's upbringing; but as she went on I began to hear that story, again, of how family life can look good, but unless the child within it feels seen and heard, the rest matters little.

Lindsay related the toll her childhood experiences have taken on her. In high school she self-mutilated ("only mildly") and developed an eating disorder. In college she suffered anxiety attacks. But always the capable, rational side of herself, so valued and cultivated by her parents, saved her from slipping far from accepted social behavior. She knew something was wrong but, echoing a familiar refrain, she assumed she was at fault. Only in adulthood did the anxieties that had dogged her all her life become unbearable.

"The anxiety would hit randomly and I'd think, 'What's going on with me?' I started going to a women's circle, tried a sweat lodge, and found a man who does what he calls 'heart-opening therapy.' I stayed in intense therapy with him for about a year. I was terrified, but he took me into deep emotional spaces. It became a whole journey about my family of origin and my lineage.

"I began to uncover what was so very wrong, for me, about my upbringing. To live in my family, I had to give away parts of myself. Any part of me that was vulnerable, circular, messy, nonlinear, confused had to go. Period. My mother didn't want to see it.

"I was the middle child, the puppy dog who tried to please. When my mother was off kilter—angry or otherwise upset—I'd look around at my family and think, 'This is all on me. I have to get Mom in a better mood. I have to get Dad in a good space so he doesn't make her angrier.'

"My older brother was no help. I thought of him as 'the stink bomb.' He'd sit through the tense times emitting a toxic stench. And my sister was the space cadet who tuned out. I had a full-time job manipulating my family.

"I began to see that with my mother there was always a price to pay if I needed her. It took a lot out of her to step forth and give to me. And if she didn't get enough payback from me, she'd call me selfish and uncaring. But if I paid too much, which meant being who she wanted me to be, then I gave away too much of myself. It was a moving, wobbling, balancing that I could never get right because it depended too much on my mother's emotional space."

Now in adulthood, with the help of a thoughtful, supportive husband, meditation and her ongoing women's circle, Lindsay's become familiar with the parts of herself she'd let go of as a child. "I'm a watery Cancer girl, a kind of wavy woman," she says. Recently she did a creative dance performance with a group of women, the first time she'd ever performed anything so free-form and self-expressive, and she loved it. With amazement in her voice, she said, "I don't have to get over this part of me. It's mine!"

After a long effort to comb through her past, Lindsay said, she's come to "take power away" from her mother and to "be more empowered in my own being." As she talked about her desires to let her own children become themselves, knowing as she does "the heavy burden it is for a child to have to be a certain way to please parents," she expressed threads of that Jungian ideal of fully embracing, without reservation, "the particular tissue in which one finds oneself embedded." She said, "I believe I got what I needed for my lessons and growth, but my mother was and is not easy for me. Some of those painful places I've gone with my mother I'm now grateful for. But I can only say that now. I don't feel like a victim any longer."

Therapist Taffel has seen in his work with children and families that the more "kids felt personally known and parented in ways that fit them, the less angry and dangerous their public statements became." He urges parents to recognize that "all kids are very different from the get-go. They have what might be called a distinct *core*—a constellation of emotional and intellectual attributes that vary dramatically from child to child." This core, he says, "struggles to be recognized and responds with anger when it isn't." He's seen in his work with families that many parents buy "off-the-rack" parenting advice because it's quicker and easier than getting to know their individual children. "The hard truth," he says, "is that many parents may love their children, but they do not create the time to pay attention to them. They do not really hear them. They do not really see them." We undermothered women seem ideally positioned to understand the importance of making the effort to know our children at each phase of their development, as their personalities unfold and their needs evolve. Often, this sense of being respected and honored for ourselves is what we missed from our mothers.

A mother has to be supportive and encouraging. She has to work all the way around the child in terms of support. Sometimes a child needs specific direction, like with safety issues, so you're in front leading the way. Other times you have to be able to judge a situation and see what your child might learn from it. You might need to stand next to or even behind him. You have to try to maximize learning and growth without exposing kids to too much risk. It keeps changing.

Different Children, Different Needs

Knowing children means, to mothers, recognizing that each of their children is different from themselves and from siblings. Some women found they were better mothers with one child than another. Both of May Hung's daughters are "quiet in the world, loud at home," but very different in the way they relate to May.

"As a young girl, my oldest child was extremely private and loved to spend hours by herself. Even when she was upset she didn't look for comfort, but solitude. She didn't jibber-jabber to me. But my second daughter, who came seven years later, provoked me at every turn. If she had been the first child, we might not have had a second! She was in my face all the time. She couldn't see the truth if I put it in capital letters. 'I want Cheerios!' 'Look in the cupboard, no Cheerios!' 'I want Cheerios!'

"My oldest child will tell a story once and be done with it; the second will repeat it in five-part harmony every time.

"As exasperating as my second child was, though, it was the older one's uncommunicative ways that sent me to find family counseling for us. I just didn't know what was *wrong* with her. Was she hiding something? Why wouldn't she interact more? The therapist talked to each of us alone and then together and then called me in and said, 'There's no problem here. Your daughter's making intentional choices. She's simply not an emotionally gratifying child. She's not one of those children who's interested in making the adults around them happy. She doesn't care about that.' I heard the message that it was *me* who needed to adapt.

"My older daughter is very like my husband. If it weren't for me, he'd never speak to anyone. He's content to stay home, play the cello and do crossword puzzles. That left me in the lurch with a big need to be gratified, but my younger daughter flowered into the same kind of social being.

"Would I want to live only with people who have the same needs I do? No. We balance each other."

Children flourish with "attentive love," according to Bonnie Ohye, clinical psychologist and mother. As May discovered, it's a "demanding kind of love" that "requires us to listen, to look, and to understand and accept before acting." This clear-sighted love, Ohye says, asks that we try to understand what a child feels not only when we recognize ourselves in the experience, but especially when we don't. To do this, a mother must choose her actions and decisions regarding her children "out of a closely observed, ever-deepening and articulate understanding" of each child.

In any relationship, the ability to see the other's point of view, including goals, feelings and intentions, makes intimacy and harmony possible. Crucial to strong relationships as well, according to Bowlby, is that each person has a "reasonably" accurate knowledge of herself and the other that is regularly updated through communication. This is so in a marriage, friendship or working relationship, and certainly between mother and child. There, however, the onus is on the adult to structure the relationship. "It is here," Bowlby wrote, "that the mothers of securely attached children excel and those of the insecure are markedly deficient."

Recognizing and accepting individual children, especially when they're very different from the mother, challenged many of the women I spoke with. Cathy Patterson saw in her own childhood that her mother wasn't able to clear this particular hurdle. Cathy and her mother shared many qualities, including their sharp-witted humor and intellectual quickness, but her sister was the family outsider.

"My sister was simply not the kind of kid my mother wanted. My mother was always popular, had a great outgoing personality, but my sister was so shy she couldn't look people in the eye. My mother couldn't stand it and would accuse my sister of being 'antisocial.' My sister made my mother scream."

Then Cathy faced this same challenge in her mothering. As a child herself, Cathy was gregarious, curious and a good student who always had interests she pursued energetically. But neither her son nor daughter have the same drive or inquisitive nature.

"There was a time when all they wanted to know was what channel *Scooby-Doo* was on. As they were growing up they were the antithesis of what I expected. I'm a major overachiever. And my kids were major underachievers. I didn't feel anything in common with either of them." Despite her disappointment, however, Cathy never wavered in her emotional support of her children or in her parental responsibilities, including remaining steadfast in her teaching of Jewish values.

"Five years ago I was thinking, 'I love them, but . . . ' And then they began moving through high school and began to mature, and I watched them develop important personal traits and unfold into fine adults with maybe the most important gift of all, which is they are both extremely kind and have marvelous social skills.

"They can go into a room of people they don't know and charm the socks off anyone there. They have a wonderful ability to be around other people, make friends and to do the right thing. That gets you a lot further in life than an A in some class. They're becoming self-reliant, responsible, centered adults.

"If you hang in there, it can turn out okay. I was determined not to do to my kids what I watched my mother do with my sister. My sister rebelled against our parents until she was thirty. I'm sorry, but that's just a waste of energy and time.

"I'm not saying my kids won't end up at a shrink someday. In fact, one of the standing jokes in our family is that we'll have a fight and then say to the kids, 'Remember this moment. It's great material for the shrink when you go in twenty years.'

"I know I'm a good mother. And I can say that now that I have lots of years of mothering behind me. I'm so proud of my children, and they know it."

Another woman, mother to an only child who is now twenty-seven, is dismayed at how different her child is from her and from how she expected him to be. She says of him: "We still have a good relationship. It just seems superficial in that I don't feel like I really know him. We love each other and spend as much time together as we can, but he doesn't seem to know much about his feelings yet or at least doesn't convey what he knows to me." She puzzles over his choices in life. He married young, at twenty-three, and promptly had a child. She doesn't understand his attraction to his wife. "If she's smart, she hides it well, and her weight keeps her lethargic. My son does everything for her, including getting her in and out of a car. Together they're the dullest people in the world," she says.

As she talked, she got up a head of steam on the topic, telling me that she brought her son up around smart, educated, motivated, creative people and is "just shocked" at how small his world is and how different he is from her. Going on, she began to express questions about whether she did something wrong in rearing him.

"Did I raise him too liberally? I didn't know how to physically get him to do something he didn't want to do, like take piano lessons, get a math tutor, go to Europe or for a walk in the woods. I felt as if we had enough battles during his high school years for him just to attend school."

Listening to this perplexed woman talk, I heard the contrast between her remarks and those of Cathy Patterson. Though sometimes exasperated at her children, Cathy didn't try to *change* them. But this woman seems baffled that she hasn't been able to make her son be what she wants. "I'm wondering if I had been more strict if I could have maybe carved out a life for him that makes more sense to me," she said. "The only thing that does make sense to me is that he's still young. It took me a long time to grow up and become the woman I am now." She hasn't quit hoping that he'll eventually come around to be a person she can relate to or that he'll eventually let her "carve out a life for him."

Thinking about the big difference in levels of satisfaction these two mothers of young adults expressed, I wondered whether this mother might know her son better and feel closer to him now if, years ago, she had tried to see him clearly, to listen to him and to value him for who he is.

What many mothers are called to accept in their children and in life circumstances ranges from the disappointing to the tragic: absent or uninvolved husbands, children who are born or become physically or mentally disabled, financial hardship, defeats, setbacks and deep losses. "This isn't what I envisioned for myself," said one young mother whose child suffered brain injuries in a car accident. "Oh, this is going to be an interesting life," said a woman with two infants when her husband walked out. No doubt, facing what's thrust upon us can be among the hardest challenges of mothering—and of life. Being able to deal with the surprises, however, often distinguishes success from failure.

The Resilient Mother

Just as resiliency allows some children to navigate the waters of childhood successfully, so too does resiliency well serve mothers who face challenges. Resiliency researchers, if they've looked at mothers at all, have tended to look at narrow groups, such as those with children who are chronically ill. But we can learn, nonetheless, from the results. Looking for resiliency, one group of investigators closely interviewed seventy-one postdivorce single women. All had been permanently separated or divorced for at least two years and had at least one preschool child. The researchers were specifically trying to tease out differences between the single mothers who coped competently and related well to their children and those who were overwhelmed by their situations. Their findings can apply to mothers who face other stresses, such as unhappy marriages, financial trouble, ill health or the ongoing struggles of juggling the demands of children, work, home and community life; and certainly, the stress of having been under-mothered can be included. Whatever risks or stresses a mother faces test her resiliency.

The description of the nonresilient in the study sounded like many of the mothers, married and not, depicted by the women I interviewed. They didn't try to reason with their children and even exacerbated difficulties with inflexible discipline or lack of follow-through and insensitivity to the child's negative feelings. These nonresilient mothers tended to express thoughts such as: "Why do you have an attitude like that?" and "You shouldn't feel that way." They tried to get their children to stop crying or expressing anger rather than trying to understand where it came from.

Our mother glossed over our genuine fears, avoided our questions. We weren't allowed to say "no," or to have choices as young children. She was frequently angry, often furious.

My mother was very controlling, abusive verbally and some physically. She was inconsistent, critical, volatile, terrifying, reactive, nonsupportive. Do I need to go on?

She was nervous and narcissistic, and we lived in fear of upsetting her. I learned to be quiet and good and to achieve as a means to validation.

The interviewers saw a "vicious circle of negativity" in the stories of mothers who either were tyrants or caved in quickly in the hope of avoiding confrontation. These mothers expressed a preponderance of frustration and dissatisfaction in their child-rearing; they lacked confidence, which kept them from parenting with authority.

In contrast, resilient mothers showed a willingness and

ability to look at conflicts from their children's points of view. They could tell a story about an interaction with the child, filling in not only what they said and felt and did, but also the child's behavior and emotional expressions. They usually noted, as well, how the situation was resolved. These mothers understood their children's personalities, abilities and emotions and could tailor their demands to what they knew was possible for the child. They could tolerate emotional outbursts, knowing they were temporary. And when they couldn't meet a child's need or demand, such as for shorter workdays, they could accept the child's negative feelings about the situation. These mothers knew their children, which allowed them to operate from that information instead of falling back on fear, anger or rigidity.

The resilient mothers used two different styles: firm and permissive. The firm types had a flexibility that made them willing to negotiate differences with their children and kept them from feeling their authority would be undermined by bending the rules. They made statements like: "It depends on the situation," and "I'll decide whether it's worth making an issue over," and "You have to make allowances once in while. You can't be hard-nosed all the time."

These mothers felt in charge. For them, discipline wasn't a big issue because their approach to mothering tended to generate cooperation in the child. Their mothering wasn't trouble-free, but they felt effective in bringing problems to a resolution. They expressed pleasure in seeing their children's behavior improve, and they could talk about changes in their *own* behavior that helped resolve a situation. They also could talk candidly about the problems and frustrations of their parenting while maintaining an overriding confidence.

I heard just this kind of realistic confidence from Cathy Patterson. She chafed under the care of her own mother, who refused to acknowledge feelings or ideas that ran counter to her own. Cathy told a story about when her teenage daughter, Eva, who had been popular, was abruptly and mysteriously ousted from her social group.

"No one would even tell Eva why. They just wouldn't speak to her. The phone just stopped ringing. At first I let her talk and ventilate. That went on for about a month. She'd walk in the door from school and break into tears and we'd go through it all again. Then I decided maybe I should interact and started asking whether she could think of anything she had done that would piss somebody off this much. We just kept talking. I was getting extremely worn down emotionally. I hurt for her and then in all honesty I got tired of listening to it.

"As the weeks wore on, Eva was beaten down and scared to death to pick up the phone and call someone. So she began to look to me to be her little friend. 'Let's go shopping. Let's go to a movie.' The first couple of times I went because I felt sucked in out of guilt and felt so sorry for her. But it didn't take me long to straighten up and remind myself that I'm not her friend, I'm her *mother*.

"She needed to dig down and uncover the internal fortitude to make new friends, to pick up that phone and ask one of the girls from school to go out with her. I knew it wouldn't happen as long as I made it comfortable for her not to. To say nothing of the fact that I have my own life and plenty to do.

"In the midst of this I was wracked with guilt. There's no black and white in mothering and you often don't know at the time whether you're doing the right thing. It's only later that you can see the outcome. This was one time I was consumed with self-doubt, but I just went ahead doing what my gut told me and it was right in the end.

"Eventually Eva got tired of being lonely and slowly got herself back into the crowds at school. She came out of it a much stronger person. I've found that the less I interfere, the more both of my kids find out what they're made of."

Other resilient mothers in the study were considerably less

demanding than the firm ones, but like them, they had confidence. They *chose* their "indulgent permissiveness" (though they didn't describe themselves that way). Their leniency didn't arise from feeling intimidated or coerced by their children or from being tired or overwhelmed or frustrated. Like the firm mothers, the lenient ones felt in charge of the situation and the relationship.

Vickie, a single mother I interviewed who revealed herself to be in this lenient, resilient camp, told me that mothering her only child, a teenage daughter, is very rewarding. "Yes! I meant it," she said. "I have a smart, responsible, funny, loving kid who still talks to me. So I'm pretty proud of my mothering at this stage."

Vickie divorced the girl's father when the child was five, which was an extremely stressful time for them all. "I found myself yelling a lot more than I wanted to," is how Vickie remembers it. "But over the years," she said, "I've seen how both the good times and the bad times have forged the special human being who is my daughter."

She sums up her mothering this way: "I've learned to listen carefully without too much judgment, and to realize that nothing stays the same. Today's drama is most often forgotten tomorrow. I don't know how her story will end so I try not to worry too much. I'm trying to let go, to allow her to make her own decisions and mistakes. I'm struggling to get out of her way."

The researchers who studied resiliency in single mothers examined the relationships between those mothers and their children, but didn't ask about the mothers' mothers. While it would be interesting to know what kind of parenting the resilient women had themselves received, what's more important to we motherless mothers is that this study reinforces the idea that it's not circumstances that determine resiliency. Both resilient and non-resilient mothers in the study described similar child-rearing issues, such as conflict over rules, dealing with their children's negative emotions, power struggles and disagreements with the fathers of their children. The difference came in the way the mothers interpreted the issues and responded to their children. As Emmy Werner found in her study of the children of Kauai, resiliency lies in the way an individual adapts to adversity. Positive factors in an individual's life circumstances or personality help balance the risk factors. Not having a partner to help rear her children is certainly a risk factor for a mother—and so is not having been well mothered herself. But just as not having a partner doesn't mean a woman can't be a good mother, not having been well mothered doesn't mean a woman can't be a good mother. Other forces, as we know, are at work.

Like the single women in the study, all of us mothers are bolstered by such positive factors as supportive friends, family and coworkers; the flexibility of our work and child-care situations; our physical and mental health; our children's health and how they functioned in school. With such support, women are able to maintain positive bonds with their children, even in adverse circumstances.

Giving and Giving Up

A key characteristic distinguishing the more resilient mothers in the study was that they knew their children's strengths and weaknesses and knew how to support them. Thinking of resilient mothers and the need to know our children took me back to Daniel Stern's "motherhood constellation" and his discussions of the new identity required of mothers. A significant force in shifting a woman's identity is her duty, and often desire, to put her baby's interests before her own. That doesn't mean she abandons her other wishes and desires, nor does it mean that striking a balance between narcissism and altruism is easy, says Stern, especially when some of the mother's central life goals, such as a career, suffer.

Being able to hold another person's well-being above her own without losing all identity appears to be a critical characteristic of effective mothers, a divider between the resilient and the nonresilient. Yet this is an area of great controversy and conflict within the lives of individual mothers and within the larger discussion of what mothers are meant to do and be. Giving too much or too little can lead to anger, resentment, fractious and fractured relationships and an unfulfilled life; and, as the mountain of attachment research attests, it can lead to sending grown children into the world to spend adulthood searching for the love, respect and security they missed in childhood. No one, however, can tell an individual mother where that line is for her and each of her children. Every mother faces the daunting task of nourishing herself without depriving her children and of nourishing her children without depriving herself.

With my first child I worked part-time and still was able to do a lot of the things I enjoy, like playing squash and other exercise. I wasn't so aware then of how important it was to fit my life to my children rather than trying to fit children into my life. Then I had twins, which gave me three children in fifteen months. A big change. I now want to and must make rearing children my life. I still try to fit in some of the things I like to do, but I've had to let go of a lot.

Anyone with more than half a brain would have fears when it comes to kids. It's scary being totally responsible for another human being. There's a lot of doubt involved. It takes a lot of maturity to put your own wants and needs on the back burner in order to take care of a screaming infant or whiny toddler.

I always keep checking in with myself and keep asking: "Would you want to have a mother like yourself?"

Most every mother decides, again and again, what she's willing to give her children and to give up on their behalf. And every mother eventually arrives at the charged concept of sacrifice. The word means to forfeit something highly valued for the sake of something of even greater value, which, to me, well describes the landscape of motherhood. Child-rearing is too difficult, exacting, demanding and complex and goes on for too long for it not to require sacrifice from the adults who have responsibility for children.

Sacrifice as merely a self-effacing, altruistic, charitable act isn't what's required of mothers. Instead, the mindful mother devises an ever-changing strategy of trade-offs to be made in her own life as her children wind their ways to maturity. Anthropologist Sarah Blaffer Hrdy urges us to take a broader view of maternity than the simple self-sacrificing image of "doting nurturers" surrounded by children. She contends that mothers have evolved to seek social and economic status in order to increase the chances that their offspring, or at least a few of them, will survive and prosper. She views the mother as a "multifaceted strategist," a term that suits modern women as well as our ancestral mothers. Maternity, in our own as well as other species, requires a female to be an ambitious, tactical, flexible opportunist in order to bring her offspring to maturity. She repeatedly makes shifts in her activities, judging what must be traded to keep her children growing. Bowlby, as usual, was blunt on this subject: "Giving time and attention to children means sacrificing other interests and other activities. Yet I believe the evidence for what I am saying is unimpeachable. Study after study . . . attest that healthy, happy, and self-reliant adolescents and young adults are the products of stable homes in which both parents give a great deal of time and attention to the children."

Part of being a mother is being caged by the dependency of others. If you know your children and what they need, you're limited by the responsibility to provide it and by an inability to go back to *not* knowing and *not* thinking of your children and their needs. Even when children grow beyond the very young years and begin to act independently, moving out into the world for longer and longer times—to school, to camp, to friends' homes—mothers are still bound, for one cannot be truly free and vigilant at once. Hrdy asks whether attachment theory restrains the lives of mothers and answers this way: "Not necessarily, but for mothers who care about their infants' well-being it often comes to the same thing." First-time mother Jane Lazarre was just twenty-one when she wrote in her memoir, *The Mother Knot*, of being faced with "the terrible choice which always confronted me in the truth-saturated middle of the night between self-sacrifice and strange baby-sitters." Every mother has to decide for herself whether she can safely delegate care of her children to others.

The working mothers of young children I interviewed expressed the conflict and confusion endemic among their peers. A young mother who had recently started working full-time said: "My son is in day care now for the first time in his life. I'm being separated from the one constant I've had twenty-four hours a day for two years, and so is he. It's the hardest thing I've ever had to do and each day I'm overcome with guilt and sadness that I have to go to work and leave him in the care of someone other than me. I feel like I am letting my son down." A twenty-three-year-old woman who became pregnant accidently right after her wedding took a short leave when the baby was born and then went back to her job. "At this point," she said, "I feel guilty about working full-time. I feel I should be home with my son, instead of letting someone I don't really know take care of him. My husband and I are in the process of making changes that we hope will make it possible, financially, for me to stay at home with our baby. But right now, that's just a wish I hope will come true."

Mothers face hard choices about self-sacrifice and children's needs; but I think that the more clearly a woman understands her role, her own needs and the child, the easier it is to find a balance between giving too much and too little. Many women, however, are faced with powerful social forces that work against their efforts to find balance. One significant factor pushing against mothers is that we live, according to Ann Crittenden, author of *The Price of Motherhood: Why the Most Important Job in the World Is Still the Least Valued,* in a society that talks "endlessly about the importance of family, yet the work it takes to make a family is utterly disregarded." The realities of the work world, where flexible full-time and meaningful, fairly compensated part-time work is scarce, mean many women must make painful, unsatisfying and often damaging choices about who will care for their children. Among the sacrifices is money. Crittenden estimates that the lifetime income gap between a college-educated American mother and a childless woman is more than $1 million. Whether a mother continues in paid employment or not, rearing children and running a household likely remain her primary responsibilities. Housework may be unskilled labor, but mothering is not, and yet it, too, holds little social and no economic value. This is true, Crittenden herself found, although it requires more patience, inner strength, intelligence, skill, wisdom and love than had ever been required of her as a network news commentator, lecturer at Yale and reporter for *The New York Times.*

Bowlby describes the conflict this way: "Man and woman power devoted to the production of material goods counts a plus in all our economic indices. Man and woman power devoted to the production of happy, healthy, and self-reliant children in their own homes does not count at all. We have created a topsy-turvy world." And it's in this topsy-turvy world that mothers today in developed countries must rear their children.

The mother-child relationship is entirely unique in the female life span. Most of a woman's relationships are predominately reciprocal and symmetrical, but those with her children are asymmetrical. As the attachment figure, she holds power and accountability. Sustaining her end of this imbalanced pairing often means that many of her desires, needs and interests will be postponed, altered or filled in less than ideal ways during her most intense years of child-rearing. Yet in the face of these necessary renunciations, she has to keep herself separate from her children. Her identity must be strong enough so that during those years when her children come first, she doesn't lose herself. A solid identity allows her to listen without needing to fix, change or feel guilty about her children's feelings. She can stand calmly as a loving supporter when her self is firmly in place. As the feminist psychoanalyst Rozsika Parker says, "Mothers find children both draining and a source of plenitude. Being a mother lends a richness and sense of power to a woman's life, but equally she feels devoured and depleted by the all-encompassing demands of motherhood." Only a strong woman can ride this day-to-day teeter-totter between richness and depletion.

In many of my conversations with mothers I heard of the individual struggle that each mother makes to walk the narrow line between sacrifice that leads to resentment, with its attendant ills, and sacrifice that provides enough love, time and support to a particular, unique child. The women who seemed most peacefully resigned to this struggle, which is inherently filled with tension, seemed to look not to an external source to tell them how much was enough, but to their own children.

One such mother was Nina, a business consultant who expected to put on her silk suits and return to her busy, fulfilling career after her daughter was born. She found, instead, that she had to put them back in the closet after a year of mothering as it became clear that her daughter was not the child she expected, the child one can hand over to a nanny or preschool or public school with equanimity. Every step of the way the girl, who in first grade was tested and found to be exceptionally gifted, has demanded special treatment and has gobbled up Nina's time and attention.

Now twelve, Nina's daughter is finally enrolled in a school that suits her unusual academic needs. Is it time for Nina to pull back and clear space for herself? Well, the school is an hour's drive away, with no suitable public transportation. That's four hours a day in the car. And Nina, who has attended her child carefully all her growing life, looks at her now and says, "It would be a mistake to think she doesn't need me now, because she does, but in totally new ways I can't quite verbalize. So before I can stake my claim to my hours, I have to get past the question that looms like some gatekeeper: What does my daughter need? *Really* need, not *apparently* need as seen from my eyes looking past her to the freedom to be self-involved, which I'd have if only I didn't spend so much time accommodating her.

"The complexity of this child is not going to go away just because she's growing older. Her interface with the world will only get more challenging, not less. Now's the time to be here, not to fade away."

Her dreams still on hold, Nina, a congenial, well-educated woman who lives with her family in an outlying suburb of Washington, D.C., says: "I feel like I blinked, and gave my life away. Blink: marriage. Blink: baby." She's had to find satisfactions in her mothering rather than in the career accomplishments she'd hoped for.

"I find myself looking back over the last ten years with wonder. I've done a mighty job with this child, a job my mother didn't do. And her not-doing is what has made me so determined to be available to my daughter.

"I know what I needed from my mother and didn't get. When I see my friends trot off to work, I feel the pang of not staking a substantial claim to my own time, but I just remember what it was like to feel so abandoned, as I did when my mother went to work with a huge sigh of relief. My brother and sister and I were difficult to parent, so she just didn't. She got a job. I refuse to do that to my child."

Nina would be the first to say the choices have been wrenching ones and that she's fortunate to have a husband who can single-handedly hold up the financial end of supporting a family.

"I felt I had no choice but to let go of my own professional goals in order to take care of my daughter. For a long time, I grieved that reality and even resented it. But recently, as my husband and I have begun to see the wonderful results of our work, I've become more philosophical about my choice, more certain that I made the right one for *us*—not only for her. Yes, she's turning out to be a great kid, but I'm even more amazed at what this effort on her behalf has done to and for me. I've grown emotionally in ways I never would have otherwise. I've experienced the simple power of my family's love and have felt empowered to grow and change as a result.

"Somehow, you don't hear about this hidden benefit of mothering, but the truth of it awes me. I'm so grateful my daughter and I have had the chance to be together this way. Of course, I say this on a *good* day. On the bad days, I wish I were an executive in a major corporation, preferably with a schedule involving fifty percent travel!"

Here Nina flashed her wide, engaging grin and added this note about her present self, the mother of a preadolescent: "I am reforming, in some odd way. I'm reshaping the way I see myself and my past, creating new meaning from the old stories. Somehow, this feels like the prep work for the life that will come after the child grows into her growing."

From another mother, Audrey, I heard the story of a completely different sort of time sacrifice made on behalf of her child and based, like Nina, on what she saw he needed from her. Audrey divorced after sixteen years of marriage, with her children ages two and nine, and came out as a lesbian. It was the mid-1980s then, and in the way of the proceedings of that time the courts gave custody of the children to their father because of Audrey's sexual orientation. By then Audrey's daughter was twelve and refused to go, but her son, only five, was placed with his father and new stepmother.

Audrey had visitations every other weekend, and they were

conflicting, difficult times as the children acted out their sadness and anger at having been assigned a parent, and as her son, who had been diagnosed with attention deficit disorder, struggled with the coming and going. "I realized my relationships with my children, especially my son, were based on anger," she said, "so I worked with them to take a positive stance when together."

Audrey found herself in continual conflict with her ex-husband and his wife over her claims on her son. Growing up, her own strategy with her nervous, easily upset mother was to be quiet and "good," so this life of confrontation challenged her. She suffered, also, knowing her son was being raised by people who were instilling values of intolerance and punishment in him. Always, she feared she would lose him forever. Audrey could not turn to her mother for help and comfort during the hard years of her struggle, but she did have the support of a women's group and a particular good friend. She also had within the memory of the unconditional love her grandmother had given her. Although that grandmother had died before Audrey had children, her inspiration and example lived on.

As the battles with her ex-husband intensified, Audrey's son often asked her not to fight, because he couldn't bear being the center of the storm. Her son's distress led her to step back.

"One survival tactic for me was to keep reminding myself that it was more important that he have a happy life than that I win any battles," she said. "So I gave in when his birthday or Mother's Day fell on my visitation weekend and his father and stepmother insisted he be with them because they were his 'real' family.

"I even bit my tongue when they forbade my son to refer to me as 'mother.' But when my ex moved away with our son, I went to court to restructure my visitation rights, even though my son asked me not to. I told him this was one I had to fight."

The rancor between the parents went on. Not long after the move, her son, then in high school, asked Audrey not to have any contact with him. "I'm being too torn," he said. She did what he asked and neither saw nor spoke to him except during their six weeks of summer together. As high school graduation approached, his father and stepmother said they would pay for him to go to school anywhere but the state where Audrey lived, but this time the boy stood his ground and insisted that he return to live near his mother. Now in their twenties, Audrey's children live within a couple of miles of her, and she has close ties to both.

"I feel powerfully affirmed as a mother," she says. "My daughter, now a mother herself, is just that strong, independent woman I envisioned when I became her mother. And I'm proud of the strong relationship my son and I maintained through those terribly painful years. My steadfast love triumphed. Both my children are fine young adults with strong values, and I acknowledge that I had a part in making that happen. I also believe that the faith and love which my son and I maintained all those years is deeply spiritual."

Sacrifice feels more like choice, it seems, when a mother knows why she's giving up her own wishes and desires, when she knows what her child needs and gives it willingly, despite the personal cost.

Time Enough

More than anything, children need to be connected to their parents, but that requires just what's in short supply in most families today: time. Interestingly, recent research indicates that both mothers and fathers, whether they work outside the home or not, spend more time with their children than parents did in the past. Yet it would be hard to find a parent, or a child, who didn't feel time-starved. Taffel says that's because family members may be in physical proximity, but engaged in parallel, separate activities. "Indeed," he says, "a long-distance phone conversation can provide a much closer and more intimate experience of connection than a typical evening in the bosom of the modern American family." Family members multitasking side by side doesn't breed connection, doesn't allow for family members to get to know one another, to share and explore their values, to fill up on the love, interaction and nurturing humans thrive on all through their lives. But how can we satisfy those needs in ourselves and our children without unhurried time, without looking one another in the eye? If we're to gain the familiarity that lets us know our children and meet them intimately, we need relaxed time with them, and lots of it.

Children today, says Taffel, yearn for what they're not getting from parents, and they're angry. "Sometimes," said one of the fifth graders in his study, "I get the feeling my parents don't know me." "Me, too," another chimed in. "We don't spend time together—we're always so busy in my house."

The kindergarteners through sixth graders Taffel has spoken with say that what they most want from their parents is focused attention. "I want my mom to stop being so busy and just play with me." "I want my mommy to lie down with me every night." Taffel says he hears this as "the heartfelt responses of children who are desperate to be *seen*, truly *known*, rather than scheduled or psychologized."

I suspect that without respite from the busy-ness of life in modern families, parents can't know themselves any more than they can know their children. Being aware of one's own feelings as they occur, aware of one's moods and thoughts about those moods, requires time and space. Being able to evaluate, control and understand the self and behave in ways that reflect that knowledge allows mothers to model for their children how to live in a healthy, self-aware way.

Whether or not a mother tries hard in appropriate ways to do well by her children, they remain uniquely themselves and may become people who are entirely different from the individuals their mothers expect or desire. Charlie Brown, the hapless main character of the "Peanuts" comic strip, once quoted his "philosopher" grandmother on the subject of children: "When they're young they step on your toes. When they grow up they step on your heart." Hearing this, his friend Lucy turned to walk away, hollering a warning all of us mothers would do well to heed: "LOOK OUT, TOES!! LOOK OUT, HEART!!!"

Bowlby had a less succinct but similar message, saying, "At some time of their lives, I believe, most human beings desire to have children and desire also that their children should grow up to be healthy, happy, and self-reliant. For those who succeed the rewards are great; but for those who have children but fail to rear them to be healthy, happy, and self-reliant the penalties in anxiety, frustration, friction, and perhaps shame or guilt, may be severe. Engaging in parenthood therefore is playing for high stakes." The stakes are different for each of us. We each have our own struggles with our selves, our present circumstances, our pasts and our children. One of mine has been overcoming my fears of specific physical dangers to my husband and children and fears of the future. While writing this book, I had a dream that has helped me move toward peacefulness. In the dream, my children and I were outdoors in a place very like the foothills near our home. We stood by a low stone wall on a hillside that sloped down and away from us into a wooded area. We looked across the hill and saw on the rolling mesa two lions and a cheetah moving slowly, stalking. Several other big cats moved our way through the tall grass in the distance. My younger son clutched my hand and said, "There's a cheetah!" I watched, paralyzed with fear, knowing the menacing felines were too close to us for me to do anything before they struck. I could not protect my children. And then the cats continued past us, down the hill toward a small herd of antelope. We were safe.

We are safe, and I try hard to hang on to the serenity and relief I felt in that dream. The message of the dream came, as grace often does, unbidden and unearned, the answer to an unasked question. Frederick Buechner says that divine grace always carries the same basic message, which is this: "Here is your life. You might never have been, but you *are* because the party wouldn't have been complete without you. Here is the world. Beautiful and terrible things will happen. Don't be afraid. I am with you." My hope and effort is to stay awake, alert to the abundant gifts given me, able to carry the security of my dream with me and to live as if I believe in it.

In talking about mothering her seven children, four born to her and three acquired in her second marriage, Hannah Frank, whose mother left when Hannah was five, repeatedly expressed the thought, "We're in this together. We can rely on each other." In spite of—or because of—the lack of love and stability in her own young life, Hannah was determined to create family solidarity for herself and her children. In her first marriage, she said, she and her four children were a "pack." Their father would not participate, but Hannah made sure she and the children stuck together. Then, when she remarried, she and her new husband made a point of saying "this is one family."

"We did a lot of what our children remember as family building. We have certain songs we sing together. We made them participate in family Sunday once a month. We made them eat one meal together every day, which was breakfast because our teenagers had such busy lives. The girls would stumble in wearing bathrobes and big curlers and not eat, but they'd sit there with us.

"Whatever disagreements and hurts went on between members of the family were sublimated, because *always* the family as a whole was more important."

Now that the children are parents themselves, Hannah goes on being deeply enriched and satisfied by her relationships with them and her grandchildren. They can be in a room together, she says, and "we'll finish each other's sentences. Someone will say a wrong word, but we'll all know what word was really meant. We'll play charades and just roar with laughter, thoroughly reveling in the joy of our connectedness."

Hannah can talk about what she regrets in her mothering, such as wishing she'd talked more about goal-setting with her children; and on the subject of what a good mother is, she'll say, "I don't know. It's a crapshoot." She makes it sound easy by saying, "I have great kids. They love us. They make a point to be with us. But we're not perfect." When I listen to her talk, I can hear how, despite her growing up without her mother's care, despite her troubles as a young single mother of four and her later experiences as the mother in a family with as many as five teenagers at once, her love for her family always dominated. Despite going back to work when the youngest was four, she always carved out time for her children, and they must have known they were her highest priority. Out of the losses of her childhood, she was able to create a family of commitment, loyalty, love and solidarity.

Listening to Hannah that winter morning as we sat at the dining table where she had shared meals with her family for many years, I remember thinking about the women who had told of the heartbreak of having grown children they seldom see and hardly know. I thought about how I don't want my mothering to be a job that ends, but instead to be an ongoing, intimate relationship with people I dearly love. The key to achieving that, I think, is as simple as this: If we choose to stand close to our children when they are small, if we take them right there, where they are, for who they are, and move along through their growing with them, maybe they later choose us. Maybe, with a bit of luck and grace thrown in, that's what happens.

In the end, we each must discover and name what it is we're able and willing to give our children. My unusual, disjointed upbringing has led me to want a simple, "normal" family life. As much as I can, I orchestrate a regular pattern of after-school snacks and homework, family meals and vacations, spiral notebooks and soccer cleats. It's an orderliness that comforts, and it's something I learned from my grandmother. Though she was unable to, I hope that I'm creating a warm, loving environment around these ordinary moments, days and years. I like to think that I'm helping craft a structure sturdy enough to support any kind of life my children might later choose. I once asked a friend to tell me a favorite memory of her mother, who had died when my friend was a young adult. She thought for a moment, then shrugged and told of a New Year's Eve. She described how she and her mother had gone to a movie together and then kissed each other good night afterward. It can be, this structure I'm talking about, as ordinary and sumptuous as that.

My time and attention in the context of a conventional family life are what I choose to give my children. I don't offer this as a recommendation for other mothers. I know that for some people, anything that speaks of routine, "normal" or ordinary is anathema. But I consider my inability to take for granted the blessings of day-to-day family life to be one of the positive legacies of my childhood. The loss of my mother and the long wait for my own children allow me to see how nourishing and essential home life can be. At our kitchen table, in our minivan, in front of the fireplace, in a church pew, face to face or side by side we sit, talk, read, pray, laugh, hike, bike. Walking to school, taking road trips, celebrating holidays with our circle of family friends, cooking on our deck, going to ball games and museums, we go on living out what sounds like the most ordinary of lives, these boys, their father and I. And to my children this is, indeed, ordinary. They know nothing else, expect nothing else. One evening at the dinner table, when our children were perhaps three and four, it came up in conversation that someone we knew didn't have a mother. Our youngest laughed out loud and said, "Oh, no. *Everyone* has a mother!" My husband and I exchanged smiles across the table, knowing that this simple evening made up of two parents who had lost mothers in childhood, who now sat loving these two children, was as exotic and precious as life gets, to be valued and protected above all else.

All of us who missed out on the attentive care we needed in our own individual ways from our own individual mothers know better than most how important it is that we help our children grow up to enter adulthood feeling loved, worthy, known and cherished, understanding who we are and who they are, and what our families stand for. This is our legacy. This awareness is our gift to our own children. From this foundation our children can go into the world prepared to live by their own values and to love, cherish and attend the families they create for themselves.

NOTES

CHAPTER ONE: **The Beginning**

page 1 . . . and what a priceless gift William Gass, "Happy Families Are All Alike," *The New York Times*, August 1, 1977.

2 "There is no such thing" D. W. Winnicott, "Anxiety Associated with Insecurity," in *Through Paediatrics to Psycho-Analysis* (New York: Basic Books, 1975), 99.

3 "the mother will feed and protect" Meredith F. Small, *Our Babies, Ourselves: How Biology and Culture Shape the Way We Parent* (New York: Anchor Books, 1998), 15.

3 one of the most distinguishing features Ibid., 14.

CHAPTER TWO: **Mothers Matter**

9 . . . there she was Virginia Woolf, "A Sketch of the Past," in Jeanne Schulkind, ed., *Moments of Being: Unpublished Autobiographical Writings* (New York: Harcourt Brace Jovanovich, 1976), 81.

10 nine in utero Meredith F. Small, *Our Babies, Ourselves: How Biology and Culture Shape the Way We Parent* (New York: Anchor Books, 1998), 6–7.

10 Through evolutionary design Ibid., 224.

11 He says that at six months Daniel N. Stern, *The First Relationship: Infant and Mother* (Cambridge, MA: Harvard University Press, 1977), 1.

11 everyday moments Ibid., 5.

11 "This biologically designed" Ibid., 1.

11 That first relationship D. W. Winnicott, *The Maturational Processes and the Facilitating Environment* (New York: International Universities Press, 1965), 57.

13 a forerunner of Winnicott Rozsika Parker, *Mother Love, Mother Hate: The Power of Maternal Ambivalence* (New York: Basic Books, 1995), 104.

13 the infant's love is remote Alice Balint, "Love for the Mother and

Mother Love," in Michael Balint, *Primary Love and Psycho-Analytic Technique* (New York: Liveright Publishing, 1965), 95–96.

13 "the ideal mother" Ibid., 93.

13 A young child might be distressed Ibid., 97.

13 The love the mother holds Ibid., 101–2.

14 When all goes well Robert Karen, *Becoming Attached: Unfolding the Mystery of the Infant-Mother Bond and Its Impact on Later Life* (New York: Warner Books, 1994), 12.

14 That's why Balint calls Balint, "Love for the Mother," 103.

15 as the child faces Ibid., 103.

16 Maslow ranked five sets A. H. Maslow, "A Theory of Human Motivation," in Richard J. Lowry, ed., *Dominance, Self-Esteem, Self-Actualization: Germinal Papers of A. H. Maslow* (Monterey, CA: Brooks/Cole Publishing, 1973), 172.

17 In Maslow's model Ibid., 156.

17 The next requirement Ibid., 159–60.

17 "Separation from mother" Judith Viorst, *Necessary Losses: The Loves, Illusions, Dependencies and Impossible Expectations That All of Us Have to Give Up in Order to Grow* (New York: Simon and Schuster, 1986), 22.

18 Love needs Maslow, "A Theory of Human Motivation," 161–62.

18 An infant's first passion H. F. Harlow, "The Nature of Love," *American Psychologist* (1958): 673.

18 "In our society" Maslow, "A Theory of Human Motivation," 161–62.

18 "The miracle is that" Harriet Lerner, *The Mother Dance: How Children Change Your Life* (New York: HarperCollins Publishers, 1998), 310.

19 Satisfaction of this need Maslow, "A Theory of Human Motivation," 162.

20 People who have been Ibid., 166–67.

20 They long to be Ibid., 163.

20 Self-actualized people Richard J. Lowry, ed., introduction to *Dominance, Self-Esteem, Self-Actualization: Germinal Papers of A. H. Maslow* (Monterey, CA: Brooks/Cole Publishing, 1973), 175.

20 Most people, however Maslow, "A Theory of Human Motivation," 167.

21 In her book Alice Miller, *The Drama of the Gifted Child: The Search for the True Self* (New York: Basic Books, 1981), 89.

22 McBride describes James McBride, *The Color of Water: A Black Man's Tribute to His White Mother* (New York: Riverhead Books, 1996), 10–11.

23 His mounds of feces Ibid., 66–69.

23 "we thrived on thought" Ibid., 94.

23 some people get stuck Maslow, "A Theory of Human Motivation," 166–67.

26 Attachment in psychology Mary Main, "Epilogue: Attachment Theory:

Eighteen Points with Suggestions for Future Studies," in Jude Cassidy and Phillip R. Shaver, eds., *Handbook of Attachment: Theory, Research, and Clinical Applications* (New York: Guilford Press, 1999), 846.

26 Bowlby was the first Sarah Blaffer Hrdy, *Mother Nature: A History of Mothers, Infants, and Natural Selection* (New York: Pantheon Books, 1999), xiii, 493.

26 This inclination John Bowlby, *A Secure Base: Parent-Child Attachment and Healthy Human Development* (New York: Basic Books, 1988), 120–21.

26 In the early 1960s This summary is adapted from Karen, *Becoming Attached,* 4.

27 With her research Ibid., 174, 212.

27 Ainsworth demonstrated Ibid., 4–5.

27 The term secure Inge Bretherton and Kristine A. Munholland, "Internal Working Models in Attachment Relationships: A Construct Revisited," in Cassidy and Shaver, eds., *Handbook of Attachment,* 91.

31 Children who are securely attached Bowlby, *A Secure Base,* 179; Karen, *Becoming Attached,* 212, 442–43.

31 Children who grow up Bowlby, *A Secure Base,* 179.

31 "an unthinking confidence" Cited in Bretherton and Munholland, "Internal Working Models," 102.

31 A central point Bowlby, *A Secure Base,* 11.

31 "it is none the less vital" Ibid., 11, 122.

31 Research has shown that Bretherton and Munholland, "Internal Working Models," 103.

32 One study of college students Karen, *Becoming Attached,* 384.

32 The behavior of anxious mothers Ibid., 159–60.

32 These insecure attachments compound Bowlby, *A Secure Base,* 126–27; Karen, *Becoming Attached,* 160.

33 a child becomes as definitively attached Main, "Epilogue," 847.

33 Some feminists have objected For a discussion of opponents to attachment, see Karen, *Becoming Attached,* especially 6–7 and 252–66.

33 They, too, act as role models Bowlby, *A Secure Base,* 10; Karen, *Becoming Attached,* 204.

33 Children who are securely attached Karen, *Becoming Attached,* 203.

34 Mother's role is so immense D. W. Winnicott, in Clare Winnicott, Ray Shepherd, and Madeleine David, comps. and eds., *Home Is Where We Start From: Essays by a Psychoanalyst* (New York: W. W. Norton, 1986), 125.

34 "I am trying" Ibid., 124.

34 What this early E. James Anthony and George H. Pollock, *Parental Influences in Health and Disease* (Boston: Little, Brown and Company, 1985), 16.

34 "Ordinary good mother" Winnicott, *Home Is Where,* 123.

35 Winnicott did not wish Ibid., 125.

35 Ordinary devotion creates Bowlby, *A Secure Base*, 11.

36 "they do not end" Therese Benedek, "Motherhood and Nurturing," in E. James Anthony and Therese Benedek, eds., *Parenthood: Its Psychology and Psychopathology* (Boston: Little, Brown and Company, 1970), 158.

37 naive egoism Balint, "Love for the Mother," 95.

37 To the infant Ibid., 96.

37 "otherwise quite normal" Ibid., 97.

38 "To be understood" Karen, *Becoming Attached*, 247.

38 her mother had an absolute Kay Redfield Jamison, *An Unquiet Mind: A Memoir of Moods and Madness* (New York: Vintage Books, 1996), 17.

38 "Without her" Ibid., 119.

40 "You don't need to be rich" Karen, *Becoming Attached*, 416.

CHAPTER THREE: Uneasy Attachments

42 Who is ever weaned? Sharon Begley, "The Parent Trap," *Newsweek*, September 7, 1998, 58.

43 The loss of a parent Maxine Harris, *The Loss That Is Forever: The Lifelong Impact of Early Death of a Mother or Father* (New York: Dutton, 1995), 21.

43 Fearing rejection Daniel N. Stern, *The Motherhood Constellation: A Unified View of Parent-Infant Psychotherapy* (New York: Basic Books, 1995), 41–42.

44 Those hurt in childhood Harris, *The Loss That Is Forever*, 201–2, 206.

44 Others grow up Ibid., 152–53.

44 Some shut down emotionally Ibid., 245.

45 trying to delay the child's development Alice Balint, "Love for the Mother and Mother Love," in Michael Balint, *Primary Love and Psycho-Analytic Technique* (New York: Liveright Publishing, 1965), 102.

47 Sometimes these failures Anna Ornstein and Paul H. Ornstein, "Parenting as a Function of the Adult Self: A Psychoanalytic Developmental Perspective," in E. James Anthony and George H. Pollock, eds., *Parental Influences in Health and Disease* (Boston: Little, Brown and Company, 1985), 202–3.

48 resulting in low self-esteem A. F. Lieberman, D. Weston, and J. H. Paul, "Preventative Intervention and Outcome with Anxiously Attached Dyads," *Child Development* 62 (1991): 199.

48 as illustrated by one clinician Stern, *The Motherhood Constellation*, 131–32.

48 When the primary caregiver John Bowlby, *A Secure Base: Parent-Child Attachment and Healthy Human Development* (New York: Basic Books, 1988), 124–25, 131.

49 Research indicates Robert Karen, *Becoming Attached: Unfolding the Mystery of the Infant-Mother Bond and Its Impact on Later Life* (New York: Warner Books, 1994), 5.

49 various difficulties Ibid., 230.

49 it often generates behaviors Ibid., 233.

49 And if the parent's psychology Ibid., 256.

50 For emotionally healthy women Therese Benedek, "Toward the Biology of the Depressive Constellation," *Journal of the American Psychoanalytic Association* 4 (1956): 421.

50 Not having a secure base Karen, *Becoming Attached*, 256.

51 Infants whose needs Byron Egeland, Deborah Jacobvitz, and L. Alan Sroufe, "Breaking the Cycle of Abuse: Relationship Predictions," *Child Development* 59 (1988): 1081.

51 Researchers have repeatedly measured Karen, *Becoming Attached*, 242–43.

52 Ambivalent attachment is characterized Bowlby, *A Secure Base*, 124; Karen, *Becoming Attached*, 176, 442.

52 "A mother who has never worked" Karen, *Becoming Attached*, 376–77.

53 His classic paper H. F. Harlow, "The Nature of Love," *American Psychologist* (1958): 673–85.

54 In his paper Ibid., 677.

54 His experiments showed Ibid., 684.

55 She's one whose love Ornstein and Ornstein, "Parenting as a Function," 204.

55 Winnicott called Ibid., 205.

55 Other theorists Deborah B. Jacobvitz et al., "The Transmission of Mother-Child Boundary Disturbances Across Three Generations," *Development and Pscyhcopathology* 3 (1991): 517, 525.

56 "rankling needs" Karen, *Becoming Attached*, 377.

56 Particularly frightening John Byng-Hall and Joan Stevenson-Hinde, "Attachment Relationships Within a Family System," *Infant Mental Health Journal* 12, no. 3 (fall 1991): 194.

56 The overinvolvement Jacobvitz et al., "The Transmission of Mother-Child," 517.

56 the child in the "inverted" Bowlby, *A Secure Base*, 18, 31.

56 The motives of smothers Therese Benedek, "Motherhood and Nurturing," in E. James Anthony and Therese Benedek, eds., *Parenthood: Its Psychology and Pscyhopathology* (Boston: Little, Brown and Company, 1970), 163–64.

57 smothering prevents Ibid., 162–63.

57 The girl growing Joyce Block, *Motherhood as Metamorphosis: Change and Continuity in the Life of a New Mother* (New York: Dutton, 1990), 56.

59 these children become Karen, *Becoming Attached*, 227.

59 "but through it all" Ibid., 227.

59 And that may be Ibid., 377–78.

59 These children are drawn Ibid., 196–97.

59 While ambivalent mothers Ibid., 159.

60 They are often unavailable Ibid., 442.

60 In clinical studies Ibid., 160.

60 "Needs and longings" Ibid., 375.

60 As Anna Freud said Anna Freud, "The Concept of the Reject-ing Mother," in E. James Anthony and Therese Benedek, eds., *Parenthood: Its Psychology and Psychopathology* (Boston: Little, Brown and Company, 1970): 378.

61 This can happen E. James Anthony and George H. Pollock, eds., *Parental Influences in Health and Disease* (Boston: Little, Brown and Company, 1985), viii.

61 "[T]he relationship of a mother" Freud, "Rejecting Mother," 378.

61 "It is the mother who" Ibid., 379–80.

62 "apathetic mothers" Benedek, "Motherhood and Nurturing," 161.

63 In a survey Louis Genevie and Eva Margolies, *The Motherhood Report: How Women Feel About Being Mothers* (New York: Macmillan, 1987), 413.

64 As babies, avoidantly Robert Karen, "Becoming Attached," *The At-lantic Monthly* (February 1990), 47.

64 In order to cope Bowlby, *A Secure Base*, 124; Karen, *Becoming At-tached*, 230–31.

64 These children often look good Karen, *Becoming Attached*, 164, 196–97.

64 The child of an avoidant Bowlby, *A Secure Base*, 124; Karen, *Becoming Attached*, 443.

65 She may even idealize Karen, *Becoming Attached*, 443.

66 In a longitudinal study Mary Main and J. Solomon, "Procedures for Identifying Infants as Disorganized/Disoriented During the Ainsworth Strange Situation," in M. Greenberg, D. Cicchetti, and E. M. Cummings, eds., *Attachment in the Preschool Years: Theory, Research, and Intervention* (Chicago: University of Chicago Press, 1990): 136–40.

67 Such behavior included Mary Main and Erik Hesse, "Parents' Un-resolved Traumatic Experiences Are Related to Infant Disorganized At-tachment Status: Is Frightened and/or Frightening Parental Behavior the Linking Mechanism?", in M. Greenberg et al., eds., *Attachment in the Preschool Years*, 175.

67 Main labeled these Ibid., 162; Karen, *Becoming Attached*, 217.

67 Main and her associates Main and Hesse, "Parents' Unresolved Trau-matic Experiences," 162.

67 mothers who had lost Main and Solomon, "Procedures for Identifying Infants," 122–23.

67 which might be a result Karen, *Becoming Attached,* 217.

67 The mother is frightened Main and Hesse, "Parents' Unresolved Traumatic Experiences," 175.

68 The reason, Main Ibid., 174.

68 The researchers were Ibid., 170.

71 The mother-daughter relationship Therese Benedek, "The Family as a Psychologic Field," in E. James Anthony and Therese Benedek, eds., *Parenthood: Its Psychology and Psychopathology* (Boston: Little, Brown and Company, 1970), 131.

71 The anxiety that arises Benedek, "The Family as a Psychologic Field," 130.

73 as Bowlby emphasized Mary Main, "Epilogue: Attachment Theory: Eighteen Points with Suggestions for Future Studies," in Jude Cassidy and Phillip R. Shaver, eds., *Handbook of Attachment: Theory, Research, and Clinical Applications* (New York: Guilford Press, 1999), 846.

73 "Nevertheless," writes Robert Karen Karen, *Becoming Attached,* 251.

CHAPTER FOUR: Ghosts

75 No past is dead Helen Hunt Jackson, "At Last," in *Verses,* H. H. (Boston: Roberts Brothers, 1890), 56–58.

78 "What else is there" Daniel N. Stern, *The Birth of a Mother: How the Motherhood Experience Changes You Forever* (New York: Basic Books, 1998), 139.

78 Freud called it Freud and Bowlby quoted in Robert Karen, *Becoming Attached: Unfolding the Mystery of the Infant-Mother Bond and Its Impact on Later Life* (New York: Warner Books, 1994), 396.

79 "In every nursery" Selma Fraiberg, with Edna Adelson and Vivian Shapiro, "Ghosts in the Nursery: A Psychoanalytic Approach to the Problems of Impaired Infant-Mother Relationships," in Louis Fraiberg, ed., *Selected Writings of Selma Fraiberg* (Columbus: Ohio State University Press, 1987), 100.

79 "magic circle of" Ibid., 134.

79 "The baby in these" Ibid., 100–01.

79 Considerable research Deborah B. Jacobvitz et al., "The Transmission of Mother-Child Boundary Disturbances Across Three Generations," *Development and Psychopathology* 3 (1991): 513–14.

79 Children of depressed E. Mark Cummings and Dante Cicchetti, "Toward a Transactional Model of Relations Between Attachment and Depression," in M. Greenberg, D. Cicchetti, and E. M. Cummings, eds., *Attachment in the Preschool Years: Theory, Research, and Intervention* (Chicago: University of Chicago Press, 1990): 340.

80 In a study Byron Egeland, Deborah Jacobvitz, and L. Alan Sroufe,

"Breaking the Cycle of Abuse: Relationship Predictions," *Child Development* 59 (1988): 1080–81.

80 Interviewers asked Ibid., 1086.

80 Eighty percent said Jacobvitz et al., "The Transmission of Mother-Child," 525.

81 Although many of the relationships Ibid., 523–24.

81 "we have mounting" Stern, *The Birth of a Mother*, 142.

82 The pattern of attachment Ibid., 139.

82 Alan Sroufe Quoted in Karen, *Becoming Attached*, 199.

82 Arietta Slade Ibid., 370.

85 In the 1980s Adapted from Erik Hesse, "The Adult Attachment Interview: Historical and Current Perspectives," in Jude Cassidy and Phillip R. Shaver, eds., *Handbook of Attachment: Theory, Research, and Clinical Applications* (New York: Guilford Press, 1999): 395–433; Karen, *Becoming Attached*, 366–69; Bonnie Ohye, *Love in Two Languages: Lessons on Mothering in a Culture of Individuality* (New York: Viking, 2001), 21–25; and Inge Bretherton and Kristine A. Munholland, "Internal Working Models in Attachment Relationships: A Construct Revisited," in Cassidy and Shaver, eds., *Handbook of Attachment*, 89–111.

86 In her research of pregnant Karen, *Becoming Attached*, 369.

86 The majority of children Hesse, "The Adult Attachment Interview," 397.

87 An insecure parent Bretherton and Munholland, "Internal Working Models," 101.

87 other researchers found Peter Fonagy et al., "The Capacity for Understanding Mental States: The Reflective Self in Parent and Child and Its Significance for Security of Attachment," *Infant Mental Health Journal* 12 (1991): 214–16.

87 Main and her colleagues Mary Main, "Epilogue: Attachment Theory: Eighteen Points with Suggestions for Future Studies," in Cassidy and Shaver, eds., *Handbook of Attachment*, 861.

92 Others associate childhood Maxine Harris, *The Loss That Is Forever: The Lifelong Impact of the Early Death of a Mother or Father* (New York: Dutton, 1995), 170–71.

93 Women have children Harriet Lerner, *The Mother Dance: How Children Change Your Life* (New York: HarperCollins Publishers, 1998), 14.

93 The authors of Louis Genevie and Eva Margolies, *The Motherhood Report: How Women Feel About Being Mothers* (New York: Macmillan, 1987), 4.

93 Despite the wide range Lerner, *The Mother Dance*, 14.

95 as it does for many women John Bowlby, *A Secure Base: Parent-Child Attachment and Healthy Human Development* (New York: Basic Books, 1988), 3–4.

97 "*Quite surprising to new*" Stern, *The Birth of a Mother*, 146.
97 *Entangled with the* Ibid., 9.
98 *Sometimes this allows* Daniel N. Stern, *The Motherhood Constellation: A Unified View of Parent-Infant Psychotherapy* (New York: Basic Books, 1995), 25.

CHAPTER FIVE: Exceptions

102 *There are those* Michael Ondaatje, *The English Patient* (New York: Vintage International, 1993), 272.
106 *it was well known* Sue Howard, "Childhood Resilience: Review and Critique of Literature," *Oxford Review of Education* 25, no.3 (1999): 308.
106 *parental mental illness* Katy Butler, "The Anatomy of Resilience," *Family Therapy Networker* (March/April 1997): 24.
107 *studied 698 men* Emmy E. Werner, "The Children of Kauai: Resiliency and Recovery in Adolescence and Adulthood," *Journal of Adolescent Health* 13 (1992): 263–64.
107 "*Problems don't predict*" Butler, "The Anatomy of Resilience," 25.
107 *Only about 15* Ibid., 25.
107 *One expert in the field* Judith S. Musick et al., "Maternal Factors Related to Vulnerability and Resiliency in Young Children at Risk," in E. James Anthony and Bertram J. Cohler, eds., *The Invulnerable Child* (New York: Guilford Press, 1987), 229.
107 *Another calls* Butler, "The Anatomy of Resilience," 25.
107 *Yet another* Ibid., 25.
107 *Children are more or less* Howard, "Childhood Resilience," 310.
107 *No child is invincible* E. James Anthony, "Risk, Vulnerability, and Resilience: An Overview," in E. James Anthony and Bertram J. Cohler, eds., *The Invulnerable Child* (New York: Guilford Press, 1987), 18.
108 *Resilience is not just* Butler, "The Anatomy of Resilience," 26.
108 *When working with* Winifred Gallagher, *I.D.: How Heredity and Experience Make You Who You Are* (New York: Random House, 1996), 102.
108 *These children seemed* Ibid., 7.
108 *Protective factors such* Howard, "Childhood Resilience," 310–11.
108 *Emmy Werner saw* Butler, "The Anatomy of Resilience," 26.
108 *Some say that* Anna Ornstein and Paul H. Ornstein, "Parenting as a Function of the Adult Self: A Psychoanalytic Developmental Perspective," in E. James Anthony and George H. Pollock, eds., *Parental Influences in Health and Disease* (Boston: Little, Brown and Company, 1985), 185.
108 "*they picked their own*" Werner, "The Children of Kauai," 265.
109 *Most of the resilient* Ibid., 266.

109 "reveal a clear pattern" J. Kirk Felsman and George E. Vaillant, "Resilient Children as Adults: A 40-Year Study," in E. James Anthony and Bertram J. Cohler, eds., *The Invulnerable Child* (New York: Guilford Press, 1987), 311.

110 One researcher involved Jane F. Gilgun, "Mapping Resilience as Process Among Adults with Childhood Adversities," in Hamilton I. McCubbin et al., eds., *The Dynamics of Resilient Families* (Thousand Oaks, CA: Sage Publications, 1999), 64.

110 She looked at adults Ibid., 41.

110 Emmy Werner also Werner, "The Children of Kauai," 267.

111 Emmy Werner found Butler, "The Anatomy of Resilience," 26.

111 other people, in Gilgun, "Mapping Resilience," 46.

112 These positive relationships Howard, "Childhood Resilience," 310.

112 Having caring adults Werner, "The Children of Kauai," 266.

112 One study of Musick et al., "Maternal Factors," 240–41.

117 Werner found that Werner, "The Children of Kauai," 264.

117–18 They're significantly more Byron Egeland, Deborah Jacobvitz, and L. Alan Sroufe, "Breaking the Cycle of Abuse: Relationship Predictions," *Child Development* 59 (1988): 1080.

119 "What is believed to be essential" John Bowlby, *Attachment*, 2d ed., vol. 1, *Attachment and Loss* (New York: Basic Books, 1982), xi–xii.

119 Women who repressed Selma Fraiberg, with Edna Adelson and Vivian Shapiro, "Ghosts in the Nursery: A Psychoanalytic Approach to the Problems of Impaired Infant-Mother Relationships," in Louis Fraiberg, ed., *Selected Writings of Selma Fraiberg* (Columbus: Ohio State University Press, 1987), 135.

122 keeping emotional distance Daniel N. Stern, *The Birth of a Mother: How the Motherhood Experience Changes You Forever* (New York: Basic Books, 1998), 145.

123 The key to the stability Erik Hesse, "The Adult Attachment Interview: Historical and Current Perspectives," in Jude Cassidy and Phillip R. Shaver, eds., *Handbook of Attachment: Theory, Research, and Clinical Applications* (New York: Guilford Press, 1999), 401.

123 "no less able to respond" John Bowlby, *A Secure Base: Parent-Child Attachment and Healthy Human Development* (New York: Basic Books, 1988), 134–35.

124 Those wounded in childhood Alice Miller, *The Drama of the Gifted Child* (New York: Basic Books, 1981), 101.

124 Someone like me, whose Bowlby, *A Secure Base*, 135.

125 They need new ways For more discussion of what therapy can do, see Robert Karen, *Becoming Attached: Unfolding the Mystery of the Infant-Mother Bond and Its Impact on Later Life* (New York: Warner Books), 401–2.

125 Counseling has been shown A. F. Lieberman, D. Weston, and J. H. Paul, "Preventative Intervention and Outcome with Anxiously Attached Dyads," *Child Development* 62 (1991): 199–201.

125 Mothers who have Egeland et al., "Breaking the Cycle," 1087.

126 "A thing which has not" Quoted in Bowlby, *A Secure Base,* 137.

126 Fraiberg demonstrated Fraiberg, "Ghosts in the Nursery," 109–11.

127 "this persisting potential" Bowlby, *A Secure Base,* 136.

128 Therapists and analysts Inge Bretherton and Kristine A. Munholland, "Internal Working Models in Attachment Relationships: A Construct Revisited," in Jude Cassidy and Phillip R. Shaver, eds., *Handbook of Attachment: Theory, Research, and Clinical Applications* (New York: Guilford Press, 1999), 105.

128 Being emotionally mature Frank J. Bruno, Ph.D., *The Family Mental Health Encyclopedia* (New York: John Wiley and Sons, 1989), 238.

128 Clinical psychologist Quoted in Karen, *Becoming Attached,* 379.

128 "fortunate exceptions" Bowlby, *A Secure Base,* 180.

128 They may not feel Felsman and Vaillant, "Resilient Children as Adults," 406.

128 Adults who have had Butler, "The Anatomy of Resilience," 27–29.

129 that special one-third Ibid., 27–29; Werner, "The Children of Kauai," 263.

129 "the fact that some" Bowlby, *A Secure Base,* 180.

130 Bowlby said this Karen, *Becoming Attached,* 110–11.

CHAPTER SIX: **Reclamations**

131 Sometimes we do not Barry Unsworth, *Morality Play* (New York: Doubleday, 1995), 61.

133 "is a woman in a" Daniel N. Stern, *The Motherhood Constellation: A Unified View of Parent-Infant Psychotherapy* (New York: Basic Books, 1995), 6.

133 "It is a unique" Ibid., 171.

133 Once a woman becomes Ibid., 24.

134 Some clinicians have Ibid., 25.

134 Parenting is often viewed Anna Ornstein and Paul H. Ornstein, "Parenting as a Function of the Adult Self: A Psychoanalytic Developmental Perspective," in E. James Anthony and George H. Pollock, eds., *Parental Influences in Health and Disease* (Boston: Little, Brown and Company, 1985), 201.

134 "Since, in becoming mothers" Joyce Block, *Mother as Metamorphosis: Change and Continuity in the Life of a New Mother* (New York: Dutton, 1990), 20.

134 Parenting encourages Ornstein and Ornstein, "Parenting as a Function of the Adult Self," 201.

135 If a woman's parents Robert Karen, *Becoming Attached: Unfolding the Mystery of the Infant-Mother Bond and Its Impact on Later Life* (New York: Warner Books, 1994), 375.

135 But on becoming Stern, *The Motherhood Constellation*, 181.

135 "The flow of evoked" Ibid., 183.

138 "Of all the people" Daniel N. Stern, *The Birth of a Mother: How the Motherhood Experience Changes You Forever* (New York: Basic Books, 1998), 147.

141 "A woman who is able to reconstruct" Ibid., 142–43.

141 When I began What began as a personal search into my mother's life was eventually incorporated into a book, *In the Shadow of Polio: A Personal and Social History* (Reading, MA: Addison-Wesley Publishing, 1996).

142 "What is at stake here" Stern, *The Motherhood Constellation*, 175.

144 Most difficult of all Naomi Ruth Lowinsky, *Stories from the Motherline: Reclaiming the Mother-Daughter Bond, Finding Our Feminine Souls* (Los Angeles: Jeremy P. Tarcher, 1992), 58.

145 "Parents learn" Karen, *Becoming Attached*, 379.

151 Jungian Lowinsky suggests Lowinsky, *Stories from the Motherline*, 18–19.

152 "ideal mother" Alice Balint, "Love for the Mother and Mother Love," in Michael Balint, *Primary Love and Psycho-Analytic Technique* (New York: Liveright Publishing, 1965), 93.

153 The nature-nurture debate Karen, *Becoming Attached*, 319.

154 Handicapped, sick and Erik Hesse, "The Adult Attachment Interview: Historical and Current Perspectives," in Jude Cassidy and Phillip R. Shaver, eds., *Handbook of Attachment: Theory, Research, and Clinical Applications* (New York: Guilford Press, 1999), 425.

154 "off the hook" Karen, *Becoming Attached*, 302.

154 Bowlby thought it important John Bowlby, *A Secure Base: Parent-Child Attachment and Healthy Human Development* (New York: Basic Books, 1988), 126.

155 In her novel Edwidge Danticat, *Breath, Eyes, Memory* (New York: Vintage Books, 1994), 203.

155 "Eventually, one must separate" Karen, *Becoming Attached*, 405–6.

157 "We are all but" Therese Benedek, "Psychobiological Aspects of Mothering," *American Journal of Orthopsychiatry* 26 (1956): 272.

158 Nietzsche, whose father This idea is explained in more depth in Maxine Harris, *The Loss That Is Forever: The Lifelong Impact of the Early Death of a Mother or Father* (New York: Dutton, 1995), 290.

158 Jung expressed this C. G. Jung, "A 'Complete' Life," in *Letters*, vol. 2 (Princeton, NJ: Princeton University Press, Bellingen Series XCV, 1973), p. 171, cited in Lowinsky, *Stories from the Motherline*, 51.

158 *"our mothers were only not so dense"* Lowinsky, *Stories from the Motherline*, 51.

159 *Along the way* Therese Benedek, "The Family as a Psychologic Field," in E. James Anthony and Therese Benedek, eds., *Parenthood: Its Psychology and Psychopathology* (Boston: Little, Brown and Company, 1970), 131.

162 *He first divided* D. W. Winnicott, in Clare Winnicott, Ray Shepherd, and Madeleine David, comps. and eds., *Home Is Where We Start From: Essays by a Psychoanalyst* (New York: W. W. Norton, 1986), 31–32.

162 *Winnicott decided* Ibid., 35–36.

162 *Healthy people* Ibid., 35–36.

163 *Maslow contended* A. H. Maslow, "Self-Actualizing People: A Study of Psychological Health," in Richard J. Lowry, ed., *Dominance, Self-Esteem, Self-Actualization: Germinal Papers of A. H. Maslow* (Monterey, CA: Brooks/Cole Publishing, 1973), 175.

163 *In his study* Ibid., 179.

163 *having a clear perception* Ibid., 182–96.

164 *"are the major"* Harriet Lerner, *The Mother Dance: How Children Change Your Life* (New York: HarperCollins Publishers, 1998), 149, 224.

164 *"I like to think"* B. Smaller, *The New Yorker*, October 18 and 25, 1999, 215.

CHAPTER SEVEN: **Mother Lore, Mother Love**

165 *Come forth* William Wordsworth, "The Tables Turned/ An Evening Scene on the Same Subject," *The Norton Anthology of English Literature*, rev. ed., vol. 2, M. H. Abrams, ed., (New York: W. W. Norton, 1968), 94.

166 *Biological instinct* Robert Karen, *Becoming Attached: Unfolding the Mystery of the Infant-Mother Bond and Its Impact on Later Life* (New York: Warner Books, 1994), 92.

166 *Biologists have found* Sarah Blaffer Hrdy, *Mother Nature: A History of Mothers, Infants, and Natural Selection* (New York: Pantheon Books, 1999), 293–94.

167 *Among humans* Ibid., 297–98.

167 *holds no credence* For a full discussion of maternal instinct, see Ibid.; and Roszika Parker, *Mother Love, Mother Hate: The Power of Maternal Ambivalence* (New York: Basic Books, 1995), especially 139–65.

167 *"hard-wired to bond"* Meredith F. Small, *Our Babies, Ourselves: How Biology and Culture Shape the Way We Parent* (New York: Anchor Books, 1998), 26–27.

167 *"Nothing blank about"* Hrdy, *Mother Nature*, 411.

167 *No one needs* Ibid., 96.

167 *babies come equipped* Ibid., 474 and throughout for further discussion.

167 *"activists and salesmen"* Ibid., 484.

167 *What makes a woman* Ibid., 500–01.

168 *Bowlby was the first* Ibid., 25.

168 *"the desperation, rage"* Ibid., 394.

168 *"Human infants"* John Bowlby, *A Secure Base: Parent-Child Attachment and Healthy Human Development* (New York: Basic Books, 1988), 9.

168 *A baby's need* Hrdy, *Mother Nature*, 411.

168 *Even when a mother-infant* Adapted from Daniel N. Stern, *The First Relationship: Infant and Mother* (Cambridge, MA: Harvard University Press, 1977), 110–14.

169 *a singular woman* G. L. Engel et al., "Monica: Infant-Feeding Behavior of a Mother Gastric Fistula–Fed as an Infant: A 30-Year Longitudinal Study of Enduring Effects," in E. James Anthony and George H. Pollock, eds., *Parental Influences in Health and Disease* (Boston: Little, Brown and Company, 1985), 29–89.

170 *"Our first view"* Ibid., 85.

172 *Her researchers concluded* Ibid., 86–87.

172 *No one has* Small, *Our Babies, Ourselves*, 23.

172 *In beings as intricate* Hrdy, *Mother Nature*, 147–48, 174, for a discussion of nature versus nurture.

172 *"Nurturing has to be"* Ibid., 174.

173 *"Every act by parents"* Small, *Our Babies, Ourselves*, 108.

173 *Even ideas* Ibid., 43.

173 *In this country* Ibid., 103–4.

173 *Parents keep a close* Ibid., 105.

173 *Mothers are expected* Ibid., 106.

173 *Our culture tells us* Ibid., 215–17.

173 *Parents fear* Ibid., 105–6.

173 *American babies* Ibid., 105–6, 215–17.

174 *Thumb sucking* Sharon Begley, "The Parent Trap," *Newsweek*, September 7, 1998, 56.

174 *Since the 1970s* Adapted from Ron Taffel, "Discovering Our Children," *Family Therapy Networker*, September/October 1999, 28.

175 *In our culture* Small, *Our Babies, Ourselves*, 104.

175 *"How odd it would be"* Ibid., 224.

176 *As members of what* Hrdy, *Mother Nature*, 90–91.

176 *Among species* Ibid., 121.

176 *They're either* Ibid., 267, 271–74.

176 *Our foraging ancestors* Ibid., xix.

176 *"is no job"* Bowlby, *A Secure Base*, 2.

176 *Beginning with* Small, *Our Babies, Ourselves*, 13–14.

176 *A sobering illustration* Hrdy, *Mother Nature*, 165.

177 Once born Adapted from Small, *Our Babies, Ourselves*, 13–14.

177 In nearly all cultures Bowlby, *A Secure Base*, 13–14.

179 Even in instances Ann Crittenden, *The Price of Motherhood: Why the Most Important Job in the World Is Still the Least Valued* (New York: Henry Holt and Company, 2001), 23–26.

180 "create, permit, accept" Daniel N. Stern, *The Motherhood Constellation: A Unified View of Parent-Infant Psychotherapy* (New York: Basic Books, 1995), 177.

180 "If the mother is" Ibid., 180.

180 "One or more members" Ibid., 179.

181 This can happen Ibid., 179.

181 especially when the infant Karen, *Becoming Attached*, 421.

181 "hundreds of instructional" Bowlby, *A Secure Base*, 19.

182 ambivalence is not Parker, *Mother Love, Mother Hate*, 5–6.

183 One study of forty Cathy Urwin, "Constructing Motherhood: The Persuasion of Normal Development," in Carolyn Steedman, Cathy Urwin, and Valerie Walkerdine, eds., *Language, Gender and Childhood* (London: Routledge & Kegan Paul, 1985), 198. Thanks to Roszika Parker's *Mother Love, Mother Hate* for leading me to this study.

183 "You sort of compare" Ibid., 198–99.

185 "Just as the fetus" Elizabeth Bing and Libby Colman, *Laughter and Tears: The Emotional Life of New Mothers* (New York: Henry Holt and Company, 1997), 30–31.

193 That survey found Louis Genevie and Eva Margolies, *The Motherhood Report: How Women Feel About Being Mothers* (New York: Macmillan, 1987), 11.

194 caring for an impaired Anna Ornstein and Paul H. Ornstein, "Parenting as a Function of the Adult Self: A Psychoanalytic Developmental Perspective," in E. James Anthony and George H. Pollock, eds., *Parental Influences in Health and Disease* (Boston: Little, Brown and Company, 1985), 199–200.

199 "To our amazement" Genevie and Margolies, *The Motherhood Report*, xxii.

CHAPTER EIGHT: **The Mother Within**

201 The nature of this work Susan Dominus, "The Venerable Bead," *The New York Times Magazine*, July 11, 1999, 15.

203 "first relationship" Daniel N. Stern, *The First Relationship: Infant and Mother* (Cambridge, MA: Harvard University Press, 1977), 133.

207 strongly urges parents Ron Taffel, "Discovering Our Children," *Family Therapy Networker*, September/October 1999, 24–35.

208 That *"second family culture"* Ibid., 27, 35.

208 *into the "psychic void"* Ibid., 29.

208 *"It's become clearer"* Richard Simon, "The Family Unplugged," interview with Mary Pipher, *Family Therapy Networker*, January/February 1997, 32.

208 *"Your life is shaped"* Quoted in John Moses, *The Desert: An Anthology for Lent* (Harrisburg, PA: Morehouse Publishing, 1997), 58.

210 *"grows in the job"* D. W. Winnicott, *Mother and Child: A Primer of First Relationships* (New York: Basic Books, 1957), 13.

210 *"endure the extremes"* Ibid., 95.

210 *"and, of course"* Quoted in E. James Anthony and George H. Pollock, eds., *Parental Influences in Health and Disease* (Boston: Little, Brown and Company, 1985) 513–14.

212 *the reason attunement* Anna Ornstein and Paul H. Ornstein, "Parenting as a Function of the Adult Self: A Psychoanalytic Developmental Perspective," in E. James Anthony and George H. Pollock, eds., *Parental Influences in Health and Disease* (Boston: Little, Brown and Company, 1985), 196.

212 *Instead her responses* Ibid., 198–99.

212 *Being able to tune* Ibid., 226.

212 *Psychiatrist Norman Paul* Norman L. Paul, "Parental Empathy," in E. James Anthony and Therese Benedek, eds., *Parenthood: Its Psychology and Psychopathology* (Boston: Little, Brown and Company, 1970), 341–43.

213 *"The child is viewed"* Ibid., 345.

213 *The empathetic parent* Ibid., 348.

214 *In America* Meredith Small, *Our Babies, Ourselves: How Biology and Culture Shape the Way We Parent* (New York: Anchor Books, 1998), 107.

217 *Therapist Taffel* Taffel, "Discovering Our Children," 35.

217 *"all kids are very different"* Ibid., 30.

217 *many parents buy* Ibid., 28–29.

219 *Children flourish* Bonnie Ohye, *Love in Two Languages: Lessons on Mothering in a Culture of Individuality* (New York: Viking, 2001), xv.

219 *"out of a closely observed"* Ibid., xvii.

219 *Crucial to strong relationships* John Bowlby, *A Secure Base: Parent-Child Attachment and Healthy Human Development* (New York: Basic Books, 1988), 131.

222 *Looking for resiliency* Barbara J. Golby and Inge Bretherton, "Resilience in Postdivorce Mother-Child Relationships," in Hamilton I. McCubbin et al., eds., *The Dynamics of Resilient Families* (Thousand Oaks, CA: Sage Publications, 1999), 243–69.

223 *They didn't try to reason* Ibid., 259–60.

223 *"vicious circle of negativity"* Ibid., 261, 264.

223 *These mothers expressed* Ibid., 253–54.

223 resilient mothers showed Ibid., 243.

224 These mothers understood Ibid., 263.

224 The resilient mothers used Ibid., 245.

224 discipline wasn't a big issue Ibid., 264.

224 They expressed pleasure Ibid., 243–44.

226 They chose *their* Ibid., 250–51.

227 such positive factors as Ibid., 265.

227 A significant force Daniel N. Stern, *The Motherhood Constellation: A Unified View of Parent-Infant Psychotherapy* (New York: Basic Books, 1995), 25.

227 That doesn't mean Ibid., 25.

229 a broader view of maternity Sarah Blaffer Hrdy, *Mother Nature: A History of Mothers, Infants, and Natural Selection* (New York: Pantheon Books, 1999), 9–10.

229 "multifaceted strategist" Ibid., 387.

229 "Giving time and attention" John Bowlby, *A Secure Base*, 2.

230 "Not necessarily, but" Hrdy, *Mother Nature*, 497.

230 "the terrible choice" Jane Lazarre, *The Mother Knot* (New York: McGraw Hill, 1976), 50.

231 "endlessly about the importance" Ann Crittenden, *The Price of Motherhood: Why the Most Important Job in the World Is Still the Least Valued* (New York: Henry Holt and Company, 2001), 5.

231 the lifetime income gap Ibid., 5.

231 although it requires more patience Ibid., 11.

231 "Man and woman" Bowlby, *A Secure Base*, 2.

232 "Mothers find children both" Rozsika Parker, *Mother Love, Mother Hate* (New York: Basic Books, 1995), 145.

236 both mothers and fathers Crittenden, *The Price of Motherhood*, 13.

236 family members may be Taffel, "Discovering Our Children," 29.

237 Children today, says Taffel Ibid., 29.

237 Being aware of one's own feelings For a thorough discussion of what it means to know one's self, see Daniel Goleman's *Emotional Intelligence* (New York: Bantam Books, 1995). This specific description is from 46–47.

238 "At some time of their lives" Bowlby, *A Secure Base*, 1.

239 "Here is your life" Frederick Buechner, *Wishful Thinking: A Seeker's ABC* (New York: HarperSanFrancisco, 1993), 39.

SELECTED BIBLIOGRAPHY

Anthony, E. James, and Therese Benedek, eds. *Parenthood: Its Psychology and Psychopathology.* Boston: Little, Brown and Company, 1970.

Anthony, E. James, and Bertram J. Cohler, eds. *The Invulnerable Child.* New York: Guilford Press, 1987.

Anthony, E. James, and George H. Pollock, eds. *Parental Influences in Health and Disease.* Boston: Little, Brown and Company, 1985.

Balint, Alice. "Love for the Mother and Mother Love," in Michael Balint, *Primary Love and Psycho-Analytic Technique.* New York: Liveright Publishing, 1965.

Bassoff, Evelyn. *Mothering Ourselves.* New York: NAL-Dutton, 1992.

Benedek, Therese. "Parenthood as a Developmental Phase." *Journal of the American Psychoanalytic Association* 7 (1959): 389–417.

———. "Psychobiological Aspects of Mothering." *American Journal of Orthopsychiatry* 26 (1956): 272–78.

———. "Toward the Biology of the Depressive Constellation." *Journal of the American Psychoanalytic Association* 4 (1956): 389–427.

Bowlby, John. *A Secure Base: Parent-Child Attachment and Healthy Human Development.* New York: Basic Books, 1988.

Butler, Katy. "The Anatomy of Resilience." *Family Therapy Networker* (March/April 1997), 22–31.

Cassidy, Jude, and Phillip R. Shaver, eds. *Handbook of Attachment: Theory, Research, and Clinical Applications.* New York: Guilford Press, 1999.

Egeland, Byron, Deborah Jacobvitz, and L. Alan Sroufe. "Breaking the Cycle of Abuse: Relationship Predictions." *Child Development* 59 (1988): 1080–88.

Engel, G. L., F. Reichsman, V. Harway, and D. Hess. "Monica: Infant-Feeding Behavior of a Mother Gastric Fistula-Fed as an Infant: A 30-Year Longitudinal Study of Enduring Effects." In E. James Anthony and George H. Pollock, eds. *Parental Influences in Health and Disease.* Boston: Little, Brown and Company, 1985.

Fonagy, Peter, Miriam Steele, George Moran, Howard Steele, and Anna Higgitt. "Measuring the Ghosts in the Nursery: An Empirical Study of the Relation Between Parents' Mental Representation of Childhood Experiences and Their Infants' Security of Attachment." *Journal of the American Psychoanalytic Association* 41 (1993): 957–89.

Fraiberg, Selma, with Edna Adelson and Vivian Shapiro. "Ghosts in the Nursery: A Psychoanalytic Approach to the Problems of Impaired Infant-Mother Relationships." In Louis Fraiberg, ed. *Selected Writings of Selma Fraiberg.* Columbus: Ohio State University Press, 1987.

Freud, Anna. "The Concept of the Rejecting Mother." In E. James Anthony and Therese Benedek, eds. *Parenthood: Its Psychology and Psychopathology.* Boston: Little, Brown and Company, 1970.

Genevie, Louis, and Eva Margolies. *The Motherhood Report: How Women Feel About Being Mothers.* New York: Macmillan, 1987.

Golby, Barbara J., and Inge Bretherton. "Resilience in Postdivorce Mother-Child Relationships." In Hamilton I. McCubbin, Elizabeth A. Thompson, Anne I. Thompson, and Jo A. Futrell, eds. *The Dynamics of Resilient Families.* Thousand Oaks, Calif.: Sage Publications, 1999.

Harlow, H. F. "The Nature of Love." *American Psychologist* (1958): 673–85.

Hrdy, Sarah Blaffer. *Mother Nature: A History of Mothers, Infants, and Natural Selection.* New York: Pantheon Books, 1999.

Karen, Robert. "Becoming Attached." *The Atlantic Monthly* (February 1990), 35–70.

———. *Becoming Attached: Unfolding the Mystery of the Infant-Mother Bond and Its Impact on Later Life.* New York: Warner Books, 1994.

Main, Mary. "Epilogue: Attachment Theory: Eighteen Points with Suggestions for Future Studies." In Jude Cassidy and Phillip R. Shaver, eds. *Handbook of Attachment: Theory, Research, and Clinical Applications.* New York: Guilford Press, 1999.

Main, Mary, and J. Solomon. "Procedures for Identifying Infants as Disorganized/Disoriented During the Ainsworth Strange Situation." In M. Greenberg, D. Cicchetti, and E. M. Cummings, eds. *Attachment in the Preschool Years: Theory, Research, and Intervention.* Chicago: University of Chicago Press, 1990.

Maslow, A. H. "A Theory of Human Motivation" and "Self-Actualizing People: A Study of Psychological Health." In Richard J. Lowry, ed. *Dominance, Self-Esteem, Self-Actualization: Germinal Papers of A. H. Maslow.* Monterey, Calif.: Brooks/Cole Publishing, 1973.

Parker, Rozsika. *Mother Love, Mother Hate: The Power of Maternal Ambivalence.* New York: Basic Books, 1995.

Small, Meredith F. *Our Babies, Ourselves: How Biology and Culture Shape the Way We Parent.* New York: Anchor Books, 1998.

Stern, Daniel N. *The First Relationship: Infant and Mother.* Cambridge, Mass.: Harvard University Press, 1977.

———. *The Motherhood Constellation: A Unified View of Parent-Infant Psychotherapy.* New York: Basic Books, 1995.

Taffel, Ron. "Discovering Our Children." *Family Therapy Networker* (September/October 1999), 24–35.

Werner, Emmy E. "The Children of Kauai: Resiliency and Recovery in Adolescence and Adulthood." *Journal of Adolescent Health* 13 (1992): 262–68.

Winnicott, D. W. *The Maturational Processes and the Facilitating Environment.* New York: International Universities Press, 1965.

Winnicott, D. W. *Through Paediatrics to Psycho-Analysis.* New York: Basic Books, 1975.

INDEX

adolescents, secure base and,
31–32
Ainsworth, Mary, 26–27, 32, 66,
85
alcoholism, 79–80
allomothers, 176, 179
ambivalence, in mothers, 182–83
ambivalent attachment, 52–59,
70, 71
and preoccupied response to
childhood experiences, 85–86,
87, 88
present-but-absent mother and,
53–55, 70
too-present mother and,
55–59
anger, 47, 48, 64, 65
Annie (interviewee), 78–79
Anthony, E. James, 108
anxious (insecure) attachment,
32–33, 48–66, 153, 169,
219
ambivalent, *see* ambivalent
attachment
avoidant, *see* avoidant
attachment
perpetuation of, 49–50
self-esteem and, 51–52
apathetic mothers, 62, 63

attachment, 26–27, 31–33, 42–74,
153–54, 168, 197, 230
ambivalent, *see* ambivalent
attachment
avoidant, *see* avoidant
attachment
category-D, 66–70
changing circumstances and,
71–73
difficulties leading to problems
in, 49
importance of, 73–74, 119
insecure (anxious), *see* insecure
attachment
and memories of childhood,
85–91
and mother's pushing away,
45–48
and mother's refusal to see child
as separate, 44–45
overlapping categories of, 70–71
present-but-absent mother and,
53–55, 70
repetition of patterns of,
82–91
secure, 32, 33, 153, 219
too-present mother and,
55–59
attentive love, 219

attunement, 211–14
Audrey (interviewee), 234–36
avoidant attachment, 59–66
  emotional withdrawal and,
    64–65
  and dismissing response to
    childhood experiences, 85, 87,
    89

babies, *see* infants
Balint, Alice, 13–16, 26, 37, 45,
    152
Beauvais, Jeanne, 72–73, 105–6,
    109–10, 129
Benedek, Therese, 36, 50, 62, 63,
    157
Bing, Elizabeth, 185
Bishop, Kit, 11–13, 29, 70–71,
    96–97, 120–21, 123, 127–28,
    129, 136–38, 144, 147, 196,
    197–98
Black, Kathryn:
  childhood relationships
    re-created by, 77
  children and motherhood of, 2,
    10, 42–43, 69, 76–77, 91–92,
    119, 131, 132, 146–47, 156,
    157–58, 158–59, 164, 165,
    184–86, 197, 198–99, 202,
    210, 241–42
  dream of, 238–39
  father of, 33–34, 42, 44, 69, 88,
    103, 104, 201, 202
  first marriage of, 76, 77, 88–89,
    91, 103–4, 201–2
  Freud's theories encountered by,
    102–3
  grandmother of, 2, 9, 10, 15–16,
    24–25, 52, 69–70, 71–72,
    75–76, 87–89, 104, 124,
    141–43, 146–47, 157, 184,

198, 201, 202, 205–6,
    241
  grandmother's Christmas gift to,
    88–89
  mother of, 1–2, 9–10, 29, 33,
    34, 42–43, 44, 69–70, 71–72,
    75–76, 87, 91–92, 101, 104,
    124, 131, 141–43, 146,
    157–58, 164, 201, 202, 241–42
  mother's life investigated by,
    141–42
  past as viewed by, 87–89
  San Francisco move of, 103–4,
    201–2
  second marriage of, 2, 42, 69,
    91, 119, 131, 185–86, 197,
    199, 242
  therapy of, 104–5, 125, 164,
    201, 202
  at university, 76
  women interviewed by, *see*
    interviewees
blame, 151–52, 153, 154, 191
Block, Joyce, 134
boundary distortions, 55–56
Bowlby, John, 26, 56, 73, 127,
    176, 181, 219, 238
  attachment theory of, 26, 27,
    31, 33, 118–19, 123, 154,
    219; *see also* attachment
  on economic value of parenting,
    231
  evolutionary theory and, 168
  on lack of love and attention,
    130
  on repetition, 78
  resilience and, 128, 129, 130
  on sacrifice, 229
Breath, Eyes, Memory (Danticat),
    155
Buechner, Frederick, 239

Carolyn (interviewee), 65–66
category-D attachment, 66–70
chain of generations, 157–58
child abuse, 80
childhood memories:
  dismissing response to, 85, 87,
    89
  motherhood and, 135
  preoccupied response to, 85–86,
    87, 88
  and repetition of mothering
    patterns, 85–91, 119–22,
    186–90
  secure-autonomous (earned-
    secure) response to, 86–87,
    89–91, 123, 188, 199–200,
    212
children:
  attachment and, *see* attachment
  differing needs among, 218–22
  fathers and, 33, 178–79
  in grandmother-mother-child
    triangle, 97–101
  as healers, 158–64
  ideal, 214–17
  impaired, caring for, 194–95
  knowledge of, in mothering,
    211–22, 223–24, 227, 229
  needs of, *see* needs
  older, mother's role for, 38
  as one with mother, 44–45
  point of view of, 211–14, 219,
    224
  resilience in, *see* resilience
  responsibility for life of, 142
  risk factors and, *see* risk factors
  secure base for, 27, 28, 31–32,
    35, 38, 41, 50–51
  unique personalities of, 237–38
  see also infants; mother;
    mothering, motherhood

cloth and wire mothers, in
  monkey experiments, 53–54,
  70, 168
Color of Water, The (McBride),
  22–23
counseling, *see* therapy
Crawford, Christina, 62
Crawford, Joan, 62
Crittenden, Ann, 231
culture:
  healthy individual and, 162
  ideal child in, 214–17
  moral education and, 208
  mothering and, 173–75, 197

Danticat, Edwidge, 155
daughter, identity as, 132, 180
death, of mother, 151
decisions, embracing of, 184,
  197
depression, 79–80
Diane (interviewee), 177–78
Dionne (interviewee), 147–50
discipline, 224
dismissing response to childhood
  experiences, 85, 87, 89
Drama of the Gifted Child, The
  (Miller), 21–22

earned-secure (secure-autonomous)
  adults, 86–87, 89–91, 123,
  188, 199–200, 212
egoism, naive, 37, 152
embracing:
  of decisions, 184, 197
  of fate, 158
empathy, 211–14
esteem (respect), need for, 16,
  19–20, 23, 26, 27, 30–31, 36,
  163
evolution, 142, 167–68

families:
  learning about mothering in,
    175
  recurring traits in, 79–81
  time crunch in, 236–37
  values taught in, 206–10
fate, embracing of, 158
fathers, 33, 178–79
firm mothers, 224, 226
forgiveness, 147–53
Fraiberg, Selma, 79, 119, 126
Frank, Hannah, 20–21, 22, 27–29,
    30, 113–14, 123, 161–62,
    239–40
Freud, Anna, 60–62
Freud, Sigmund, 78, 102–3, 126,
    128
"frightened" mother, 67–69

Gass, William, 1
generations, chain of, 157–58
Genevie, Louis, 63
ghosts, 75–101, 119, 126
girlhood, end of, 134
give-and-take, between mother and
    child, 50
giving and giving up, by mother for
    children, 227–36
grandmother-mother-child
    triangle, 97–101, 138, 184

Haarhoff, Dorian, xi
Harlow, Harry, 53–54
healing, children's role in, 158–64
healthy individual, characteristics
    of, 162–63
Hrdy, Sarah Blaffer, 167–68, 172,
    176–77, 229, 230
Hung, May, 100–101, 126–27,
    160–61, 218–19
husbands, support from, 178–79

identity:
  as daughter, 132, 180
  as mother, 132–33, 180, 227,
    232
income, 231
infanticide, 167
infants:
  evolution and, 142, 167–68
  instincts of, 167–68
  intense care needed by, 2–3,
    10–11
  interactions between mothers
    and, 168–69
  love of, for mother, 13–16, 18,
    45
  mother as viewed by, 37, 152
  mother's love for, 13–16, 45
  socialization of, 11
insecure (anxious) attachment,
    32–33, 48–66, 153, 169, 219
  ambivalent, *see* ambivalent
    attachment
  avoidant, *see* avoidant
    attachment
  perpetuation of, 49–50
  self-esteem and, 51–52
instinct, 166–67
interviewees:
  Alexandra Reed, 83–85,
    116–17, 118, 129
  Annie, 78–79
  Audrey, 234–36
  Carolyn, 65–66
  Cathy Patterson, 144–45, 146,
    188–90, 209, 219–20, 221,
    224–25
  Diane, 177–78
  Dionne, 147–50
  Hannah Frank, 20–21, 22,
    27–29, 30, 113–14, 123,
    161–62, 239–40

Jeanne Beauvais, 72–73, 105–6, 109–10, 129
Kim, 63, 64
Kit Bishop, 11–13, 29, 70–71, 96–97, 120–21, 123, 127–28, 129, 136–38, 144, 147, 196, 197–98
Laura, 39
Leanne, 89–90
Lindsay, 214–17
May Hung, 100–101, 126–27, 160–61, 218–19
Melinda Morales, 36–37, 40, 191–95
Michelle Struthers, 94–96, 97, 134
Nina, 232–34
Rachel, 63–64
Sheila, 45–47, 51
Susan Wiseman, 47–48, 50, 79–80, 90–91, 113, 123, 129, 151
Vickie, 226
Wendy, 58–59
intimacy, avoidance of, 43–44
inverted relationship, 56

Jackson, Helen Hunt, 75
Jamison, Kay Redfield, 38
Jung, Carl, 158, 216–17

Karen, Robert, 14, 32, 38, 40, 49, 52–53, 56, 59, 60, 73–74, 135, 145–46, 154, 155
Kim (interviewee), 63, 64
!Kung San, 175, 183

Laura (interviewee), 39
Lazarre, Jane, 230
Leanne (interviewee), 89–90
Lerner, Harriet, 18, 93, 164

Lindsay (interviewee), 214–17
Lou, Liza, 201
love:
    attentive, 219
    avoidance of, 44, 64–65
    of infant for mother, 13–16, 18, 45
    initial archaic, 45
    of mother for infant, 13–16, 45
    need for, 16, 18–19, 20, 21, 23, 26, 27, 30–31, 36, 163
Lowinsky, Naomi Ruth, 144, 151–52, 158

McBride, James, 22–23, 110
McCourt, Frank, 42
Main, Mary, 66–68, 85, 86, 87, 212
Margolies, Eva, 63
Maslow, Abraham H., 16–17, 18, 19, 20, 23, 26, 162–63, 197, 208
maternal instinct, 166–67
mental health, meaning of, 162–63
Merton, Thomas, 208–9
Miller, Alice, 21–22, 124
"missing mother photo," 29–30
Mommie Dearest (Crawford), 62
money, 231
Monica (research subject), 169–72
monkeys, Harlow's experiments with, 53–54, 168
moral education, 206, 207–8
Morales, Melinda, 36–37, 40, 191–95
mother(s):
    adolescents' communication with, 31–32
    ambivalence in, 182–83
    American, 173–74
    apathetic, 62, 63

mother(s) (*cont.*)
availability and responsiveness
of, 40–41
blaming of, 151–52, 153, 154,
191
daughter's view of, when
becoming a mother, 91–97
death of, 151
forgiving of, 147–53
"frightened," 67–69
good, characteristics of, 163
in grandmother-mother-child
triangle, 97–101, 138
identity as, 132–33, 180, 227,
232
infant's love for, 13–16,
18, 45
infant's narrow view of, 37
interactions between babies and,
168–69
love of, for infant, 13–16, 45
nonresilient, 223, 226, 228
as one with child, 44–45
ordinary devoted, 34–40, 204
perspective on, after becoming a
mother oneself, 136–39,
143–46, 189–90
possessive, 61–62
rejection by, 60–66
resilient, 222–27, 228
role of, for older children, 38
secure base provided by, 27, 28,
31–32, 35, 38, 41, 50–51
and uniqueness of mother-child
relationship, 231–32
see also mothering, motherhood
motherhood constellation, 133–35,
227
Motherhood Report, The (Margolies
and Genevie), 63, 93, 193,
199

mothering, learning of, 165–200
authorities and, 174–75, 217
creating the mother within,
203–5
cultural influences on, 173–75
families and, 175
and "growing in the job," 210
and help from others, 175–79
instinct and, 166–67
lessons learned from one's own
mother in, 186–90
Monica and, 169–72
other mothers and, 179–86
overcompensating and, 190–95
mothering, motherhood:
attachment and, *see* attachment
benefits of inadequate maternal
model in, 195–200
childhood memories and,
91–97, 119–22, 135
children's needs and, *see* needs
and culture of affluence, 197
and differences between
children, 218–22
diversity in, 172
evolution and, 142
giving and giving up in,
227–36
healing and, 158–64
help needed for, 175–79
husbands and, 178–79
ideal child and, 214–17
impaired children and, 194–95
and infants' need for intense
care, 2–3, 10–11
give-and-take in, 50
and knowing the child, 211–22,
223–24, 227, 229
nature and nurture in, 33, 153,
172
overcompensation in, 190–95

and perspective on one's own
    mother, 136–39, 143–46,
    189–90
    romanticization of, 193
    self-awareness and, 122–28, 146,
    196, 203, 212
    smothering in, 55–59
    social and economic value of,
    231
    time and, 236–37
    values in, 206–10
    see also children; mother
mothering patterns, repetition of,
    78–81, 128, 155, 162, 164,
    186–90, 200
    anxious attachment and, 49–50
    childhood memories and,
    85–91, 119–22, 186–90
    Monica and, 171–72
    overcompensating and, 190–95
    self-awareness and, 122–28, 196
Mother Knot, The (Lazarre), 230
Mother Nature (Hrdy), 177

naive egoism, 37, 152
nature and nurture, 33, 153, 172
"Nature of Love, The" (Harlow),
    53–54
Necessary Losses (Viorst), 17
needs, 16–25, 26, 36, 40, 163, 167
    differing, for different children,
    218–22
    for esteem (respect), 16, 19–20,
    23, 26, 27, 30–31, 36, 163
    for love, 16, 18–19, 20, 21, 23,
    26, 27, 30–31, 36, 163
    physiological, 16, 17, 18, 19, 36,
    163
    for safety, 16, 17, 18, 19, 20, 23,
    24, 26, 27, 36, 51, 163
    values and, 208

New Yorker, The 164
Nietzsche, Friedrich, 158
Nina (interviewee), 232–34

Ohye, Bonnie, 219
Ondaatje, Michael, 102
ordinary devoted mother, 34–40,
    204
Ornstein, Anna, 194–95, 212
Ornstein, Paul, 194–95, 212
orphans, Romanian, 108
overcompensating, 190–95

parenting:
    attachment in, 73–74; *see also*
    attachment
    availability and responsiveness
    in, 40–41
    cultural influences on, 173
    by fathers, 33, 178–79
    personal growth and,
    134–35
    sacrifice in, 229–36
    secure base and, 31
    stakes in, 238
    see also mothering, motherhood
Parker, Roszika, 182, 232
Patterson, Cathy, 144–45, 146,
    188–90, 209, 219–20, 221,
    224–25
Paul, Norman, 212, 213
"Peanuts," 238
permissive mothers, 224, 226
physiological needs, 16, 17, 18, 19,
    36, 163
Pipher, Mary, 208
possessiveness, rejection and,
    61–62
pregnancy, 91–97
preoccupied response to childhood
    experiences, 85–86, 87, 88

present-but-absent mother, 53–55,
70
*Price of Motherhood, The: Why the
Most Important Job in the
World Is Still the Least Valued*
(Crittenden), 231
psychotherapy, *see* therapy
purgation, 156

Rachel (interviewee), 63–64
Reed, Alexandra, 83–85, 116–17,
118, 129
rejection, by mother, 60–66
relationships:
resilience and, 111–18
and seeing other person's point
of view, 219
repetition, 78
of mothering patterns, *see*
mothering patterns,
repetition of
resentment, 158
resilience, 107–18, 162, 227
price of, 128–30
relationships and, 111–18
temperament and, 109
will and, 110
resilient mothers, 222–27, 228
firm and permissive styles in,
224, 226
respect (esteem), need for, 16,
19–20, 23, 26, 27, 30–31, 36,
163
responsibility:
for life of child, 142
for one's own life, 155
risk factors, 106–7
resilience and, *see* resilience
Romanian orphans, 108
romanticization of motherhood,
193

sacrifice, 229–36
safety, need for, 16, 17, 18, 19, 20,
23, 24, 26, 27, 36, 51, 163
saudade, 101
secure attachment, 32, 33, 153,
219
secure-autonomous (earned-secure)
adults, 86–87, 89–91, 123,
188, 199–200, 212
secure base, 27, 28, 31–32, 35, 38,
41, 50–51
self, formation of, parenting and,
134–35
self-actualization, 16, 20, 162–64
good mother and, 163
self-awareness, motherhood and,
122–28, 146, 196, 203, 212
self-esteem:
insecure attachment and, 51–52
need for, 16, 19–20, 23, 26, 27,
30–31, 36
self-sacrifice, 229–36
shadow, 144
Sheila (interviewee), 45–47, 51
Slade, Arietta, 82, 86, 128
Small, Meredith, 3, 11, 167, 173,
175
smothers, 55–59
Sroufe, Alan, 82
Stern, Daniel, 11, 78, 97, 108,
133–34, 135, 138, 141, 142,
168, 180–81, 203, 227
strength, *see* resilience
Struthers, Michelle, 94–96, 97,
134
substance abuse, 79–80

Taffel, Ron, 207–8, 217, 236–37
temperament, in resilience, 108
therapy, 124, 125–28, 148–49,
150, 154, 161, 164, 189

author's experiences in, 104–5, 125, 164, 201, 202
time, 236–37
too-present mother, 55–59
Tortoise Voices (Haarhoff), xi
triangle, grandmother-mother-child, 97–101, 138, 184

Unquiet Mind, An (Jamison), 38
Unsworth, Barry, 131

values, teaching of, 206–10
Vickie (interviewee), 226
Viorst, Judith, 17

Wendy (interviewee), 58–59
Werner, Emmy, 107, 108, 109, 110–11, 117–18, 128–29, 227
will, in resilience, 110
Winnicott, D. W., 2, 13, 34–35, 55, 162, 203, 204, 210
wire and cloth mothers, in monkey experiments, 53–54, 70, 168
Wiseman, Susan, 47–48, 50, 79–80, 90–91, 113, 123, 129, 151
Woolf, Virginia, 9
Wordsworth, William, 165